LIVING BEYOND
the
Daily Grind

LIVING BEYOND
the
Daily Grind

Reflections on the Songs and Sayings in Scripture

CHARLES SWINDOLL

Inspirational Press • New York

Previously published in two separate volumes as

LIVING BEYOND THE DAILY GRIND: REFLECTIONS ON THE SONGS
AND SAYINGS OF SCRIPTURE (BOOK I) Copyright © 1988 by Charles R. Swindoll.

LIVING BEYOND THE DAILY GRIND: REFLECTIONS ON THE SONGS
AND SAYINGS OF SCRIPTURE (BOOK II) Copyright © 1988 by Charles R. Swindoll.

First Inspirational Press edition published in 1994.

Inspirational Press
A division of BBS Publishing Corporation
386 Park Avenue South
New York, NY 10016

Inspirational Press is a registered trademark of
BBS Publishing Corporation.

Published by arrangement with Word, Inc.,
a division of Thomas Nelson Inc.

Library of Congress Catalog Card Number: 93-80458

ISBN: 0-88486-095-7

Printed in the United States of America.

CONTENTS

LIVING BEYOND THE DAILY GRIND

BOOK I

It is with deep feelings of gratitude that I dedicate this volume to the men who served on the faculty at Dallas Theological Seminary during my years of training from 1959 to 1963.

Their competent scholarship, insightful instruction, unfailing dedication to Christ as Lord, and relentless commitment to the Scriptures as the inerrant Word of God have marked me for life.

CONTENTS

INTRODUCTION

Without a song the day would never end;
Without a song the road would never bend;
When things go wrong a man ain't got a friend,
Without a song.

. . . .

I got my trouble and woe,
But sure as I know the Jordan will roll,
I'll get along as long as a song is strong
In my soul. . . .[1]

Even though this song was composed before I was born (which makes it a *real* oldie), I often find myself returning to the tune. It slips out in places like my shower at the beginning of a busy day, between appointments and assignments in the middle of a hectic day, and on the road home at the end of a tiring day. Somehow it adds a touch of oil to the grind, smoothing things up a bit. Willie Nelson recently blew the dust off the old lyrics. I still sing them to myself . . .

Without a song the day would never end;
Without a song the road would never bend;
When things go wrong a man ain't got a friend,
Without a song.

True, isn't it? The right combination of words, melody, and rhythm seldom fails to work like magic. And given the pressures and demands folks like us are forced to cope with on a daily basis, we could use a little magic. Most of the people I know are never totally free of a relentless daily grind.

—The homemaker with ever-present children at her feet faces fourteen or more hours a day in the grind of meeting deadlines, making decisions, competing with strong wills, and completing an endless list of chores.

—The professional experiences a grind of a different type: people, people, people . . . especially dissatisfied people who would rather scream and sue than smile and solve, which only intensifies the drain brought on by increasing expectations and decreasing energy.

—The truck driver has an altogether different but equally exhausting routine: the grind of traffic snarls, weather hazards, thoughtless drivers, and monotonous miles.

—Then there is the grind of repetition the athlete must live with: unending hours of practice, weight training, road work, watching films, perfecting technique, fierce competition, injuries, loneliness, boredom, exhaustion . . . only to wake up to another day of the same song, fifth verse.

—And who can deny the exacting requirements of academic pursuits? Students and faculty alike must live with the ceaseless, cyclical grind of daily preparation and assignments, attending class, doing projects, choosing electives, cramming for exams, grading papers, and (hopefully) earning a degree or tenure.

Fact is, the grind is not going away! The salesperson has to live with a quota. The performer must constantly rehearse. The therapist can't escape one depressed soul after another. The pilot has to stay strapped in for hours. The preacher is never free of sermon preparation. The broadcaster cannot get away from the clock any more than the bureaucrat can escape the hassle of red tape. Days don't end . . . roads don't bend. . . . Help!

Instead of belaboring the point, since we cannot escape the grind, we must find a way to live beyond it. The question is, how? The answer is, a song. Remember? "Without a song the day would never end." But not just any song! Certainly not some mindless, earsplitting tune yelled at us by a bunch of weird-looking jerks with blue and orange hair, dressed in black leather and spikes, and microphones stuffed halfway down their throats. No, not that. I have in mind some songs that are really old. We're talking ancient. In fact, they are the ones inspired and composed by our Creator-God—the original Rock music with a capital *R*. They're called psalms.

These are timeless songs—that have yielded delicious fruit in every generation. They're not silly ditties, but strong, melodious messages written with life's daily grind in mind and specially designed to help us live beyond it. That's right, *beyond* it. To borrow again from the songwriter, "We'll get along as long as a *psalm* is strong in our souls." I really do believe that. Why else would God have inspired those age-old compositions? Surely, He realized the lasting value of each musical masterpiece and therefore preserved them to help us persevere. They drip with the oil of glory that enables us to live beyond the grind.

Along with the songs, Scripture provides us with wise sayings as well. David's brilliant son Solomon, the man of wisdom, left in his legacy one axiom after another which, when applied, gives us the wisdom we need to cope with life's daily grind. These sayings are known as proverbs.

Interestingly, the original term *proverbs* is a Latin derivative, meaning "to represent something." It conveys the thought of similarity: *pro*, meaning "for" or "in the place of" and *verba*, meaning "words." A proverb, therefore, is a statement in the place of many words . . . a crisp saying, briefly stated, given to regulate our lives. The Book of Proverbs is a rich treasure house of short sentences drawn from long experiences.

When they are woven into the fabric of our daily hassles, it is remarkable how much oil they add to our gears. And when these sayings are coupled with the songs in Scripture, who can possibly measure the benefits? The daily grind of life can be greatly reduced by an application of God's songs and sayings.

• Who hasn't been comforted, when frightened and alone, by the quiet reminder that "The Lord is my shepherd, / I shall not want"? Those are lyrics from an ancient song of David—Psalm 23.

• Who hasn't been calmed and refreshed from the reminder to "Trust in the Lord with all your heart, / And do not lean on your own understanding. / In all your ways acknowledge Him, / And He will make your paths straight"? Beautiful words! Wonderful words of life! They represent a saying from Solomon's inspired pen found in Proverbs 3.

• Again, who hasn't felt strangled by the grip of guilt . . . only to find soothing relief from "Be gracious to me, O God, according to Thy lovingkindness; / According to the greatness of Thy compassion blot out my transgressions / . . . Wash me, and I shall be whiter than snow"? Another song of David, hymn 51.

• And, again, who hasn't felt the finger of God pushing against his sternum when reading off the seven things the Lord hates: "Haughty eyes, a lying tongue, / And hands that shed innocent blood, / A heart that devises wicked plans, / Feet that run rapidly to evil, / A false witness who utters lies, / And one who spreads strife . . ."? Talk about a powerful saying! Solomon wrote it in Proverbs 6.

I could go on for pages. In fact, that is exactly what I intend to do! Since God's Book is full of such songs and sayings, I am convinced it is worth our while to spend our time pondering and applying these wise words and timeless principles.

To help make them stick, let's not try to digest too great a meal in one sitting. Seems to me these songs and sayings are like rich food, to be eaten slowly. Too much, too fast would be counterproductive. I realize the grinds we live with are of a daily nature . . . but I'm suggesting that we deal with each one on a weekly basis. That is why I have provided fifty-two songs and sayings in this two-volume set rather than three hundred sixty-five of them.

Let me urge you to take your time . . . to read each section carefully . . . to give your mind time to digest each weekly provision slowly . . . and to enter into my reflections methodically and meaningfully. I have kept the twenty-six readings in each volume practical and in touch with very real issues, which I have called daily grinds. I have also alternated the songs and sayings, using two thirteen-week segments of each to make sure we maintain a balance between the two throughout our fifty-two-week year.

Let's sing David's song through each day of the week. Let's also remember Solomon's saying with equal commitment. I believe these time-tested lyrics and axioms will add just enough oil to our days to enable us to live beyond the daily grind. Otherwise, our long days would never end and the wearisome road before us would never bend. How grateful I am for these inspired songs and sayings!

Before getting under way, I must pause and express my gratitude to Kip Jordon and Ernie Owen of Word Books. These men have become more than distant, professional associates in the publishing business. They are my friends whose sincere affirmation fuels my fire. Along with them I thank Beverly Phillips, my editor. Her careful attention to detail has been of inestimable value. And then I also want to mention Helen Peters, who has worked alongside me with each of my books. As a secretary she has no equal in diligence or in commitment.

If my numbering is correct, *Living Beyond the Daily Grind* is my twenty-fifth book . . . a milestone in my twelve-year publishing career. Words fail me as I attempt to describe the depth of my gratitude to my family for their understanding, their unselfishness, and their encouragement. Without their willingness to adapt to my writing addiction; to listen patiently to my incessant reading of what I have written; to prod me on during the dry spells; and to tolerate the late-night, middle-of-the-night, and early-morning flashes of insight that kept the light burning over the desk in my home study—there is no way I could have reached this milestone.

And now . . . let's press on. The year stretches out in front of us, and God's insightful songs and sayings await our appropriation. My desire is that this year of study and reflection of His Word will enable us to do more than plod along a tiresome path. If my weekly game plan works, we'll soon be living beyond the daily grind.

Chuck Swindoll
Fullerton, California

THE
SONGS
IN
SCRIPTURE

WEEK 1
THROUGH
WEEK 13

Psalm

How blessed is the man who
does not walk in the counsel
of the wicked,
Nor stand in the path of
sinners,
Nor sit in the seat of scoffers!
But his delight is in the law of the Lord,
And in His law he meditates day and
night.
And he will be like a tree firmly planted
by streams of water,
Which yields its fruit in its season,
And its leaf does not wither;
And in whatever he does, he prospers.

The wicked are not so,
But they are like chaff which the wind
drives away.
Therefore the wicked will not stand in
the judgment,
Nor sinners in the assembly of the
righteous.
For the Lord knows the way of the
righteous,
But the way of the wicked will
perish.   [1:1–6]

THE GRIND OF
COMPROMISE

One of the best-loved portions of God's Book is the Psalms. For centuries these songs have comforted, calmed, and consoled the hearts of readers. We shall turn to them during the first thirteen weeks of our journey together for the purpose of having our lives enriched by being exposed to their lyrics. Our interest is primarily a devotional one. We shall seek first to know the meaning of the psalm, and then grasp the practical significance of that psalm in light of some daily grind all of us must cope with. I will conclude each reading with a section entitled Reflections . . . which will include three practical suggestions to help you apply the oil of Scripture to that particular grind.

The Hebrews' ancient hymnal begins with a song that addresses one of life's most common grinds—compromise. Please understand, I'm not referring to those give-and-take times so necessary for living in harmony with one another. Without that healthy kind of compromise, nations could never find a meeting ground for peaceful coexistence. Furthermore, growing family members would seldom enjoy the freedom involved in giving one another room to be different were it not for the tolerance such compromise encourages.

I'm thinking, rather, of compromising with wrong . . . allowing the slow-moving tentacles of evil to wrap themselves around us, squeezing the joys and rewards of obedience from our lives. It happens so silently, so subtly, we hardly realize it's taking place. Like an enormous oak that has decayed for years from within then suddenly falls, those who permit the eroding grind of compromise can expect an ultimate collapse.

Years ago I recall reading of the construction of a city hall and fire station in a small northern Pennsylvania community. All the citizens were so proud of their new red brick structure—a long-awaited dream come true. Not too many weeks after moving in, however, strange things began to happen. Several doors failed to shut completely and a few windows wouldn't slide open very easily. As time passed, ominous cracks began to appear in the walls. Within a few months, the front door couldn't be locked since the foundation had shifted, and the roof began to leak. By and by, the little building that was once the source of great civic pride had to be condemned. An intense investigation revealed that deep mining blasts several miles away caused underground shock waves which subsequently weakened the earth beneath the building foundation, resulting in its virtual self-destruction.

So it is with compromise in a life. Slowly, almost imperceptibly, one rationalization leads to another, which triggers a series of equally damaging alterations in a life that was once stable, strong and reliable. That seems to be the concern of the psalmist as he composes his first song which encourages us to resist even the slightest temptation to compromise our convictions.

OUTLINE

Next to the Twenty-third Psalm, the First Psalm is perhaps the most familiar. It is brief and simple, direct and profound. Even a casual reading of these six verses leads us to see that it is filled with contrasts between two different walks of life— the godly and the ungodly. A simple yet acceptable outline of Psalm 1 would be:

   I. The Godly Life (vv. 1–3)
  II. The Ungodly Life (vv. 4–6)

Written between the lines of this ancient song is evidence of the age-old battle in which all of us are engaged: compromise— the erosion of our good intentions.

THE GODLY LIFE

In the first three verses the psalmist describes the one who chooses to live a righteous life . . . who consciously resists the subtle inroads of compromise that erode commitment to a godly life. He begins in verse 1 by illustrating (with three negatives) the importance of allowing absolutely no compromise with evil, lest the evil become a habit of life. Then, in verse 2, he shows the positive side of godliness and the means by which it may be attained, followed in verse 3 with a description of what results when a righteous walk is practiced. Now let's do some in-depth analysis:

> How blessed is the man who does not walk in the counsel of the
>   wicked,
> Nor stand in the path of sinners,
> Nor sit in the seat of scoffers! [v. 1]

The first word, *blessed,* is somewhat bland in our English language. The Hebrew term is much more descriptive, especially with its plural ending. Perhaps a workable rendering would be, "Oh, the happiness, many times over. . . . "

What is it that causes such an abundance of happiness? It is the uncompromising purity of a righteous walk with God. We see this by analyzing the three categories of remaining terms in this verse.

walk	counsel	ungodly
stand	path	sinners
sit	seat	scoffers

The psalmist has spiritual erosion in mind. The word pictures give us the concept of how easy it is for our intentions toward righteousness to slow to a standstill or a complete stop as they are worn away by the company we choose to keep.

Walk

Walk is a term that suggests passing by or "a casual movement along the way." With its entire phrase, it implies the idea of one who does not imitate or "go through the casual motions" of wickedness. The word translated *counsel* comes from the Hebrew term meaning "hard, firm." Here, it means a definite, firm, planned direction. Consider this paraphrase of verse 1:

> Oh the happiness, many times over, of the one who does not even casually go through the motions or imitate the plan of life of those who live in ungodliness. . . .

It is not uncommon to flirt with the wicked life, periodically imitating the motions of one without Christ. We may, in jest, refer to the fun and excitement of ungodliness—or chuckle at our children's questionable actions. David warns us against that. He tells us that we will be abundantly more happy if we steer clear of anything that could give the erosion of spiritual compromise a head start.

Stand

The Hebrew word for *stand* has the idea of coming and taking one's stand. The word *path* comes from the word meaning "a marked-out path, a certain and precise way of life." Can you see the progressive deterioration toward more involvement in sinful living? The casual passerby slows down and before you know it, he takes his stand.

On the other hand, by taking a firm stand for righteousness, we will be "like a tree firmly planted by streams of water"— one that cannot be eroded by the winds of wickedness and unrighteousness.

Sit

The next word the psalmist emphasizes is *sit*. This suggests a permanent settling down, an abiding, even a permanent dwelling. It is made even clearer by the use of *seat,* meaning "habitation" or "permanent residence." Don't miss this: The way of life is in the sphere of "the scornful," the one who continually makes light of that which is sacred—the blasphemous crowd.

Can you see the picture in the writer's mind? We shall be happy many times over if we maintain a pure walk, free from even the slightest flirtation with evil. If we begin to "walk" in "the counsel of the wicked," it is easy to slip slowly into the habitation of the scornful. Three illustrations from the Bible flash into my mind. Two men flirted with evil, then fell; but there was one other who refused to begin a "walk in the way of the ungodly."

The first two I'm thinking of are Lot and Samson, and the third is Joseph. People the world over are familiar with Samson, whose life is best described in Proverbs 5:20–23:

> For why should you, my son, be exhilarated with an adulteress,
> And embrace the bosom of a foreigner?
> For the ways of a man are before the eyes of the Lord,
> And He watches all his paths.
> His own iniquities will capture the wicked,
> And he will be held with the cords of his sin.
> He will die for lack of instruction,
> And in the greatness of his folly he will go astray.

Most people are not as well-acquainted with Lot, Abraham's nephew. With Psalm 1:1 in mind, note Genesis 13:

> So Lot chose for himself all the valley of the Jordan; and Lot journeyed eastward. Thus they separated from each other. [v. 11]

He *"walked in the way of the ungodly."*

> Abram settled in the land of Canaan, while Lot settled in the cities of the valley, and moved his tents as far as Sodom. Now the men of Sodom were wicked exceedingly and sinners against the Lord. [vv. 12–13]

He *"came and took his stand among sinners."*

And in Genesis 19:

Now the two angels came to Sodom in the evening as Lot was sitting in the gate of Sodom. . . . [v. 1]

He now lived among them with his dwelling in "the seat of the scornful."

How different was Joseph! He refused to allow the daily grind of compromise to take its toll even though Potiphar's wife continued to make her moves. Please stop and read Genesis 39:1–12. The man literally ran from her alluring advances. I find it most significant that every time sexual sins are mentioned in the New Testament we are told to "flee." Psalm 1:1 assures us we will be happy many times over if we check the first signals of compromise with evil. Happiness is maintaining unblemished, moral purity.

The song goes on: "But his delight is in the law of the Lord, / And in His law he meditates day and night (v. 2)."

This verse begins with *but,* a word of contrast. While the first verse was negative, this is positive. In contrast to compromise and erosion, the godly believer occupies himself with God's Word.

Why does David mention the Law here? Because in order to change our path of living, we need an absolute standard, clear direction. God's Word gives us that sense of direction. We understand the Law to be a reference to God's written Word, the Bible.

In Psalm 119:9, 11 we read:

> How can a young man keep his way pure?
> By keeping it according to Thy word. . . .
> Thy word I have treasured in my heart,
> That I may not sin against Thee.

The psalmist claims that the godly person "delights" in the Lord's Word. He doesn't look upon the Word as irksome or a burden or an interruption in his day. Rather, day and night he meditates on it. Even though he was busy and dedicated to the leadership of God's nation, Israel, David meditated on—placed his mind upon, mused, pondered, thought upon—the Scriptures day and night. He testifies to this in Psalm 119:97: "O how I love Thy law! / It is my meditation all the day."

Verse 1 of Psalm 1 gives us a promise of happiness; verse 2 provides the means for experiencing it. Now verse 3 declares the end result:

> And he will be like a tree firmly planted by streams of water,
> Which yields its fruit in its season,
> And its leaf does not wither;
> And in whatever he does, he prospers.

I am impressed that we shall *be* something rather than *do* something as a result of delighting in and meditating on God's Word. Without any fanfare, yet surely as the rising of the morning sun, we shall become treelike.

As I read the vivid lyrics of this verse, I discover four treelike characteristics of a godly life:

1. Planted—fortified, stable, rooted, solid, and strong
2. Fruitful—production naturally follows being planted and growing
3. Unwithered—even during days of difficulty, the treelike soul is undaunted
4. Prosperous—fulfills the goals God has designed for his life

I have said for years: "The roots grow deep when the winds are strong."

The prophet Jeremiah verifies this:

> Thus says the Lord,
> "Cursed is the man who trusts in mankind
> And makes flesh his strength,
> And whose heart turns away from the Lord.
> For he will be like a bush in the desert
> And will not see when prosperity comes,
> But will live in stony wastes in the wilderness,
> A land of salt without inhabitant.
> Blessed is the man who trusts in the Lord
> And whose trust is the Lord.

> For he will be like a tree planted by the water,
> That extends its roots by a stream
> And will not fear when the heat comes;
> But its leaves will be green,
> And it will not be anxious in a year of drought
> Nor cease to yield fruit." [Jer. 17:5–8]

Let me encourage you today to maintain a pure, uncompromising walk; delight yourself in His Word, and you'll grow into a stable, reliable "spiritual tree." There is no shortcut to spiritual growth. Like physical growth, it occurs on a daily basis, depending upon the food and proper surroundings.

With the right kind of spiritual diet and climate, *you can experience* "happiness many times over." And best of all, the daily grind of compromise and its erosive effects can be checked.

THE UNGODLY LIFE

A key observation in these verses is contrast. Don't miss the many things that are different from the preceding verses. "The wicked are not so, / But they are like chaff which the wind drives away."

"Not so!" That is exactly how verse 4 begins in the Hebrew Bible. It is an emphatic negative assertion. Literally, it says, "Not so, the wicked!"

It refers back to the three preceding verses describing the righteous, godly believer, who:

- is happy many times over (but "not so, the wicked!")
- delights and meditates in the Word (but "not so, the wicked!")
- is like a tree (but "not so, the wicked!")
- is fruitful and prosperous (but "not so, the wicked!")

In other words, none of the previously mentioned characteristics describes the lifestyle of the ungodly. Instead, the psalmist uses a single term that portrays the life of the ungodly—"chaff."

What is chaff? It is that outer part of the grain seeds which separates at the time of threshing—the husks and grasses which fall and blow about during harvest time. Chaff is completely worthless. It is the refuse and impurities blown away in the winnowing process. Chaff stands in contrast to the tree mentioned in verse 3. And to make this even more descriptive, look at the picturesque phrase which follows: ". . . like chaff which the wind drives away."

The Hebrew term translated "drives away" is the word which means "to drive asunder, disseminate, diffuse, strike, or beat." It is a harsh, buffeting picture.

Call to mind our Savior's words in Matthew 7:26–27:

And every one who hears these words of Mine, and does not act upon them, will be like a foolish man, who built his house upon the sand. And the rain descended, and the floods came, and the winds blew, and burst against that house; and it fell, and great was its fall.

Just as the winds and rains caused that house to fall because of an unstable foundation, so it will occur among the ungodly. Solomon's words provide a mental picture of the emptiness of life lived apart from fellowship with God:

And all that my eyes desired I did not refuse them. I did not withhold my heart from any pleasure, for my heart was pleased because of all my labor and this was my reward for all my labor. Thus I considered all my activities which my hands had done and the labor which I had exerted, and behold all was vanity and striving after wind and there was no profit under the sun. [Eccles. 2:10–11]

For what does a man get in all his labor and in his striving with which he labors under the sun? Because all his days his task is painful and grievous; even at night his mind does not rest. This too is vanity. [Eccles. 2:22–23]

Do you know the Lord Jesus Christ as your Savior? Are you building your life on His firm foundation? Or are you trying to construct order out of your inner chaos by the works of your own hands? Everything you produce this way falls in the category of "chaff."

Remember the warning in the First Psalm: "Therefore the wicked will not stand in the judgment, / Nor sinners in the assembly of the righteous" (v. 5).

The first word connects this verse with the previous verse—"Therefore [or on account of their inner worthlessness and instability] . . . the wicked will not stand in the judgment. . . ."

The Hebrew verb translated "stand" is not the same as the previous term rendered "stand" in verse 1. This particular Hebrew term means "to stand erect, to arise." The idea in the mind of the songwriter is an inability to stand erect before God's judgment. A parallel statement follows: ". . . Nor sinners in the assembly of the righteous."

The one who has never come by faith to the Lord and trusted Him alone for eternal life and a position of righteousness in God's eyes has no part among the assembly of believers. Again, let me remind you of yet another contrast. In destiny there is a great difference between the godly and the ungodly. But so many unbelievers live healthy, moral lives, even sacrificial and dedicated lives. How can anyone say they won't be among the eternal assembly of the righteous? Verse 6 answers that question: "For the Lord knows the way of the righteous, / But the way of the wicked will perish."

You'll observe it is *the Lord* who does the judging. He alone—not man—is capable of being just and fair. But doesn't the first part of this verse bring a question to your mind? Doesn't He know the way of the ungodly as well? He certainly does! But this sixth verse is explaining why the ungodly will not be able to stand up under judgment nor stand among the righteous assembly (v. 5). Why? Because the Lord takes special interest in the righteous. Because the Lord is inclined and bound to the righteous by special love, He will not allow an intermingling between the righteous and the unrighteous. That is not His plan.

The verse concludes with the severe reminder that the way of the unrighteous will perish. What a jolting climax to the psalm! Again, another vivid contrast. Instead of prospering, the ungodly will ultimately perish just as the little red brick city hall was ultimately condemned.

The central lesson in Psalm 1 is this: There is not the slightest similarity between the spiritually accelerating life of the righteous and the slowly eroding life of the wicked. Take time to ponder the bold contrasts:

Godly	Ungodly
Happiness many times over	Not so!
Uncompromised purity	Driven by the wind
Has a guide—Word of God	No guide mentioned
Like a tree	Like chaff
Stands erect before God	Unable to stand erect
Special object of God's care	No right to stand among righteous assembly
Destiny secure, safe, prosperous	Perish

Let's bring this week's study of Psalm 1 to a close with an expanded paraphrase:

Oh, the happiness, many times over, of the man who does not temporarily or even casually imitate the plan of life of those living in the activity of sinful confusion, nor comes and takes his stand in the midst of those who miss the mark spiritually, nor settles down and dwells in the habitation of the blasphemous crowd. But (in contrast to that kind of lifestyle) in God's Word he takes great pleasure, thinking upon it and pondering it every waking moment, day or night. The result: He will become treelike-firm, fruitful, unwithered, and fulfilling the goals in life that God has designed for him.

Not so, the ungodly! They are like worthless husks beaten about and battered by the winds of life (drifting and roaming without purpose). Therefore—on account of their inner worthlessness without the Lord—the ungodly are not able to stand erect on the day of judgment, nor do they possess any right to be numbered among the assembly of those declared righteous by God, because the Lord is inclined toward and bound to His righteous ones by special love and care; but the way of the one without the Lord will lead only to eternal ruin.

R EFLECTIONS ON COMPROMISE

1. Pause several times during this week and give yourself time to think deeply. Ask yourself a few probing questions such as:

   - Are areas of my life showing signs of spiritual, ethical, or moral compromise?
   - Am I really "happy many times over"?
   - Does my life resemble the kind of tree described in Psalm 1?
   - Should I put an end to some things that are dragging me down?

2. Read Psalm 1 again, this time aloud. Pay close attention to the "walk . . . stand . . . sit . . ." picture in the first verse. Honestly now, have you begun to tolerate a few compromises you once rejected? What will it take to get that cleared up? Never doubt the dangers brought on by spiritual, ethical, or moral erosion. Ponder the analogies between a building whose foundation is weakened and a person whose convictions are compromised.

3. This week, spend a few minutes each day—perhaps not more than two or three—delighting in the Lord. Tell Him in prayer how much you love Him and appreciate Him. Spell out why. Thank Him for removing most of the "chaff" that once weighed you down. And while you're at it, don't hide your relief; you might even smile more this week!

Psalm

For the choir director; for flute accompaniment.
A Psalm of David.

Give ear to my words, O Lord,
Consider my groaning.
Heed the sound of my cry for
help, my King and my God,
For to Thee do I pray.
In the morning, O Lord, Thou wilt hear
my voice;
In the morning I will order my prayer to
Thee and eagerly watch.

For Thou art not a God who takes
pleasure in wickedness;
No evil dwells with Thee.
The boastful shall not stand before Thine
eyes;
Thou dost hate all who do iniquity.
Thou dost destroy those who speak
falsehood;
The Lord abhors the man of bloodshed
and deceit.
But as for me, by Thine abundant
lovingkindness I will enter Thy house,
At Thy holy temple I will bow in
reverence for Thee.

O Lord, lead me in Thy righteousness
    because of my foes;
Make Thy way straight before me.
There is nothing reliable in what they
    say;
Their inward part is destruction itself;
Their throat is an open grave;
They flatter with their tongue.
Hold them guilty, O God;
By their own devices let them fall!
In the multitude of their transgressions
    thrust them out,
For they are rebellious against Thee.

But let all who take refuge in Thee be
    glad,
Let them ever sing for joy;
And mayest Thou shelter them,
That those who love Thy name may exult
    in Thee.
For it is Thou who dost bless the
    righteous man, O Lord,
Thou dost surround him with favor as
    with a shield.   [5:1–12]

THE GRIND OF
DISCOURAGEMENT

The Book of Psalms is the oldest hymnal known to man. This ancient hymnal contains some of the most moving and meaningful expressions of the human heart.

Songs are usually born out of surrounding circumstances that so affect the thinking of the composer, he cannot help but burst forth with a melody and an accompanying set of lyrics describing his plight. This is certainly the case with the blues and jazz of yesteryear as well as the old spirituals of days gone by and the romantic love songs of any era. The same has often been true of gospel songs and sacred hymns; their historical settings explain their message.

Psalm 5 is no exception. As we read it, we can detect that it emerged out of an atmosphere of strife and oppression. David is down in the dumps . . . discouraged. Whatever his pressures were, they prompted him to compose an ancient hymn in the minor key.

I seriously doubt that there is any subject more timely than discouragement. So many folks I meet are playing out their entire lives in a minor key. There is the grinding discouragement that follows an unachieved goal or a failed romance. Some are discouraged over their marriage which began with such promise but now seems hopeless. Lingering ill-health can discourage and demoralize its victim, especially when the pain won't go away. And who can't identify with the individual who gave it his best shot yet took it on the chin from a few self-appointed critics? The discouragement brought on by several back-to-back criticisms can scarcely be exaggerated. It could be that David was just picking himself up off the mat when another sharp-worded comment knocked him back to his knees . . . hence the birth of Psalm 5.

Many a discouraged soul has identified with this song down through the centuries. Frequently, the words just above the first verse (which comprise the *superscription*) set forth the historical backdrop of the song.

If you glance just above verse 1 in the King James Version of the Bible, you will see that David desired this song to be played "upon Nehiloth." A nehiloth was an ancient woodwind instrument, something like today's flute or oboe. An oboe is a double-reed instrument giving a sad-sounding whine as it is being played. Its penetrating tone causes it to be used frequently as a solo instrument.

Interestingly, David did not play the nehiloth, but rather an ancient stringed instrument called the harp (see 1 Samuel 16:23, KJV). My point is simply this: David wrote this sad song of discouragement for someone else to play—not himself. Perhaps the surrounding circumstances were too overwhelming for him to participate in the playing of this piece. It could be rendered better by one who was skilled on the nehiloth. The sad tone of that instrument would enhance the feeling of discouragement which gave birth to this song.

OUTLINE

Some psalms are difficult to outline; others easily lend themselves to an organized layout. Psalm 5 falls in the latter category. It begins with a *plea* (vv. 1–3) directed to the Lord, whom David addresses, "O Lord . . . my King . . . my God . . . O Lord." It concludes with a *promise* (v. 12).

Sandwiched between the plea and the promise are four descriptions. An outline would look something like this:

   I. A Plea (vv. 1–3)
  II. Four Descriptions (vv. 4–11)
     A. What the Lord is like (vv. 4–6)

B. What the psalmist is like (vv. 7–8)
C. What the enemies are like (vv. 9–10)
D. What the righteous are like (v. 11)
III. A Promise (v. 12)

Take a look at David's introductory plea:

> Give ear to my words, O Lord,
> Consider my groaning.
> Heed the sound of my cry for help, my King and my God,
> For to Thee do I pray.
> In the morning, O Lord, Thou wilt hear my voice;
> In the morning I will order my prayer to Thee and eagerly
>   watch. [vv. 1–3]

I observe three things in this plea.

First, it was a "morning" prayer. Twice in verse 3 David mentions that it was "in the morning" that he met with his Lord.

Second, it came from one who was becoming increasingly more discouraged. Look at the first two verses and notice how they grow in intensity: "Give ear to my words . . . consider my groaning . . . heed my cry!"

Hebrew poetry can be a complicated study, but some things about it are easy to grasp. One rather simple yet meaningful technique used in these two verses is what we might call synonymous parallelism. As the line progresses, the thoughts (though similar) increase in intensity. If this were played by an orchestra, there would perhaps be a crescendo sign appearing in the score. David is pleading: "Give ear!" Next, he becomes more burdened: "Consider!" He then grows stronger in his plea with the request that the Lord: "Heed the sound of my cry for help!" To enter into the depth of this hymn, you cannot afford to miss the growing discouragement in the writer's heart. Let yourself imagine his inner groaning. Picture the misery as you mentally relive his situation.

The third thing I observe in the psalmist's plea is that he anticipated God's intervention. By faith, he counted on it. I see two statements in verse 3 that reveal this: (1) "I will order my prayer to Thee" and (2) "I will eagerly watch."

The Hebrew verb translated *order* means "to make an order." The statement could read, "In the morning I will make my order to Thee." It is almost as if the composer had a menu in his hands. David looked upon the morning as the time to "place his order" with the Lord.

He then said, "I will eagerly watch" (literally, "look forward"). After placing his order, he eagerly anticipated an answer from his Lord.

David refused to stumble about stoop-shouldered, carrying his burdens throughout the day. On the contrary, he took his needs to the Lord each morning. When we think of "placing an order," we remember one thing that is essential: We have to be specific. Are you specific when you place your morning order? If there is one thing that plagues our prayer meetings and personal prayers it is vagueness. Could it be our generalities that keep us from witnessing direct and specific answers?

After David placed a specific order each morning, he anticipated answers. He expected God to "fill his order" and looked forward to that throughout the day. When our outlook is dim in the morning, when discouragement worms its way in, a good remedy is to focus our attention upward. And what a difference it makes in our day!

Frequently, the morning times are mentioned in Scripture as being especially meaningful to our spiritual lives. Let's review several examples:

> For His anger is but for a moment,
> His favor is for a lifetime;
> Weeping may last for the night,
> But a shout of joy comes in the morning. [Ps. 30:5]

> Evening and morning and at noon, I will complain and murmur,
> And He will hear my voice. [Ps. 55:17]

> But I, O Lord, have cried out to Thee for help,
> And in the morning my prayer comes before Thee. [Ps. 88:13]

> The Lord's lovingkindnesses indeed never cease,
> For His compassions never fail.
> They are new every morning;
> Great is Thy faithfulness. [Lam. 3:22–23]

And in the early morning, while it was still dark, He arose and went out and departed to a lonely place, and was praying there. [Mark 1:35]

After the plea in Psalm 5:1–3, David begins to think through the day that spreads out before him, and especially of those whom he would encounter. His song addresses four specific realms of interest (vv. 4–11). Let's look at each one of them:

1. David meditates on the Lord Himself (vv. 4–6).

> For Thou art not a God who takes pleasure in wickedness;
> No evil dwells with Thee.
> The boastful shall not stand before Thine eyes;
> Thou dost hate all who do iniquity.
> Thou dost destroy those who speak falsehood;
> The Lord abhors the man of bloodshed and deceit.

He mentions seven specific things about his Lord:

a. He takes no pleasure in wickedness.
b. No evil will "sojourn" with Him (literally).
c. Arrogant boasters will not stand before Him.
d. He hates workers of iniquity.
e. He destroys those who lie.
f. He abhors murderers.
g. He abhors deceivers.

Why does David review these things? Because it is a therapy to review the magnificent attributes of God. Many of the pent-up angry feelings and frustrations of our inner emotional tank are diffused as we spell out God's abilities. Focusing on His character helps dispel discouragement! Furthermore, we are reminded that *our* enemies are really *God's* enemies. And He is far more capable of dealing with them than we are.

2. David describes himself (vv. 7–8).

> But as for me, by Thine abundant lovingkindness I will
>   enter Thy house,
> At Thy holy temple I will bow in reverence for Thee.

> O Lord, lead me in Thy righteousness because of my foes;
> Make Thy way straight before me.

Verse 7 begins with a strong contrast. The Hebrew is exceptionally strong, literally: "But me . . . as for me!"

In contrast to those whom the Lord would destroy (v. 6), David enjoyed a spiritual position, which is mentioned in the latter part of verse 7 as "Thy holy temple," a poetic reference to intimate fellowship with the Lord.

Verse 8 is the major prayer of this song. Everything before this verse could be considered preliminary. Here is the kernel of his request: "O Lord, lead me in Thy righteousness because of my foes; / Make Thy way straight before me."

What does this mean? David didn't want to resort to the tactics of his enemies, so he prayed that the Lord would lead him *His way* throughout the conflict. He wanted God's righteous way first and foremost. Not too many years later, the princely prophet Isaiah wrote similar words:

> "For My thoughts are not your thoughts,
> Neither are your ways My ways," declares the Lord.
> "For as the heavens are higher than the earth,
> So are My ways higher than your ways,
> And My thoughts than your thoughts." [Isa. 55:8–9]

3. David then describes his enemies (Ps. 5:9–10).

> There is nothing reliable in what they say;
> Their inward part is destruction itself;
> Their throat is an open grave;
> They flatter with their tongue.
> Hold them guilty, O God;
> By their own devices let them fall!
> In the multitude of their transgressions thrust them out,
> For they are rebellious against Thee.

In his mind, David deliberately hands his enemies over to God, who could handle them with no problem. He also asks God to allow them to "fall by their own devices." A very significant lesson to learn, when dealing with those who oppose righteousness, is to realize that they are fighting God, not you . . . therefore He is to be relied upon for your defense. Furthermore, if left alone in their own counsel, they will fall by themselves! Do you need the reminder from Romans 12:17–19? It says it straight.

> Never pay back evil for evil to anyone. Respect what is right in the sight of all men. If possible, so far as it depends on you, be at peace with all men. Never take your own revenge, beloved, but leave room for the wrath of God, for it is written, "Vengeance is Mine, I will repay," says the Lord.

The daily grind of discouragement is lessened when we focus on the Lord's fighting our battles for us.

4. Finally, he describes the righteous (Ps. 5:11).

> But let all who take refuge in Thee be glad,
> Let them ever sing for joy;
> And mayest Thou shelter them,
> That those who love Thy name may exult in Thee.

The key thought through this verse is obvious; it is joy. How are you doing regarding your countenance—is it joyful? Do you really live above the pressures? Is there an evidence of peace written across your face? If you fight your own battles without the Lord, you'll become bitter, severe, cranky, and your face will bear the marks of the battle.

Have you ever taken note of Cain's response to God's refusal of his offering? A most significant statement appears in Genesis 4:5: "So Cain became very angry and his countenance fell." Another way of translating the Hebrew text adds a bit more color: "And Cain burned with anger exceedingly and his face fell."

When anger and resentment are harbored, our faces show it. Our lips droop. Our eyes become sad. It is impossible to hide inner discouragement! "Fallen" faces are telltale signs of discouraged hearts. David wanted God to take his inner burden and replace it with inner joy.

Finally, the composer mentions in Psalm 5:12 a promise we frequently forget: "For it is Thou who dost bless the righteous man, O Lord, / Thou dost surround him with favor as with a shield."

David closes his song occupied with the Lord, having given Him his "morning burden." His discouragement has fled away. The shield he mentions at the end of his song here in verse 12 was the largest of warriors' shields, covering the entire body. So what is the promise? God will bless the one who looks to Him for protection. How? He will do this by giving him favor and by providing him with His large, protective (yet invisible) shield.

Up with the shield . . . out with discouragement!

REFLECTIONS ON DISCOURAGEMENT

1. Each morning of this week squeeze in some time to meet alone with the Lord. Just you and Him. If you are discouraged, admit it. Spell it out in detail. Take time to express the depth of your pain. Don't deny the reality of your sorrow. State your honest feelings. God can handle it!

2. While there, alone with the Lord, follow the guidelines of Psalm 5. Do you remember them?

   - Place your order. Be specific.
   - Review His attributes.
   - Tell Him how deeply you hurt. Describe why your face has "fallen" lately.
   - Remind yourself of His defense.
   - Call to mind two or three of His promises.
   - Stand firm on the Rock with a joyful countenance.

3. At least twice this week, tell someone why you are grateful to be alive . . . why you are more encouraged than you used to be. It will not only be therapy for you, it will lift that person's spirits as well. Wonderful changes can occur in us and others when we spread a few cheer germs around.

Psalm

For the choir director; on the Gittith.
A Psalm of David.

O Lord, our Lord,
How majestic is Thy name in
all the earth,
Who hast displayed Thy
splendor above the heavens!
From the mouth of infants and nursing
babes Thou hast established strength,
Because of Thine adversaries,
To make the enemy and the revengeful
cease.

When I consider Thy heavens, the work
of Thy fingers,
The moon and the stars, which Thou hast
ordained;
What is man, that Thou dost take thought
of him?
And the son of man, that Thou dost care
for him?

Yet Thou hast made him a little lower
than God,
And dost crown him with glory and
majesty!
Thou dost make him to rule over the
works of Thy hands;
Thou hast put all things under his feet,
All sheep and oxen,
And also the beasts of the field,
The birds of the heavens, and the fish of
the sea,
Whatever passes through the paths of the
seas.

O Lord, our Lord,
How majestic is Thy name in all the
earth!   [8:1–9]

THE GRIND OF
FEELING
OVERLOOKED

All of us need to be needed. It is satisfying to know that we can make a contribution or assist others in their need. Being in the swirl of activity, resourceful and responsive, we tend to think it'll never end. But it does. Sometimes ever so slowly through a chain of events or sometimes abruptly without warning, we find ourselves sidelined and no longer in demand. A tiny blood clot in the brain can seize our usefulness and leave us in its devastating wake. Another factor is age . . . merely growing older can move us away from the fast lane. By being passed over for a promotion or by being benched because a stronger player joins the team, we feel overlooked. It hurts.

The eighth song in God's ancient hymnal is a great one for those times in our lives when we feel bypassed, set aside, overlooked. It highlights the value God places upon His creatures, especially mankind.

There are three introductory observations that leap off the page as I read through the Eighth Psalm:

First, it is a psalm of David, written under the Holy Spirit's direction.

Second, it was designed to be "on the Gittith" (note the superscription, those words above verse 1). The etymology of this Hebrew term is questionable. Most probably *Gittith* is derived from Gath, an ancient Philistine city.

Do you remember David's most famous victory? Goliath, the

giant he slew, was from Gath (1 Sam. 17:4, 23). You, too, may have a giant to slay—that personal giant of feeling insignificant. So take heart; this song is for you.

The Scriptures also tell us that after David's victory over Goliath the people of Israel sang and danced as they celebrated the triumph (1 Sam. 18:6–7). I suggest—and it is only a suggestion—that this psalm was composed by David as a hymn of praise in honor of God who gave David that epochal triumph over Goliath of Gath. As you read the Eighth Psalm, you'll see that it seems to fit that historical backdrop.

My third observation is that Psalm 8 begins and ends with identical statements: "O Lord, our Lord, / How majestic is Thy name in all the earth. . . . " I find several interesting things about this repeated statement:

1. The psalmist speaks on behalf of the people of God, not just himself, hence *our* instead of *my*. This tells us he represents the people as he composes this song of victory.

2. The name of Jehovah is identified with *majestic*. This is from the Hebrew word *ah-daar*, meaning "wide, great, high, noble." David pictures our Lord as One who is gloriously magnificent, absolutely majestic!

3. The Lord's works and attributes are not limited to Israel or to the Land of Canaan. They are universal in scope. The Lord God is no national or tribal deity secluded from all else.

OUTLINE

Since seven and a half verses of Psalm 8 fall between repetitions of the same statement, we should understand that the twice-repeated statement is the central theme of the psalm. David worships the living Lord as the majestic and glorious Lord of all. Perhaps an outline of the song could resemble a public worship service all of us have attended:

    I. Doxology (v. 1a)
   II. Worship (vv. 1b–8)

    A. Praise (vv. 1b–2)
    B. Message (vv. 3–8)
       1. Man's Insignificance: "What is man?"
       2. God's Grace: "Thou . . . hast crowned him."
III. Benediction (v. 9)

DOXOLOGY

"O Lord, our Lord,
How majestic is Thy name in all the earth. . . . " [v. 1]

This first section declares the transcendent majesty and glory of God. Such a thought sets the tone of the psalm.

WORSHIP

As though standing before a congregation of believers, the songwriter reflects upon God's greatness and, in doing so, offers praise.

Praise

Who hast displayed Thy splendor above the heavens!
From the mouth of infants and nursing babes Thou hast
   established strength,
Because of Thine adversaries,
To make the enemy and the revengeful cease. [vv. 1–2]

The difference between praise and petition is the absence of self. David leaves himself out of the picture in this expression of praise. He declares that the majesty and glory of God are "displayed" in the heavens. The Lord has invested the physical universe with an awesome splendor of His majesty. Psalm 19:1 verifies this fact: "The heavens are telling of the glory of God; / And their expanse is declaring the work of His hands." And, again, Romans 1:20:

> For since the creation of the world His invisible attributes, His
> eternal power and divine nature, have been clearly seen, being
> understood through what has been made.

David then goes on to illustrate his concept of God's glory by the
other extreme—babes and infants. As tiny babies—even those
still nursing—gurgle and smile, God shows Himself majestic
and glorious.

I have an obstetrician friend who testifies that even before he
became a Christian he could not ignore the power of God as he
delivered and then held in his hands one tiny, screaming infant
after another. He testifies that this ultimately led him to search
for answers in the Bible and finally to find salvation through
faith in Jesus Christ. In a very real sense, therefore, "infants and
nursing babes" declare God's power and majesty. When we
hear an infant's prattle, we have living proof of God's creative
might. When we study the delicate little features of their newborn state, we marvel at His attention to detail. Verse 2 concludes with the reminder that even God's enemies are silenced
when the heavens are observed . . . or when little ones are
considered. Neither could reflect man's doing.

Infants may be small and the stellar spaces silent, but both
convey a profound significance to the observer. So it is at those
times in our lives when we may think we are no longer that
valuable, that necessary. As long as we are alive, God can use
us. There is an overwhelming comfort in the message that follows—the Creator loves His creation . . . He cares about
us . . . we are special to Him.

Message

As though he were leading a worship service, David opens
his mouth and shares a message from God, which is the major
theme of his composition. We can imagine his standing before
the people and preaching about man and God's grace.

1. Man's Insignificance.

"What is man?" Read verses 3–4 slowly. Think them over and
enter into the mental picture David has in mind.

When I consider Thy heavens, the work of Thy fingers,
The moon and the stars, which Thou hast ordained,
What is man that Thou dost take thought of him?
And the son of man, that Thou dost care for him?

Let me call several things to your attention:

• The Hebrew word translated "consider" is the common verb meaning "to see, behold, take a look." David was out among the splendor of natural phenomena. As he looked about him he was gripped with the startling realization of God's greatness. Every one of us has had that experience. When we glance heavenward, we are struck with awe. We "take a look" at the expanse and, invariably, we are overwhelmed!

• David refers to God's creation as "the work of Thy fingers." Creation was merely the "fingerwork" of God, while salvation was His "armwork" (Isa. 52:10; 53:1; 59:16; Ps. 77:15, KJV).

• Based on his use of the words *the moon and the stars,*" I think we can conclude that it was at night when he wrote the psalm. Some of our best times for meditation present themselves in the night hours.

• In asking the question, "what is man?" David uses a rather uncommon term for man—*enosh,* from the Hebrew verb which means "to be weak, sick, frail." In other words: "In comparison to your splendor and majesty, O Lord—what is puny, weak, frail humanity?"

• God is said to perform two specific acts toward frail mankind:

(a) Thou dost take thought of him.
(b) Thou dost take care of him.

What do these things mean? The first statement means that God remembers us, while the second phrase means He pays attention to us. What an amazing thing! If the daily grind of feeling overlooked has you in its grip, here is a thought worth massaging. The God who created all the magnificent surroundings of the universe actually remembers and pays attention to puny individuals like you and me. It is easy to believe that God has too many other things to concern Himself with than to care about us. Peter reminds us, however, that "[God] cares for you" (1 Pet. 5:7). God never overlooks His own!

   2. <u>God's Grace.</u>

> Yet Thou hast made him a little lower than God,
> And dost crown him with glory and majesty!
> Thou dost make him to rule over the works of Thy hands;
> Thou hast put all things under his feet,
> All sheep and oxen,
> And also the beasts of the field,
> The birds of the heavens, and the fish of the sea,
> Whatever passes through the paths of the seas. [Ps. 8:5–8]

In spite of the vast difference between God and man, David declares that the Lord has set His love upon us and has given humanity a place of dignity and importance in this world:

- We are made lesser than angels.
- We are nevertheless crowned with glory and majesty.
- We were made to rule over other earthly creatures (Gen. 1:28–30).

Hebrews 2:6–9 applies these verses to Jesus Christ, making this section of Psalm 8 messianic and prophetic. Historically, however, it is applicable to all humans. These three things are true of us.

When we stop and consider the impact of these verses, we quickly become humbled. Just to think that the Sovereign, Creator-God of the vast universe takes personal care of me is more than I can fathom. We who have large families sometimes find it difficult to stay current on all our little ones. (I embarrassingly confess I have even found it difficult to remember all their names in a hurried moment.) But never with God! He takes a personal interest in each one who trusts in Him. He adds oil to our grind of feeling overlooked by reminding us of His personal interest.

Perhaps as you read this you feel alone, deserted. What a distressing, barren valley is loneliness! But listen! If you have the Lord Jesus Christ as your personal Savior, you have a constant Companion and Friend. He never leaves you in the lurch. This psalm is proof positive that He does not consider you as unimportant or overlooked. He isn't irritated by our coming to Him with our needs. He never looks upon your prayers or requests as interruptions. Even as James reminds us: He gives "generously and without reproach" (1:5). He provides good gifts without "variation or shifting shadow" (1:17).

Do you know why? The answer is <u>Grace</u>—sheer, undeserved, unmerited, unearned favor. Therefore, right now cast your feeling of insignificance and despair on Him. Tell Him that you are claiming this Eighth Psalm as a promise of His personal grace, concern, and love for you.

Remember, this is a psalm "on the Gittith." David composed it perhaps as a victory hymn after defeating the giant Goliath. I challenge you to take that personal "giant" of feeling overlooked and ask God to give you victory over it today. Who knows? Another Goliath could fall by sundown.

BENEDICTION

David ends his song as he began it: "O Lord, our Lord, / How majestic is Thy name in all the earth" (v. 9). We add to David's benediction our own affirming response: Amen.

REFLECTIONS ON FEELING OVERLOOKED

1. This week, commit to memory the repeated phrase at the beginning and ending of the Eighth Psalm: "O Lord, our Lord, / How majestic is Thy name in all the earth."

2. Take the time late one night this week to walk out under the stars and look up. As you study the vast stellar spaces, give God praise for His wondrous works in the universe. Though silent, they reflect our God's majesty. You might be inclined to sing that great chorus of worship, "O Lord, our Lord, / How majestic is Thy name in all the earth." Be my guest!

3. Toward the end of the week, call to mind several recent occasions when He came to your rescue or gave you assistance or perhaps answered your prayer(s). Pause and thank Him because He cares for you. Tell Him how grateful you are for His attention to detail in every area of your life. Remind yourself of two or three specifics. The next time you are tempted to feel overlooked or passed by, remind yourself of His numerous kindnesses.

Psalm

For the choir director.
A Psalm of David.

How long, O Lord? Wilt Thou
   forget me forever?
How long wilt Thou hide Thy
   face from me?
How long shall I take counsel in my soul,
Having sorrow in my heart all the day?
How long will my enemy be exalted over
   me?

Consider and answer me, O Lord, my
   God;
Enlighten my eyes, lest I sleep the sleep
   of death,
Lest my enemy say, "I have overcome
   him,"
Lest my adversaries rejoice when I am
   shaken.

But I have trusted in Thy lovingkindness;
My heart shall rejoice in Thy salvation.
I will sing to the Lord,
Because He has dealt bountifully with
   me.   [13:1–6]

THE GRIND OF DESPONDENCY

Many years ago when I was living in Dallas, I received a phone call which led me to a tiny and dirty garage apartment. I was met at the screen door by a man with a 12-gauge shotgun. He invited me in. We sat for over an hour at a tiny kitchen table with a naked light bulb hanging above it. He poured out a heart-breaking story. He had just been released from the hospital, recovering from back surgery. He was alone, having lost contact with his wife (and their only son) when his marriage failed many years before. As we talked of the man's intense struggles, I noticed that his small apartment was full of pictures—all of them of his son at various stages of growth.

There were photos taken of the boy when he was still in diapers. Others were with his dad when the lad was graduating from kindergarten. Still others showed him in his Little-League uniform with a bat over his shoulder . . . on and on, right up through high school. The man's entire focus centered upon a marriage that had failed and especially a boy he no longer was able to enjoy. Those nostalgic "misty, water-colored memories of the way we were" held him captive in a prison-house of despondency. Unfortunately, my attempts to help him see beyond the walls of his anguish proved futile. In less than a week, he shot himself to death in his car which he had driven deep into the woods in East Texas. To him, life was no longer worth the fight.

It is not necessary to read Psalm 13 many times to detect a despondency in David. Like my lonely friend in the apartment, the psalmist feels down. Forgotten. It is that age-old "nobody seems to care" syndrome. Despair may not be too strong a description of his emotional temperature. Obviously, he is "under the pile." We understand! I'm convinced it is these mutual feelings that cause us to be drawn to the Psalms on our blue days. David feels miserable. We wonder why. No one can say for sure, for the background of many of the psalms remains a mystery.

We do know, however, that some of David's darkest days came before he was officially promoted to the throne of Israel. God was preparing him for an immense task, and He used the trials to shape him into a man of maturity and inner strength. It may help us to look back into 1 Samuel for what might have been the circumstances which led David to write this song. (See 1 Sam. 18:9–15, 28–29; 20:30–33.)

He had just slain Goliath of Gath. The Philistines, therefore, had become a defeated foe of Israel and David had become the most famous (though still youthful) hero in the land. As a result, the people sang his praises which, in the process, aroused King Saul's jealousy. How he hated David's popularity! As a result, Saul fell into such a fit of hostility he became dead set on murdering David. Exit: harmony. Enter: despondency.

Think of it! From that time on, David became the object of Saul's diabolical plan. Though innocent before God and loyal to King Saul, David literally ran for his life and lived as an escaped fugitive in the hills of Judea for over a dozen years.

Hunted and haunted by madman Saul, David must have entertained doubts at times. He often had no one but the Lord to turn to in his despondent moments. There he was, the anointed king-elect, existing like a beast in the wilderness, running for his life. (That would disillusion anyone!) I can imagine David slumped beside several large bushes or hidden beneath a boulder alongside some mountain—dirty and despondent, wondering if the chase would ever end.

With that as a backdrop, Psalm 13 makes a lot of sense.

OUTLINE

This psalm, as so many, is a prayer directed to Jehovah. It includes six verses that build toward a climax. It begins in the pit of despondency and concludes on the mountain peaks of ecstasy.

    I. David is down, flat *on his face*—focused on his misery and complaints (vv. 1–2).
       A. He focuses on the depth of the trial.
       B. He focuses on the length of the trial.
   II. David is *on his knees*—taking his burden to the Lord and admitting his own dependence upon Him (vv. 3–4).
 III. David is *on his feet*, rejoicing and singing (vv. 5–6).

DAVID ON HIS FACE

> How long, O Lord? Wilt Thou forget me forever?
> How long wilt Thou hide Thy face from me?
> How long shall I take counsel in my soul,
> Having sorrow in my heart all the day?
> How long will my enemy be exalted over me? [vv. 1–2]

Swamped by the overwhelming trials of life, David resorts to four common and human ways to handle despondency. In these two verses he reminds us of ourselves and four mental escape routes we often take under pressure.

1. God has forgotten me—forever. (Remember the last time you felt that abandoned?) "How long, O Lord? Wilt Thou forget me forever?"

Since the testing had continued so long without hope of relief, David finally became emotionally crushed beneath the load and wondered if God had abandoned him.

2. God doesn't care about me. (Gross self-pity.) "How long wilt Thou hide Thy face from me?"

This inevitably accompanies feelings of abandonment. God has simply lost interest. He said He would take care of me and bear my burdens and lift my load, but that isn't the case! (Sound a little familiar?) God's Word is so very practical. How often we see ourselves reflected on the pages of the Bible.

3. I'm going to have to work things out for myself. (No faith in God's promises.) "How long shall I take counsel in my soul? . . ."

The Hebrew term translated *take counsel* means to "plan." David had begun to plan a way out, adjust matters himself. "After all," he might have said, "God gave me a mind and He expects me to use it. God helps those who help themselves!"

Hold it! Is that true? That statement never appears in Scripture! Let's pause and remind ourselves of several of Solomon's sayings:

Trust in the Lord with all your heart,
And do not lean on your own understanding.
In all your ways acknowledge Him,
And He will make your paths straight. [Prov. 3:5–6]

Commit your works to the Lord,
And your plans will be established. [Prov. 16:3]

When a man's ways are pleasing to the Lord,
He makes even his enemies to be at peace with him. [Prov. 16:7]

The lot is cast into the lap,
But its every decision is from the Lord. [Prov. 16:33]

What happens when we try to work things out in our own flesh? Exactly what happened to David. And what was that? Look at the next part of Psalm 13:2, "Having sorrow in my heart all the day."

Sorrow, strain, frustration, and worry became his constant companions. Such are the byproducts of do-it-yourself activities. WHEN WILL WE EVER LEARN TO LEAVE OUR BURDENS WITH THE LORD AND LET HIM WORK OUT THE DETAILS?

4. I resent this trial! It's humiliating to endure being stepped on. (Pride has now been wounded, so it retaliates.) "How long will my enemy be exalted over me?"

Isn't this a typical complaint? Again, I remind you, it comes from pride. It says, in effect, that I have the right to defend the truth, especially when it comes to some enemy taking advantage of me. How we fight to maintain our pride! How we long to be appreciated and well-thought-of! David was having to learn that the truth will defend itself. It will emerge as the champion in God's own time.

Immediately, I see two strategic areas of application:

1. "How long" occurs four times in two brief verses. It was the length of the test that began to weary David. Let us remember that God not only designs the depth of our trials but also their length. Sometime soon, read the words of the ancient prophet Habakkuk, chapter 1. He, too, asked, "How long?"

2. In the first two verses of Psalm 13 David turns against everyone and everything except himself. What I learn from this is that when I try to handle a test in the flesh, I turn against God, my enemy, or my circumstance rather than first asking the Lord what He is trying to teach me in this situation. What wonderful lessons God wishes to teach us if our proud hearts would only be willing to melt in the furnace of affliction.

DAVID ON HIS KNEES

Consider and answer me, O Lord, my God;
Enlighten my eyes, lest I sleep the sleep of death,
Lest my enemy say, "I have overcome him,"
Lest my adversaries rejoice when I am shaken. [vv. 3–4]

Something happened to David between stanzas 2 and 3 of his hymn. Perhaps he listened to his own complaints and realized it was self-pity. (I've done that, haven't you?) Maybe he paused in his composition and looked back over what he had just written . . . and became alarmed at the unbelief that began to surface before his eyes. We observe a genuine and marked difference now. He is up off his face. His despondency is beginning to lift. We find him, at last, on his knees—the place of victory. The martyred missionary, Jim Elliot, once wrote: "The saint who advances on his knees never retreats."

Please observe how closely verses 3 and 4 are connected with verses 1 and 2. David seems to recollect and redirect his complaints as he talks to the Lord about them. Three changes become apparent:

First, instead of viewing the Lord as being removed and unconcerned (v. 1), David requests that He "consider and answer" him (v. 3). And don't miss what he calls the Lord in verse 3—"my God!" The distance is now gone in David's mind. He is embracing an altogether different outlook.

Second, instead of the despondency and distress that had become his heart attitude due to his attempts to work things out (v. 2), he now asks the Lord to "enlighten my eyes."

Again, the Hebrew gives us a clearer understanding of this. The word translated *enlighten* in verse 3 is in the causative stem, meaning literally "to cause to shine." In Numbers 6:24–26 the identical term occurs in a benediction we've heard many times:

> The Lord bless you, and keep you;
> The Lord *make His face* shine on you,
> And be gracious to you;
> The Lord lift up His countenance on you,
> And give you peace. [Emphasis is mine.]

David's countenance had lost its "shine." His face, and especially his eyes, had become hard, flat, and dull. He longed for God's brightness to reflect itself once again from his eyes—his face had fallen.

When trials are dealt with in the flesh, I want to state once again that the eyes bear the marks of that fact. We cannot hide it. Our entire countenance becomes rigid and inflexible, lacking the "sparkle" and the "light" that once manifested itself from our hearts. When inner joy leaves, so does the "shine" from our eyes.

Third, instead of worrying about his exalted enemy (v. 2), David now mentally releases his enemy to the Lord and lets Him take care of the results (v. 4).

I notice this marked change in David occurred when he decided to lay it all out before God in prayer. Although it sounds like a cliché, our fervent petition is still the most effective oil to reduce the friction from the daily grind of despondency. A portion of an old Christian hymn states:

> O what peace we often forfeit,
> O what needless pain we bear,
> All because we do not carry
> Ev'rything to God in prayer.[1]

Yes, *everything*.

DAVID ON HIS FEET

> But I have trusted in Thy lovingkindness;
> My heart shall rejoice in Thy salvation.
> I will sing to the Lord,
> Because He has dealt bountifully with me. [vv. 5–6]

The first word in verse 5 is *but*. That little word usually introduces a contrast to the reader. It's as if David were saying, "In contrast to my earlier complaints and fears, my dull eyes and proud heart. . . . I have trusted! . . . My heart shall rejoice! . . . I will sing!"

Notice his exclamations of praise? What a delightful difference! This sounds more like the David we know, doesn't it? We dare not overlook the last part of the final verse: "Because He has dealt bountifully with me."

How significant! Read it again, then stop and think. David's circumstances had not changed. Saul still hunted him. The barren slopes of Judea were still barren. His hunger, if present before he wrote the psalm, was still a reality. *Nothing around the man was different*, and yet David's conclusions were 180 degrees from his original thoughts. Why? Because *David* had changed. God had "dealt bountifully" with him.

APPLICATION

Trials are designed for *us*, not for our surroundings. God wishes to train us, to mold us. He uses the distressing circumstances of life as His tools. He allows the icy feelings of despondency to linger within us. In doing so, He deals bountifully with us . . . deep within where no one else can see or touch.

We have not learned the most basic and essential lessons God has designed for us in any given trial until we can say, "He has dealt bountifully with me."

In the magnificent Psalm 119, David declares this same conclusion in verses 71 and 75. In fact, he says such trials are *good* for us!

> It is good for me that I was afflicted,
> That I may learn Thy statutes. . . .
> I know, O Lord, that Thy judgments are righteous,
> And that in faithfulness Thou hast afflicted me.

This is what the apostle Paul came to realize from his "thorn in the flesh" as he wrote in 2 Corinthians 12:9–10 (KJV):

> And he said unto me, "My grace is sufficient for thee: for my strength is made perfect in weakness." Most gladly therefore will I rather glory in my infirmities, that the power of Christ may rest upon me. Therefore I take pleasure in infirmities, in reproaches, in necessities, in persecutions, in distresses for Christ's sake: for when I am weak, then I am strong.

Weakness is not a symptom of a terminal disease. It is simply tangible proof of our humanity. Better still, it is the platform upon which God does some of His most magnificent work.

If the daily grind of despondency has begun to wrap its clammy fingers around you and drag you under, let me encourage you to get better acquainted with this unique song of new hope. It can be not only a comfort to your soul . . . very likely it will lift you off your face and put you back on your feet.

REFLECTIONS ON DESPONDENCY

1. Has despondency begun to dog your steps? If so, it might be helpful to retrace your path and locate what prompted your discouraged feelings. Is your focus on "The way we were"? Do you have some Saul making your life miserable? Are you struggling with a subtle pressure that increases each day? Starting to feel abandoned and alone? Has something aroused your anger? Now is a good time to get on your knees (yes, literally on your knees) and unload your burden from your shoulders and into the Lord's lap—where it belongs. Don't worry, He can handle it!

2. Let's be painfully honest, okay? Take stock of how you have handled the stress in recent days. Have you attempted to work things out in the energy of the flesh? If so, say so. Have you been protecting your pride? Come on . . . admit it. In fact, go a step further and tell the Lord you are weary of fighting your own battles. Ask Him to step in, take charge, and be your defense.

3. As David concludes his song, he writes, "I will sing to the Lord. . . ." Do that. Choose a different hymn of praise each day this week and sing it aloud to the Lord. Without a song, remember, life gets pretty grim.

Psalm

A Psalm of David.

O Lord, who may abide in Thy
    tent?
Who may dwell on Thy holy
    hill?
He who walks with integrity, and works
    righteousness,
And speaks truth in his heart.
He does not slander with his tongue,
Nor does evil to his neighbor,
Nor takes up a reproach against his
    friend;
In whose eyes a reprobate is despised,
But who honors those who fear the Lord;
He swears to his own hurt, and does not
    change;
He does not put out his money at
    interest,
Nor does he take a bribe against the
    innocent.
He who does these things will never be
    shaken.   [15:1–5]

THE GRIND OF
WEAKENED
INTEGRITY

Benjamin Franklin once called this song the "Gentlemen's Psalm." To him, it represented the standard of life after which a gentleman should pattern his walk. As fine a description as that may be, David's song goes even deeper than that—it is indeed the "Christian's Psalm." It sets forth, not so much the way a person finds the Lord, as it does the way we are to live after the Lord has entered our life. In other words, it doesn't deal with how someone becomes a Christian, but rather how a Christian should maintain a life of integrity. It sets forth many of the moral and ethical characteristics God desires in His children's day-to-day lifestyle, both in public and in private.

It should come as a surprise to no one that ours is a day of weakened integrity. Pause for a moment and call to mind a few of the more prominent examples:

- U.S. Marines stationed at our embassy in Russia whose duty it was to protect confidential documents traded our secrets for sexual gratification.
- A couple of high-profile politicians who had begun their move toward the presidency were forced to pull out . . . one because of blatant acts of plagiarism, the other because of questionable morals.
- Our space program took a giant step backward as the Challenger exploded shortly after being launched, killing the entire crew. Critical-thinking engineers who had said no

during the countdown were outvoted by several bureau-
crats who ignored the warnings regarding a leaky seal.

- Even the religious world has not escaped a breakdown in
  integrity. Sex scandals and the misuse of ministry funds
  have put a black eye on the face of several televangelists,
  which cannot help but bruise the testimony of other media
  ministries even though they may be squeaky clean. When a
  cloud of suspicion appears over several well-knowns, even
  the obscure are affected by the shadow.

If your daily grind is a weakened integrity, this song will
speak volumes to you.

BACKGROUND

No one knows what prompted David to write this song. All
we know is that he did, in fact, write it. There is a broader
biblical background, however, that causes the psalm to take on
real significance. Let me explain.

The moment a believing sinner gives his heart to Jesus Christ,
he is declared to be the recipient of numerous spiritual blessings.
These make up our eternal inheritance, which never changes.
We become a child of God (John 1:12), adopted into His family
forever (Rom. 8:14–17), sealed and secure (Eph. 1:13), delivered
from darkness into God's love (Col. 1:13), a priest (1 Pet. 2:9),
and on and on! These things never change regardless of our
walk. They become our permanent inheritance. In that way, they
represent our unchanged eternal position in God's eyes.

But something else is also true—we have temporal fellowship with our Lord. From salvation onward, the child of God
has the privilege of living under the control of the Holy Spirit.
The flip side of that arrangement introduces a possibility: He
may choose to sin and walk under the energy of his own flesh
and thus break this temporal fellowship that is his to claim.
When he does, he chooses to reject God's power and blessing
and moves immediately out of the realm of fellowship into the
realm of divine discipline. Let me hasten to add that his tragic

loss of temporal fellowship need not be extended. If the believer will confess his sins (1 John 1:9) and begin to walk in dependence upon the Holy Spirit (Gal. 5:16; Eph. 5:18), temporal fellowship will immediately be restored.

How does all this tie in with Psalm 15? Simply that this divine song has to do with our walking in the realm of temporal fellowship. In fact, it mentions some of the things we should be doing within the framework of that fellowship. It deals with those works of righteousness which are prompted by the Holy Spirit while we are walking in dependence upon our God. When these things begin to fade from our lives, our integrity is inevitably weakened—ultimately, our testimony is hurt.

OUTLINE

If you read Psalm 15 carefully, you will discover that it all hangs upon the first verse. Verse 1 is crucial in that it asks a key question. Answering it becomes the object of the rest of the verses. The song then concludes with a wonderful promise. A simple outline could be:

    I. Question: "Who may abide in Thy tent? . . . " (v. 1)
   II. Answer: "He who walks with integrity . . . " (vv. 2–5)
  III. Promise: "He will never be shaken" (v. 5)

THE QUESTION

O Lord, who may abide in Thy tent?
Who may dwell on Thy holy hill? [v. 1]

The song opens with a prayer directed to Jehovah. Two questions are asked with the same thought in mind. Literally, they read: "Jehovah, who shall dwell in your tent? Who shall settle down on your holy mountain?"

The references to God's "tent" and "holy mountain" are symbols of God's presence—descriptive expressions of intimate fellowship. In other words, David is asking, "What kind of an individual does it take to maintain and enjoy intimate fellowship with You, Lord?"

THE ANSWER

He who walks with integrity, and works righteousness,
And speaks truth in his heart.
He does not slander with his tongue,
Nor does evil to his neighbor,
Nor takes up a reproach against his friend;
In whose eyes a reprobate is despised,
But who honors those who fear the Lord;
He swears to his own hurt, and does not change;
He does not put out his money at interest,
Nor does he take a bribe against the innocent. [vv. 2–5]

Now David sets out to answer that key question. I count eleven specific characteristics, each of which is worth our attention this week.

1. He who walks with integrity. This has to do with *who we are* as well as *where we go.* The word *integrity* means "to be solid, wholesome, complete." The believer who is interested in maintaining temporal fellowship is careful about how he lives and where he goes—he walks in the realm of truth. He refuses to live a lie.

2. He who works righteousness. This has to do with *what we do.* Righteousness is to be the habit of our conscious life. Our dealings are to be honest, our activities clear of compromise. In today's vernacular, we're to "keep our nose clean." To do less is to weaken our integrity.

3. He who speaks truth in his heart. This has to do with *how we think.* Notice that the truth mentioned here is spoken "in the heart"—attitudes, reactions, and motives are in David's mind. The source of these things (the heart—Prov. 23:7, KJV) is to be a bedrock of truth, no place for deception or lies or a hidden agenda!

4. <u>He who does not slander with his tongue.</u> This and the next two characteristics have to do with *what we say*. The Hebrew word translated *slander* literally means "to go about, to foot it"—we might even say "to hoof it." It would include one who walks here and there spreading malicious slander, pouring out verbal venom and poisoning others behind their backs.

This is an excellent time for me to pose a direct question. Does this describe you? Are you a gossip? Do you inwardly enjoy hearing or passing on some juicy tale that colors another's reputation? It is interesting that in the list of seven things God hates (Prov. 6:16–19) three have to do with the tongue.

Several years ago I was given wise counsel regarding the use of my tongue. I hope it will help you as much as it has helped me:

> Before you pass along information or comments about someone else, let it first pass through four gates for approval. If all four give you a green light, share it without hesitation:
>
> > Gate 1: Is it confidential? (If so, never mention it.)
> > Gate 2: Is it true? (This may take some investigation.)
> > Gate 3: Is it necessary? (So many words are useless.)
> > Gate 4: Is it kind? (Does it serve a wholesome purpose?)

Here's another good piece of advice: If you ever have to say, "I really shouldn't say this . . . ," *don't!* Few statements from Scripture are more pointed on this subject than Ephesians 4:29. Look at it as it is recorded in The Modern Language Bible, The Berkeley Version in Modern English:

> Let no foul speech come out of your mouth, but only such as will build up where it is necessary, so as to add a blessing to the listeners.

5. <u>He who does not do evil to his neighbor.</u> The Spirit-filled believer is loyal and consistent—not fickle, not erratic. He does not consciously bring difficulty upon others.

6. <u>Nor takes up a reproach against his friend.</u> This means he does not say sharp, cutting, and scornful things about others,

either behind their back or to their face. There is honesty yet gentleness (Gal. 5:22–23) in his character.

7. In whose eyes a reprobate is despised. This has to do with *who we are with.* A reprobate mentioned here is literally a "worthless reprobate," someone who is totally disinterested in spiritual things. The genuine believer with strong integrity will discern the impact such a person can have on his own walk with the Lord, and will not cultivate an association with him. "Do not be deceived: 'Bad company corrupts good morals'" (1 Cor. 15:33).

8. He honors those who fear the Lord. Like the preceding phrase, this is still dealing with our associates, only this phrase is the other side of the coin. It addresses those with whom we *should* keep company. The believer who walks with the Lord has a scale of values that is determined by biblical principles. Since we become like those with whom we spend our time, a Christlike friend needs to be sought out for companionship.

9. He swears to his own hurt, and does not change. This means that we perform what we promise, even when keeping our word is difficult to achieve. Our word should be our bond. The Christian with integrity makes it his aim to do what he says he will do, even when it hurts—even when it is inconvenient.

10. He does not put out his money at interest. According to Deuteronomy 23:19–20 and Leviticus 25:35–38, the Jew was commanded not to loan a needy Jewish brother money on interest. He was to assist generously and unselfishly. The believer in Christ who offers to extend personal financial assistance to his brother in Christ should do so without interest, love being his only motive. (Needless to say, discernment must accompany love . . . or we will have more love than money!) Not every financial need among believers is a "need." Some "needs" stem from careless spending.

11. Nor does he take a bribe against the innocent. My Webster's dictionary defines a bribe as "money or favor bestowed on

or promised to a person in a position of trust to pervert his judgment or corrupt his conduct." We have all read about what has come to be known as "influence peddling." Not even Wall Street has been protected from such schemes. The psalmist's point is clear: One with integrity won't stoop to that level.

THE PROMISE

. . . he who does these things will never be shaken. [v. 5]

We are promised that if these things become our practice, we will live stable, solid, dependable lives. Those who bring these areas under the control of the Holy Spirit will live wholesome lives as solid citizens of heaven. Or, using Ben Franklin's suggestion, whoever lives like this will be considered a "Christian gentleman." Such people are rare, indeed. No wonder they are not easily shaken! Integrity reinforces a life with steel.

REFLECTIONS ON WEAKENED INTEGRITY

1. Get a dictionary, look up *integrity*, and write the definition below:

   _____

   _____

   _____

   Study that definition with an eye on applying it to your life. What stands out?

2. Spend this week reviewing the eleven marks of solid Christian integrity. Does one or two of them bring an extra pang of conviction? Go ahead and admit it. Ask the Lord to assist you this week as you think of ways to strengthen those weaknesses.

3. As the week passes, look for these eleven qualities of integrity in others. Whenever you witness them, thank the person for demonstrating such fine character. Let me add a further suggestion. When you hear or read of someone in the public arena who resisted the temptation to weaken his or her integrity, write that person and express your respect. Affirmation fuels the fire of strong character.

Psalm

For the choir director.
A Psalm of David.

The heavens are telling of the
 glory of God;
 And their expanse is declaring
 the work of His hands.
Day to day pours forth speech,
And night to night reveals knowledge.
There is no speech, nor are there words;
Their voice is not heard.
Their line has gone out through all the
 earth,
And their utterances to the end of the
 world.
In them He has placed a tent for the sun,
Which is as a bridegroom coming out of
 his chamber;
It rejoices as a strong man to run his
 course.
Its rising is from one end of the heavens,
And its circuit to the other end of them;
And there is nothing hidden from its
 heat.

The law of the Lord is perfect, restoring
 the soul;
The testimony of the Lord is sure, making
 wise the simple.
The precepts of the Lord are right,
 rejoicing the heart;

The commandment of the Lord is pure,
  enlightening the eyes.
The fear of the Lord is clean, enduring
  forever;
The judgments of the Lord are true; they
  are righteous altogether.
They are more desirable than gold, yes,
  than much fine gold;
Sweeter also than honey and the
  drippings of the honeycomb.
Moreover, by them Thy servant is
  warned;
In keeping them there is great reward.
Who can discern his errors? Acquit me of
  hidden faults.
Also keep back Thy servant from
  presumptuous sins;
Let them not rule over me;
Then I shall be blameless,
And I shall be acquitted of great
  transgression.
Let the words of my mouth and the
  meditation of my heart
Be acceptable in Thy sight,
O Lord, my rock and my
  redeemer. [19:1–14]

THE GRIND OF
DIVINE
SILENCE

Ever felt totally removed from God's awareness? It's almost like you are standing at the bottom of a long stairway looking up. The light is off, and even though you knock or call out for a response, nothing happens. There isn't even a stir.

You are not alone. Many a soul struggles at this very moment with divine silence. And to make matters worse, it grinds on for days, sometimes weeks. Following a calamity, the victim crawls out, cries out, and expects overnight relief. It doesn't come. A mate who has been there for years suddenly packs it in and walks out. The one who is left alone to face what seems to be endless responsibilities turns to God for His intervention—for His comforting reassurance only to be met with silence. That awful silence! Equally difficult is a lingering illness. No prayer, it seems, is effective. As the deafening silence continues from above, pain intensifies below.

Believe it or not, this grand song that directs our attention to the skies has something to say about those anguishing times of silence on earth. In beautiful ways the heavens above us speak with profound wisdom.

The philosopher Kant once wrote:

> There are two things that fill my soul with holy reverence and evergrowing wonder—the spectacle of the starry sky that virtually annihilates us as physical beings, and the moral law which raises us to infinite dignity as intelligent agents.[2]

Kant could have been influenced by the Nineteenth Psalm when he wrote that statement, for this song describes both of the things that filled his soul with reverence and wonder.

If you read the lyrics carefully, you will discover that they fall naturally into two sections. So obvious is the dividing line that some have come to the conclusion it was composed by two different people—each emphasizing a particular subject. Such is not the case, however, for David is named as the single writer.

OUTLINE

The dividing line falls between verses 6 and 7. The first section (vv. 1–6) deals with the world God has created. It describes in vivid fashion the fact that His creative work sets forth His power and His glory. The second section (vv. 7–13) deals with the truth God has communicated. It describes some of the benefits derived from the Scriptures as well as the discernment it can bring to one's personal life. The song concludes with a prayer (v. 14). What a message of hope it brings to all who struggle with the grind of divine silence. All the way through the song, David reminds us that the Lord is not only close to His creatures, He cares for us as well.

I. The World God Has Created (vv. 1–6)
    A. Overall Declaration (vv. 1–4)
        1. Consistent (vv. 1–2)
        2. Silent (v. 3)
        3. Universal (v. 4)
    B. Specific Illustration—the Sun (vv. 4–6)
        1. Appearance Described (vv. 4–5)
            a. "tent"
            b. "bridegroom"
            c. "strong man"
        2. Activity Described (v. 6)
            a. "its rising"
            b. "its circuit"
            c. "its heat"

II. The Truth God Has Communicated (vv. 7–13)
- A. Its Presence among Us (vv. 7–9)
  1. Titles (five are given)
  2. Characteristics (six are given)
  3. Benefits (four are given)
- B. Its Value to Us (v. 10)
  1. Gold . . . fine gold
  2. Honey . . . honeycomb
- C. Its Work within Us (vv. 11–13)
  1. Warning
  2. Rewarding
  3. Discerning
  4. Revealing

III. Closing prayer (v. 14)

We will hit only the highlights of these fourteen verses because neither time nor space permits us to dig into the depths of each one. However, I urge you to take the outline and use it as a guide in your own, personal study of this magnificent composition. It is a veritable treasure house of truth.

THE WORLD GOD HAS CREATED

The heavens are telling of the glory of God;
And their expanse is declaring the work of His hands.
Day to day pours forth speech,
And night to night reveals knowledge.
There is no speech, nor are there words;
Their voice is not heard.
Their line has gone out through all the earth,
And their utterances to the end of the world.
In them He has placed a tent for the sun,
Which is as a bridegroom coming out of his chamber;
It rejoices as a strong man to run his course.
Its rising is from one end of the heavens,
And its circuit to the other end of them;
And there is nothing hidden from its heat. [vv. 1–6]

For six verses David looks heavenward. He ponders the vast spaces beyond, that realm we call natural phenomena. He tells us that God uses "the heavens" and "their expanse" to declare His glory and His power (v. 1).

After this general statement, David reminds us that this declaration is (1) consistent—"day to day . . . night to night," (2) silent—"no speech, nor . . . words . . . Their voice is not heard," and (3) universal—"all the earth . . . to the end of the world."

God's majestic universe contains a message. It is, in fact, a bold announcement! Regardless of the time of day, location, or our native language, if we look up, we are able to "hear" His message! And what, specifically, is the message? The answer is in Romans 1:18–20:

> For the wrath of God is revealed from heaven against all ungodliness and unrighteousness of men, who suppress the truth in unrighteousness, because that which is known about God is evident within them; for God made it evident to them. For since the creation of the world His invisible attributes, His eternal power and divine nature, have been clearly seen, being understood through what has been made, so that they are without excuse.

Did you grasp that? God reveals "His eternal power and divine nature" so clearly that everyone is left "without excuse." Don't tell me that God has hidden Himself from the world! Every intelligent being lives every waking moment under the constant reminder of God's presence, sovereignty, and power. Stubborn unbelief causes humanity to miss God's persistent message. Anyone who struggles with the mystery of divine silence—whether it's while picking up the pieces after a disaster, or recovering from the loss of a loved one, or trying to find a burst of hope to go on beyond a divorce—needs only to look up. God is speaking!

More specifically, consider the sun's symbolism in Psalm 19:4–6: Both its appearance and activity provide ample information to anyone who asks: "Is there a God?" No one other than our God could create, sustain, and employ such a heavenly body as the sun. Its size, temperature, and distance from us (thanks to the perfect filter system of our atmosphere) provide us with just the right level of heat and light.

THE TRUTH GOD HAS COMMUNICATED

The law of the Lord is perfect, restoring the soul;
The testimony of the Lord is sure, making wise the simple.
The precepts of the Lord are right, rejoicing the heart;
The commandment of the Lord is pure, enlightening the eyes.
The fear of the Lord is clean, enduring forever;
The judgments of the Lord are true; they are righteous
    altogether.
They are more desirable than gold, yes, than much fine gold;
Sweeter also than honey and the drippings of the honeycomb.
Moreover, by them Thy servant is warned;
In keeping them there is great reward.
Who can discern his errors? Acquit me of hidden faults.
Also keep back Thy servant from presumptuous sins;
Let them not rule over me;
Then I shall be blameless,
And I shall be acquitted of great transgression.
Let the words of my mouth and the meditation of my heart
Be acceptable in Thy sight,
O Lord, my rock and my redeemer. [vv. 7–13]

The heavens may declare God's power and glory, but they do not declare His will or His plan and promise of salvation. God has communicated those marvelous truths in His Word—the living Scriptures, the Bible. Notice the change from God (vv. 1–6) to Lord (vv. 7–14). David includes in this second part of the song a more personal example of *God's presence.*

Observe first the titles God gives His Word—"law . . . testimony . . . precepts . . . commandments . . . judgments." Next, observe the characteristics of Scripture—"perfect . . . sure . . . right . . . pure . . . true . . . righteous." Then, observe the benefits it provides—"restoring the soul . . . making wise the simple . . . rejoicing the heart . . . enlightening the eyes." Talk about communicating something with effectiveness! No one could name another book or any other piece of literature that can do such an effective job in the life of mankind. God is not silent!

Then, as you would expect, David sets forth the *value of Scripture*. He uses two illustrations for the purpose of comparison:

1. Gold . . . fine gold (v. 10). In David's day, this was considered among the most precious of possessions. Man's wealth was based on the amount of gold he owned. The "fine gold" is purified gold . . . gold that had been melted down with maximum impurities and alloy removed.

2. Honey . . . honeycomb (v. 10). Turning from a precious element to a food, David declares God's Word to be sweeter than the most delectable of foods. Note that it is not just honey, but honey flowing from the combs. Makes my mouth water! Consider honey momentarily.

- It is provided through the work of someone other than ourselves; the bee virtually lays it on our platter.

- It is a natural food that doesn't need a lengthy time of digestion before it goes to work. Immediately, honey provides energy.

- Its taste is altogether unique. No other sweetness is quite like the rich taste of honey.

Honey—what a fitting analogy!

Read those three things again with God's Word in mind. Through the efforts of another, we have His Word. It goes to work immediately upon entering our spiritual system. And no other piece of literature can even compare with its uniqueness. No wonder God's Word is said to be "living and active and sharper than any two-edged sword" (Heb. 4:12).

Finally, verses 11–13 tell us of specific ways God's truth works within us. Through the Scriptures we are warned of evil and potential dangers. The individual who really knows (and applies!) his Bible is kept from numerous sins simply because he believes God's warning signals. Then, biblical truths assure us of personal <u>reward</u>—"great reward." Furthermore, they provide us with <u>discernment</u>—the ability to know right from wrong. Simple though that may sound, that is one of the signs of maturity, according to Hebrews 5:14. "But solid food is for the mature, who because of practice have their senses trained to discern good and evil."

God's Word also <u>reveals</u> error, sin, presumption, and transgression to those who ponder the pages of Scripture.

CLOSING PRAYER

Verse 14, one of the most familiar verses in the entire Book of Psalms, adequately sums up the psalmist's feelings in the form of a prayer:

> Let the words of my mouth and the meditation of my heart
> Be acceptable in Thy sight,
> O Lord, my rock and my redeemer. [v. 14]

God has revealed Himself. We constantly bask in the sunlight of His presence. We have His Word in our language—clearly printed and conveniently punctuated, bound, and preserved for our use. Added to this, He stands as our Rock (stability, One on whom we can rely) and our Redeemer (deliverance from evil acts, evil men, and our own evil nature).

Stay in the Word this week, my friend. Claim His blessings—dare Him to fulfill His promises. The "words of your mouth" and "meditation of your heart" will take on a whole new pattern of godliness and power. Furthermore, He will no longer seem distant from you or silent to you.

REFLECTIONS ON DIVINE SILENCE

1. How often we are tempted to think of our God as being distant and silent! According to the song we just studied, He is neither. This week pay closer attention to the natural phenomena that surround you, all of which speak of God's presence. Look up. Look around. Look down. Meditate on the many ways He makes His presence known. Weave those thoughts into your moments of solitude and ask Him to comfort you in tangible ways.

2. Since this song uses gold and honey as illustrations of the value of God's Word, let's focus on both. Perhaps you will want to discuss the analogies with your family or a friend. Eat some honey and remind yourself of its sweetness. Examine the beauty of a gold necklace or ring. Draw a few conclusions of your own. Talk about them.

3. Go back into Psalm 19. Locate the mention of "errors" and "hidden faults" (v. 12) as well as "presumptuous sins" (v. 13). Think about the difference during the week. By the end of the week, talk to the Lord about each in your own life.

Psalm

A Psalm of David.

The Lord is my shepherd,
I shall not want.
He makes me lie down in green
pastures;
He leads me beside quiet waters.
He restores my soul;
He guides me in the paths of
righteousness
For His name's sake.

Even though I walk through the valley of
the shadow of death,
I fear no evil; for Thou art with me;
Thy rod and Thy staff, they comfort me.
Thou dost prepare a table before me in
the presence of my enemies;
Thou hast anointed my head with oil;
My cup overflows.
Surely goodness and lovingkindness will
follow me all the days of my life,
And I will dwell in the house of the Lord
forever.   [23:1–6]

THE GRIND OF
UNCERTAINTY

No one would deny that Psalm 23 is the most familiar, best-loved portion of the Book of Psalms—perhaps of the entire Bible! It has endeared itself to people in every circumstance of life:

- The soldier in battle, fearing injury and possible death
- The grieving widow standing before a fresh grave, wondering how she can go on with her life
- The guilty wanderer seeking forgiveness and direction
- The lonely stranger longing for love and companionship
- The suffering saint strapped to a bed of pain
- The orphan and the forgotten
- The depressed and the jobless
- The prison inmate and the persecuted
- The prodigal and the divorced

All have felt the stinging daily grind of uncertainty. To each one (and thousands more) Psalm 23 brings solace and peace. When the "chips are down" and our hearts are heaviest, it is to this magnificent "Psalm of the Shepherd" we most often turn. The preschooler knows it by heart, yet it is a silent partner of the retired—and always fitting at a funeral. From the cradle to the grave, Psalm 23 provides timeless comfort and endless assurance for those who lack the secure feeling of God's perpetual presence.

I have observed that few inner battles are more fierce than the daily grind of uncertainty. No doubt you too have encountered one or more of its many faces as you have struggled with a career choice, direction in life, purpose in pain, job security, financial pressures, physical handicaps, relational snags, and a dozen other confusing puzzles not quickly or easily solved.

Because of the popularity of this song and the numerous truths that are hidden in it, we will want to spend more time on it than we have on the others. Therefore, I've chosen not to give a formal outline. Instead we will consider the analogy of sheep to the children of God, the theme of constant provision by our Shepherd-Lord, and an explanation of each verse.

ANALOGY

One cannot read Psalm 23 without realizing that it is written from the viewpoint of a sheep. It is as though a sheep were considering its life among the flock with its shepherd and recording its feelings and observations. Consider some of the analogies between helpless sheep and God's frail children:

1. Sheep lack a sense of direction. Unlike cats and dogs, sheep can get lost easily—even in the familiar environment of their own territory. So it is with believers—we cannot guide ourselves. We must rely completely on the Word of God and the voice of our Shepherd-Savior.

2. Sheep are virtually defenseless. Most animals have a rather effective means of defense—sharp claws; teeth; speed; ability to hide; keenness of smell, sight, and hearing; great strength; ferocity. But sheep are awkward, weak, and ignorant; they have spindle legs and tiny hoofs, and are pitifully slow, even devoid of an angry growl. Defenseless! The only

sure protection for the sheep is the ever-watchful shepherd. So it is with the believer, who is admonished to be strong—"in the Lord" (Eph. 6:10).

3. <u>Sheep are easily frightened</u>. Being ignorant, unimpressive in stature, and very much aware of their weakness, sheep find comfort only in their shepherd's presence and reassuring songs in the night. Psalm 27:1 also refers to this type of Shepherd-Lord relationship which we have with God.

4. <u>Sheep are, by nature, unclean</u>. Other animals lick, scrape, and roll in the grass to cleanse themselves—but not sheep. They will remain filthy indefinitely unless the shepherd cleanses them. We, too, by nature, are unclean and filthy. Apart from our tender Shepherd's cleansing (1 John 1:7–9) we would remain perpetually dirty.

5. <u>Sheep cannot find food or water</u>. While most animals have a keen sense of smell, sheep depend upon their shepherd completely. If left to themselves, sheep will eat poisonous weeds and die—and when one does it the others will follow the leader. Again, as children of God, we are equally dependent.

6. <u>The sheep's wool does not belong to the sheep</u>. While sheep may produce wool, the shepherd owns their wool. All bona fide spiritual production in the life of the Christian belongs to the Lord. The Lord, by means of the Holy Spirit, provides for all such production. In every way, you see, we are indeed "His people and the sheep of His pasture" (Ps. 100:3).

THEME

Like many of the psalms, Psalm 23 states its case in the first verse and simply verifies it in the remainder of the song.

The key thought is this: Because the Lord is my Shepherd, I shall not want for anything—I shall lack nothing! No uncertainty should frighten me. Here is the way the theme of Psalm 23 is played out in the balance of David's famous song:

I shall not lack rest or provision—why?
He makes me lie down in green pastures.
I shall not lack peace—why?
He leads me beside quiet waters.
I shall not lack restoration or encouragement when I faint, fail, or
  fall—why?
He restores my soul.
I shall not lack guidance or fellowship—why?
He guides me in the paths of righteousness.
I shall not lack courage when my way is dark—why?
Even though I walk through the valley of the shadow of death, I
  fear no evil.
I shall not lack companionship—why?
For Thou art with me.
I shall not lack constant comfort—why?
Thy rod and Thy staff, they comfort me.
I shall not lack protection or honor—why?
Thou dost prepare a table before me in the presence of my enemies.
I shall not lack power—why?
Thou hast anointed my head with oil.
I shall not lack abundance—why?
My cup overflows.
I shall not lack God's perpetual presence—why?
Surely goodness and mercy shall follow me all the days of my life.
I shall not lack security—why?
And I will dwell in the house of the Lord forever.

EXPLANATION

Although familiar in its form, Psalm 23 develops an unfamiliar metaphor throughout. I am referring to the shepherd-sheep experience. Few people in America have even seen a flock of sheep under a shepherd's care, much less experienced the everyday occurrences common to that mode of life. Because the scene is unfamiliar, many are at a loss to explain this song in its basic sense, for David drew his words from the memory of those years he had spent on the Judean hillside with his father's flock. I suggest you get hold of a book that describes the life of a shepherd—or better still, talk with someone who has worked with sheep. Believe me; the psalm will burst into life for you. No one can adequately enter into the depths of this beloved psalm unless he or she first becomes familiar with the way a shepherd relates to his sheep.

Verse 1

As I've already stated, this verse gives us the theme of the song. But for now I call your attention to two things in this sentence:

1. David refers to God as "the Lord." This is the translation of *Jehovah*—the most respected, loftiest title a Jew could utter. The Hebrews stood in awe before it—it was so holy that they substituted it with some lesser title for God whenever it occurred in their public reading of sacred Scripture. *Jehovah* means "the I AM," the self-existent Being; He who was and is and is to come, who inhabits eternity, who has life in Himself.

F. B. Meyer writes of this title:

> . . . All other life, from the aphid on the rose-leaf to the archangel before the throne, is dependent and derived. All others waste and change and grow old; He only is unchangeably the same. All others are fires, which He supplies with fuel; He alone is self-sustained. This mighty Being is our Shepherd![3]

From our perspective today, the Lord Jesus Christ is the Shepherd of this psalm.

2. David calls Jehovah "*my* Shepherd." To David (the sheep), God was his own, personal Shepherd. Millions of people know that the Lord is *a* Shepherd, but they really don't know that He is *their* Shepherd.

Who, by the way, is *your* Shepherd? In whom do you trust when you are feeling caught in the daily grind of uncertainty? To whom do you turn for direction? You have many choices. Do you go first to your pastor? Your psychologist? Your close friend? Your coach? Your priest? Your teacher? How easy to forget that they are sheep, too! As important and necessary as each of these people may be, they can never take the place of the Good Shepherd in your life. When you finally come to the place where *all* of your life—in all its detail—is placed in Christ's care, you can say with a deep, abiding certainty, "The Lord is *my* Shepherd, I shall not want."

Verse 2

Now the number-one composer of Israel begins to develop the theme he stated in verse 1. He starts with the pastoral picture of sheep under a shepherd's care. I am told that sheep, being stupid animals, frequently are alarmed and actually run over each other, racing away from something that startles them. The shepherd corrects the problem by catching a sheep and gently, yet firmly, forcing it to lie down and feed quietly on the grass beneath its feet. David remembers such an occasion as he says, "He makes me lie down. . . ."

In our hectic, hurried, harassed age in which headache medications have become the best-selling national product, we must occasionally be *made* to lie down by our Shepherd-Savior. When He steps into our helter-skelter world, He often *forces* us to rest. If that has occurred, give thanks—the pastures are green!

This verse concludes with another pleasant picture: "He leads me beside quiet waters." Look at that phrase. Literally, it refers to waters that have been stilled. Mentally capture the peaceful scene. The sheep are weary and worn. They need a long, refreshing drink from the rapid stream nearby. But sheep are instinctively afraid of running water. Perhaps they think that if water should get on their heavy coats of wool, they would become waterlogged and sink beneath the surface of a stream. As a result, even though tired and hot from a blistering day, thirsty sheep will only stand and stare at the fast-flowing stream but never drink. Uncertainty keeps them from needed refreshment.

The shepherd then steps in. With his rod and staff he loosens a few large stones and dams up a place, causing the rushing waters to slow their current. The now quiet waters immediately attract the sheep. In the midst of a rushing stream, the shepherd has provided refreshment for the flock with water he has stilled.

Has your Shepherd done this? Has He recently stepped in and made those busy currents of your life a source of refreshment by stilling them, by bringing order out of chaos? Isn't it true that we frequently receive spiritual refreshment from uncertain circumstances we dreaded most?

Verse 3

"He restores my soul. . . ." *Restoration.* What a full, meaningful term! Again, there is that familiar scene along the hillside. Sheep have a bad habit of wandering. When one is attracted to a clump of grass away from the flock, off he goes, and sometimes he's followed by several other woolly wanderers. Soon, night falls. Lurking in the darkness are hungry wolves, four-legged savages, looking for a supper of mutton! The shepherd counts his sheep, calling them by name.

Realizing he has a wanderer missing, he strikes out to "restore" that wandering member of his flock . . . calling its name and awaiting an answering bleat out in the wilderness beneath the eerie glow of the moon.

Occasionally, one particular young sheep will get into a habit of wandering. Again and again the shepherd will have to go and find the wandering lamb. When such occurs too often, the shepherd will lift the lamb from the thistles and cactus, hold it close, and abruptly break its leg. He will make a splint for the shattered leg and then carry that once-wayward lamb near his heart. That sheep learns a bitter lesson and all the while depends completely upon its shepherd during the period of *restoration.*

Do I write to a wandering sheep? Do my words fall upon one of God's children who has gotten into a habit of drifting from the flock? Let me remind you of one important word—*He.* It is *He,* the Shepherd-Savior who will restore you. He is looking for you if you have strayed away. He is jealous for your love.

He wants you back . . . and I must warn you—He will stop at nothing in order to restore you. God doesn't play games—especially with His wayward woollies!

Finally, verse 3 promises guidance. Look at the last part of this verse. Literally, it means: "He guides me in the right tracks for His name's sake."

The Palestinian shepherd was a master at reading tracks. Many marks and paths sprawled across the rugged terrain. Some were made by wilderness beasts, others by robbers lying in wait. The wind also etched its subtle "track" in the sand. To the untrained, dull eye of the sheep, they all looked alike—like real paths. But they led nowhere. The sheep were wise to follow only their shepherd, who always led them along the "right track." After all, it was the shepherd's reputation that was at stake: ". . . for His name's sake."

The application is obvious. Many voices shout for our attention. Many religions plead for a hearing. Many media ministries beg for the public's involvement (especially our financial support). Many "new doctrines" seduce us to listen . . . and, alas, many are led astray! When we follow our Shepherd, however, we follow along the "right tracks." His written Word gives us the guidance we need so desperately.

The tone changes in the latter half of Psalm 23 . . . but not the Shepherd! From the verdant, fertile slopes and bubbling brooks of verses 2 and 3, we are plunged immediately down into the "valley of the shadow of death"—literally translated the "valley of deep darkness." How does this tie in with verse 3? You'll observe that verse 3 promises that our Shepherd-Savior guides us along "right tracks." Verse 4 is simply saying that one of these tracks or paths winds along the steep, downward valley below. There is a reason for this.

Verse 4

This scene is familiar to those who know the habit of shepherds. Early in the year the flocks graze leisurely in the lowlands, but as summer's sun begins to melt the high mountain snow, the shepherd leads his flock to better grazing land above. This trip inevitably includes some dangerous paths filled with uncertainties and fearful sights. The way is dark, unfamiliar, difficult. The "valley of deep darkness" leads along turbid waters crashing and foaming over jagged rocks. The trees periodically blot out the sunlight and there are serpents coiled to strike as well as hungry wolves lurking in the shadows. But the sheep walking beside his shepherd is secure, though naturally frightened, because the shepherd is near, leading the way, fully aware of the valley's path. Such a scene was as familiar to David as a sheet of music is to an orchestra conductor . . . or a mechanical drawing to an engineer. The ancient shepherd-made-king mentally sifts through those earlier days as a lad in the wilderness with his father's flock and pictures himself as a sheep: "Even though *I* walk through the valley. . . ."

We, as God's sheep, are sometimes led by Him into the valley of darkness, where there is fear, danger, uncertainty, and the unexpected. He knows that the only way we can reach the higher places of Christian experience and maturity is not on the playground of prosperity but in the schoolroom of suffering. Along those dark, narrow, pinching, uncomfortable valleys of difficulty we learn volumes! We keep our courage simply because our Shepherd is leading the way. Perhaps that is what the writer had in mind when he exhorted us to keep ". . . fixing our eyes on Jesus. . . . For consider Him . . . so that you may not grow weary and lose heart" (Heb. 12:2–3).

Notice that the psalmist says because "Thou art with me" he is kept from being afraid. Mark it down, my friend. There is *no* experience, *no* valley (no matter how severe or uncertain) that we must journey alone.

Take special note of what David claims as his source of comfort: the Lord's rod and staff. The shepherd's rod was a symbol of his power. Actually, it was an oak club about two feet in length. It was used to defend the flock against wild beasts. The head of this rod was round, usually whittled from the knot of a tree—in which the shepherd had pounded sharp bits of metal. One expositor remarks:

A skillful shepherd not only swung the club to smash the head of an attacker, but he could also hurl the club like a missile over the heads of his flock to strike a wolf lurking in the distance.[4]

The shepherd, by being well-armed with this heavy club, could deal death-giving blows to a lion or bear or stealthy thief imperiling the safety of one of his charges.

The shepherd's staff was his crook, which was bent or hooked at one end. It provided the shepherd with an instrument for prying a sheep loose from a thicket, pushing branches aside along the narrow path, and pulling wandering sheep out of holes into which they had fallen. He also used it to beat down high grass to drive out snakes and wild beasts. Like the rod, the staff was a symbol of the shepherd's power and strength.

The sheep took comfort in the strength of its shepherd. No need to be uncomfortable with the power of God. We are to find relief and peace of mind in the fact that *He is able.* When surrounded and outnumbered by enemies, it should bring relief to us in realizing that He will use His "rod" and "staff" to protect us.

Verse 5

In spite of the fact that this song has many full and meaningful phrases, the first portion of this verse initially seems difficult to understand. Suddenly, the analogy breaks down. No sheep ever ate at a literal "table" prepared for it. And what does it mean "in the presence of my enemies . . ."? Abruptly, we are transported from the green pastures, the valley, and the rugged mountainside to "a table" in the enemy's presence. The picture may appear to change, but again, the common experience of a shepherd with his flock brings us understanding.

I have Charles W. Slemming to thank for help with this verse. He has done a masterful piece of work in his writings concerning shepherds in the Middle East.[5]

In this case he tells of the shepherd who comes to a new field in which he plans to graze his flock. The shepherd doesn't just turn them loose, he inspects the field for vipers—small brown adders that live under the ground. They frequently pop up out of their tiny holes and nip the sheep on their noses. The bite from these natural enemies sometimes causes an inflammation which can, on occasion, kill the stricken sheep.

Knowing this danger, the shepherd restrains his sheep from a new field (which may be infested) until he can inspect it. He walks up and down, looking for the small holes. Upon finding these holes, he takes a bottle of thick oil from his girdle.

Then, raking down the long grass with his staff, he pours a circle of oil at the top of each viper's hole. Before he leads the sheep into the new, green field, he also spreads the oil over each sheep's head—in that sense he "anoints" them (rubbing their heads) with his oil. When the vipers beneath the surface sense the presence of sheep and attempt to attack from their holes, they are unable to do so. Their smooth bodies cannot pass over the slippery oil—they become prisoners inside their own holes.

The oil on the sheep's head also acts as a repellent, so if a viper does manage to come near, the smell drives the serpent away. Therefore, in a very literal sense, by oiling the vipers' burrows, the shepherd has prepared the table—the meadow—and the sheep are able to graze in abundance right in the enemy's presence.

The Lord does that for His people. He frequently sends us on missions that include some danger and overt peril, but even then we bask in His protective mercy and Spirit-directed security. It is good for us to remember that our Lord prayed *not* that we would be taken "out of the world" but that we might be kept "from the evil one" (John 17:15). God's plan for us is not isolation—it's *insulation*.

We dare not overlook "My cup overflows." This refers not to oil, but to water—cool well water so refreshing to a weary sheep's parched tongue.

When there were no streams, a shepherd quenched his flock's thirst beside a well—rather rare in the wilderness. Some wells were deep—as much as a hundred feet down to the water. To draw the water, the shepherd used a long rope with a leather bucket at the end. Since the bucket held less than a gallon and had to be drawn by hand, then poured into large stone cups beside the well, the process was long and laborious. If the flock numbered a hundred, the shepherd could easily spend two hours or more if he allowed them to drink all they wished. Sheep do not like to get wet—and it was a mark of special kindness to keep the cups filled to the brim so they could drink with ease. Only a kind, considerate shepherd satisfied his thirsty sheep with overflowing cups.

How lavishly our Father provides! What bounty! What abundance! Ephesians 3:20 describes our Shepherd-God as One who does "exceeding abundantly beyond all that we ask or think." Not just barely, but abundantly!

I like the way Haddon Robinson expresses this thought:

> With Him the calf is always the fatted calf; the robe is always the best robe; the joy is unspeakable; and the peace passes understanding. There is no grudging in God's goodness. He does not measure His goodness by drops like a druggist filling a prescription. It comes to us in floods. If only we recognized the lavish abundance of His gifts, what a difference it would make in our lives! If every meal were taken as a gift from His hand, it would be almost a sacrament.[6]

May God give us a fresh realization of the overwhelming abundance He provides. Indeed, our cup overflows.

Verse 6

In his book *The Shepherd Psalm,* F. B. Meyer refers to "goodness and lovingkindness" as our "celestial escort."[7] Another quaint commentator suggests that these are "God's sheepdogs" ever near His flock, ever nipping at our heels, always available.[8] Perhaps that is a fitting analogy, especially when we consider that they "follow" us. Because we are "prone to wander, prone to leave the God we love." He sends His faithful companions out after us—goodness and mercy—kindness and *loving*kindness. Our Lord deals with us so kindly, so graciously. What a difference between God and man! Let *man* go on a search for a wayward soul and there is often bitterness and revenge and impatience in his steps, especially if the search is lengthy. But with God, there is goodness and lovingkindness.

I am convinced that one of the reasons the prodigal son "came to himself" and finally returned home was because of the kind of father he had. There is no magnet with a stronger pull than genuine love. Love has drawn back more wanderers and broken more hard hearts than this world will ever know.

It is fitting, then, that you and I are followed "all the days" of our lives by goodness and lovingkindness. God knows what will best do the job! How varied are our Lord's methods.

When God wants to drill a man
  And thrill a man
  And skill a man,
When God wants to mold a man
  To plan the noblest part;
When He yearns with all His heart
  To create so great and bold a man
That all the world shall be amazed,
  Watch His methods, watch His ways!

How He ruthlessly perfects
  Whom He royally elects!
How He hammers him and hurts him,
  And with mighty blows converts him
Into trial shapes of clay which
  Only God understands;
While his tortured heart is crying
  And he lifts beseeching hands!
How He bends but never breaks
  When his good He undertakes;
How He uses whom He chooses
  And with every purpose fuses him;
  By every act induces him
To try His splendour out—
  God knows what He's about![9]

Mark it down, my friend—God knows how to deal with His children. More specifically, He knows how to deal with you. His dealings follow you all the days of your life. Your circumstances *right now* are part of His plan for you.

. . . for it is God who is at work in you, both to will and to work for His good pleasure. [Phil. 2:13]

And we know that God causes all things to work together for good to those who love God, to those who are called according to His purpose. [Rom. 8:28]

This wonderful song concludes with a familiar and comforting thought—"I will dwell in the house of the Lord forever." The psalmist is not referring to a *place* as much as he is to a *Person*. Notice that the Twenty-third Psalm begins and ends with "the Lord." David longed to be in his Lord's house, because he could then be in his Lord's presence.

You see, the ultimate goal in David's heart was a face-to-face relationship with His Lord forever. Instead of vague uncertainty, he had confidence. We Christians will enjoy a never-ending fellowship with God the moment we draw our last earthly breath. What assurance!

That is exactly what Jesus Christ promises those who believe in Him . . . not merely "I hope so" but "I know!" In Him we truly have everything we need.

R EFLECTIONS ON UNCERTAINTY

1. Meditate on the analogy of the shepherd and his flock of sheep. All week long, think of the Lord as your Shepherd. Give Him thanks for meeting your every need. List a few of them here:

_____

_____

_____

_____

_____

2. Have you felt uncertain lately? Maybe a little insecure about the future? Does some "valley of deep darkness" stretch out in front of you? Spend at least five minutes each day this week in prayer. If you can find a place to be all alone so you can get on your knees, do that. Tell God all that is on your heart. Hold nothing back.

3. Goodness and lovingkindness . . . "God's sheepdogs." Have they been staying near you lately? Pick up the phone several times this week and affirm a family member or friend. Remind each one that the Lord's goodness and mercy are keeping watch over them day and night. You might mention the source of your encouragement. Psalm 23 never fails to bring a special touch of comfort.

Psalm

A Psalm of David.

Vindicate me, O Lord, for I have
    walked in my integrity;
    And I have trusted in the Lord
    without wavering.
Examine me, O Lord, and try me;
Test my mind and my heart.
For Thy lovingkindness is before my
    eyes,
And I have walked in Thy truth.
I do not sit with deceitful men,
Nor will I go with pretenders.
I hate the assembly of evildoers,
And I will not sit with the wicked.
I shall wash my hands in innocence,
And I will go about Thine altar, O Lord,
That I may proclaim with the voice of
    thanksgiving,
And declare all Thy wonders.

O Lord, I love the habitation of Thy
    house,
And the place where Thy glory dwells.
Do not take my soul away along with
    sinners,
Nor my life with men of bloodshed,
In whose hands is a wicked scheme,
And whose right hand is full of bribes.
But as for me, I shall walk in my
    integrity;
Redeem me, and be gracious to me.
My foot stands on a level place;
In the congregations I shall bless the
    Lord.   [26:1–12]

THE GRIND OF
MISTREATMENT

If I were asked to give a popular title to this song, it would be: "How to Do Right When You've Been Done Wrong."

We have all been "done wrong," haven't we? Maybe that describes your circumstance right now: an intolerable working situation; a husband, wife, parent, or child who takes advantage of you even when you treat him (or her) kindly; a friend who has turned against you due to a misunderstanding of something you did with only the purest of motives. Such feelings grind away at our peace so severely we wonder how we can continue. Whatever the mistreatment you are having to endure, please accept this warning: DON'T BECOME BITTER! DON'T BACKSLIDE!

The whole thrust of David's ancient composition, according to verse 1, has to do with some undeserved wrong he was enduring—and his determination to trust in his Lord "without wavering." Read the first verse again, only this time more slowly, to sense the feeling behind it: "Vindicate me, O Lord, for I have walked in my integrity; / And I have trusted in the Lord without wavering."

Descriptive phrase, "without wavering." The Hebrew verb which is translated "wavering" means "to slip, slide, totter, shake." David is saying that in spite of the daily grind of mistreatment he was living under, he was so determined to trust the Lord he would not slip or slide under the load! That explains why he begins the psalm with such an emotional plea: "Vindicate me, O Lord." You see, by his own honest admission, he was right; he was walking in integrity. That was not pride; he was stating a fact to his Lord. As he continues, he reviews the specific things that kept him upright while under unfair attacks.

Let's move through the song, keeping its theme in mind. As we do so, we will uncover six things David mentions which kept him (and will keep us) from slipping into bitterness and resentment during times of mistreatment.

1. Be open before the Lord: "Examine me, O Lord, and try me; / Test my mind and my heart" (v. 2). In three different ways David encourages His Lord to prove his inner being: "Examine . . . try . . . test. . . ."

These three English terms represent three different Hebrew terms. The first one is *bah-chan,* meaning "to examine, prove, scrutinize." It is clearly portrayed in Psalm 139:23–24 by the word *search.*

> Search me, O God, and know my heart;
> Try me and know my anxious thoughts;
> And see if there be any hurtful way in me,
> And lead me in the everlasting way.

Literally, he is asking God to "make an examination" of his inner being, to "scrutinize" him through and through.

The next term, translated "try" in verse 2, is the Hebrew *nah-sah,* which means to "test, try, prove." Deuteronomy 8:2 uses the term with its intensive (Piel) stem, meaning "an intensive test":

> And you shall remember all the way which the Lord your God has led you in the wilderness these forty years, that He might humble you, *testing* you, to know what was in your heart, whether you would keep His commandments or not. [Emphasis mine.]

God put the Israelites to an intensive test so that the real condition of their heart might be exposed.

The third term, rendered "test" in verse 2, is yet another Hebrew verb—*tzah-raff.* This is such a vivid word! Literally, it means "to smelt, refine, test." Of the thirty-two times in the Old

Testament it appears in verb form, twenty-two of those times it is linked with the activity of refining gold or silver, removing the dross and impurities.

Do you grasp the principle? When wrong comes your way, be open before the Lord. Invite Him (1) to make an internal search and examination of your life, for the purpose of determining your character, (2) to undertake an intensive, in-depth process of revealing to you the real condition of your heart, and (3) to melt and refine you . . . remove the dross and impurities which this particular mistreatment has brought to the surface. In other words, openly welcome His internal divine surgery on your innermost being. Look upon the wrong that comes your way as a choice opportunity to become increasingly more transparent and pure before the Lord. Ask Him for insight—for a full disclosure of your inner person.

Consider James 1:2–4 from J. B. Phillips' paraphrase:

> When all kinds of trials and temptations crowd into your lives, my brothers, don't resent them as intruders, but welcome them as friends! Realize that they come to test your faith and to produce in you the quality of endurance. But let the process go on until that endurance is fully developed, and you will find you have become men of mature character with the right sort of independence.

2. <u>Remember his love and continue to obey His word</u>: "For Thy lovingkindness is before my eyes, / And I have walked in Thy truth" (Ps. 26:3).

That statement implies two very subtle yet common temptations that occur when mistreatment comes our way:

    a. We doubt God's love.
    b. We drift into disobedience.

David declares, "Thy lovingkindness is before my eyes. . . ." How descriptive! He is admitting whatever comes before him; he looks at it through the lovingkindness of His Lord. It was God's lovingkindness that served as his mental "filter." Then, lest he drift into the ugly yet common temptation to strike back, he states that it is "in Thy truth" he continues to walk. Do you see this? His eyes are on the Lord's *love* for him . . . and his guide through the maze of mistreatment is the Lord's *truth.*

Are you aware of the best proof of love? It is obedience. Our Lord reminds us of that in John 14:15, 21, 23:

> "If you love Me, you will keep My commandments." [v. 15]

> "He who has My commandments and keeps them, he it is who loves Me; and he who loves Me shall be loved by My Father, and I will love him, and will disclose Myself to him." [v. 21]

> Jesus answered and said to him, "If anyone loves Me, he will keep My word; and my Father will love him, and We will come to him, and make Our abode with him." [v. 23]

If you are confident that someone really loves you, you will neither doubt nor drift in your response. Instead, you will find great delight in pleasing that individual. There is nothing quite like love to motivate us from within.

3. Refuse the temptation to get even:

> I do not sit with deceitful men,
> Nor will I go with pretenders.
> I hate the assembly of evildoers,
> And I will not sit with the wicked. [vv. 4–5]

This matter of getting involved with the wrong crowd is a byproduct of doubting and drifting. We are especially vulnerable to this trap when we have been mistreated. You will always find a group of people who will encourage your compromising and rebelling—those who say, "Why put up with that? Listen, you've got your rights; *fight back!*"

Consider David's plight. Perhaps it was when Saul hunted for him out of jealousy. David did not deserve such unfair treatment. Surely he had well-meaning friends who encouraged him to retaliate, to "get back" at Saul. On more than one occasion he deliberately resisted getting even, though a few of his friends urged him to do so. David felt that if the Lord was able to protect him, He was able to handle his enemies as well. (You may wish to stop and read 1 Samuel 24:1–20 and 26:6–12).

Then again, David may have written this song while he was going through the torment of those days when his favored son Absalom conspired against him and unfairly attempted to take the throne of Israel away from him (2 Sam. 15:1–6). This finally resulted in David's having to run for his life. Wisely, even though mistreated, David never did attempt to "get back" at his son or listen to the carnal advice of men around him.

Perhaps you have fallen prey to the unwise counsel of wrong associates. In the words of Psalm 26, when this happens you "sit with deceitful [worthless] men" and "go with pretenders [hypocrites]." Consider also the words of 1 Corinthians 15:33: "Do not be deceived: 'Bad company corrupts good morals.'"

How very true! You cannot identify yourself with wrong associates and walk away unaffected. The point is clear: Do not let mistreatment cause you to turn to the godless crowd or adopt their way of handling things. It may seem logical, but getting even often backfires; and it never glorifies God!

4. Maintain a positive attitude:

> I shall wash my hands in innocence,
> And I will go about Thine altar, O Lord,
> That I may proclaim with the voice of thanksgiving,
> And declare all Thy wonders. [vv. 6–7]

David is so concerned that his heart remain right, he refers to "washing his hands" and staying near "Thine altar." These are word pictures familiar to the Jews. In Exodus 30:17–21 the laver (basin) of bronze that belonged in the Tabernacle is mentioned. It was used for the washing of the priests' hands and feet before they approached the altar to minister. If they failed to wash, they were killed by the Lord!

David picks up that very important and serious principle in his song on mistreatment and applies it to his situation. He stayed very near his Lord at this time, making sure his sins were confessed and his heart attitude was clean. By doing so, he remained positive. This did not guarantee, however, that the mistreatment suddenly ended. Listen to Psalm 73:13–14:

> Surely in vain I have kept my heart pure,
> And washed my hands in innocence;
> For I have been stricken all day long,
> And chastened every morning.

Let's not think that a clean, godly life is always immediately blessed with pleasant circumstances. But rest assured that maintaining the proper relationship with the Lord is still the very best way to endure mistreatment.

Also note that Psalm 26:7 refers to an attitude of *thanksgiving*. David actually proclaimed words of thanksgiving to God for being mistreated. Talk about a positive attitude! The crucial test of giving thanks in everything (1 Thessalonians 5:18) occurs when we suffer mistreatment. That is the supreme test on our attitude of thanksgiving.

I'm thinking of another account much later in biblical times that has to do with the courageous, first-century apostles who were thrown in jail for preaching Christ and doing His work publicly (Acts 5:17–18). After being humiliated and rebuked for their convictions by the religious leaders (v. 28), they were beaten unmercifully and warned not to continue in their ministry of teaching, healing, and casting out demons (v. 40). What is incredible to me is their indomitable, positive attitude:

> So they went on their way from the presence of the Council, rejoicing that they had been considered worthy to suffer shame for His name. And every day, in the temple and from house to house, they kept right on teaching and preaching Jesus as the Christ. [vv. 41–42]

There is every temptation to forget to give God thanks for the privilege of being His example to others when we have been "done wrong." Learn to respond *first* with a genuine "thanks, Lord," when some undeserved attack comes your way. If you do this, you will be unique. Furthermore, a positive attitude clears our minds of needless debris, mental garbage which never fails to counteract all scriptural counsel.

5. Be faithful in public worship: "O Lord, I love the habitation of Thy house, / And the place where Thy glory dwells" (v. 8).

David was quite a man! As I read this verse, I can see why he was known as "a man after God's own heart." Even while he was under the pile, feeling more like a punching bag than a child of the Lord, he remained faithful to the place where he could sense God's glory—the tabernacle (v. 8). You must pause and read three stanzas from three ancient Psalms: 27:4, 65:4, and 84:10. To him, worship was no religious habit, no ritualistic, boring process; it was something essential, something vital. When undergoing mistreatment, David looked up in worship.

Unfortunately, we live in a day of de-emphasis regarding the value and necessity of public worship. I realize that some churches may fail to point the worshiper to the living Christ and to teach His marvelous Word. But this does not mean that all churches and all public worship gatherings are to be ignored! Hebrews 10:23–25 leaves us no option—we are to assemble together for the purpose of mutual stimulation toward the expression of love and good deeds . . . for encouragement! This is so important when undergoing mistreatment. We *need* each other. Christian friend, do not neglect this God-ordained, healthy expression of your faith.

Let me add one more thought here. Show me a believer who consistently neglects the regular services of a church that faithfully preaches and teaches the Word, and I'll show you one whose cutting edge on spiritual things is getting dull—one who is losing ground, spiritually speaking. I detect from my reading of the Book of Acts that the healthy yet persecuted believers mentioned therein absolutely craved every opportunity to meet and worship together. What a healthy example to follow!

6. Patiently stand and wait for relief:

> Do not take my soul away along with sinners,
> Nor my life with men of bloodshed,

> In whose hands is a wicked scheme,
> And whose right hand is full of bribes.
> But as for me, I shall walk in my integrity;
> Redeem me, and be gracious to me.
> My foot stands on a level place;
> In the congregations I shall bless the Lord. [vv. 9–12]

There is something about human nature that prompts us to get busy and quickly work things out. In this section of his song, David implies that such was the activity of those around him. The majority said that they "wouldn't stand for such a thing." All sorts of "wicked schemes" and hands "full of bribes" were implemented by others. Not David!

"But as for me. . . ." In Hebrew, the pronoun is extremely emphatic: "But *me* . . . as for *me!*"

He wanted it known that he wasn't going to panic and, like the majority, get all involved in those anxieties and ulcer-producing activities of self-vindication. No way! What does he say?

> . . . I shall walk in my integrity;
> Redeem me, and be gracious to me.
> My foot stands on a level place; . . .

There's a calmness, a quiet confidence in those words.

- As for my present course: "I . . . walk in integrity."
- As for my defense: "Redeem me . . . be gracious to me."
- As for my inner feelings: "My foot stands. . . ."

What stability! What patience! What assurance and faith! No sleepless nights, no doubts—just patient waiting.

Look back at that term *redeem*. The Hebrew is *rah-dah*, meaning "to ransom, deliver." It is a term of relief—as if in exile. It is the idea of delivering someone from terrible stress and even death. And don't miss that intriguing phrase in verse 12: "My foot stands on a level place. . . ." What interests me is the "level place." It is from a single Hebrew term, *mee-shore*, which can be traced back to the verb *yah-shaar*, meaning "to be smooth, straight." The first term, *mee-shore*, means "level country, a plain." It conveys the idea of a place that has a commanding view—a broad range of vision, in contrast to a place that is down in a deep gorge all shut in.

Do you get the picture? David is pleased to wait quietly on the Lord and remain totally objective. When he waits for God to deliver him, he maintains a panoramic perspective; he is able to look upon the entire process from God's viewpoint, not from his own limited human perspective. In brief, he is able to maintain *wisdom*. We'll examine that term much more in depth when we come to the sayings in Scripture—the Proverbs of Solomon.

You probably anticipate the application. When we patiently wait on the Lord's deliverance, we are able to stay calm and wise in the midst of mistreatment. We can count on Him to be gracious and to deliver us at the right time. All the while, waiting enables us to keep His perspective.

Look back over the six things that will make mistreatment bearable:

1. Be open before the Lord.
2. Remember His love. Continue to obey His Word.
3. Refuse the temptation to get even.
4. Maintain a positive attitude.
5. Be faithful in public worship.
6. Patiently stand and wait for relief.

Do you remember the words of 1 Peter 2:19–21?

> For this finds favor, if for the sake of conscience toward God a man bears up under sorrows when suffering unjustly. For what credit is there if, when you sin and are harshly treated, you endure it with patience? But if when you do what is right and suffer for it you patiently endure it, this finds favor with God. For you have been called for this purpose, since Christ also suffered for you, leaving you an example for you to follow in His steps.

May the thoughts from David's ancient song equip you to do right when you've been done wrong.

R EFLECTIONS ON MISTREATMENT

1. Think of the last time you were mistreated. Now then
   . . . answer these questions very honestly. They may
   hurt, but they deserve an answer:

   a. Have you completely released the offense to God?
   b. Do you hold a grudge?
   c. Are you waiting for the right moment to get even?
   d. Is your walk with the Lord stronger than ever before?

2. Look back over the six principles from David's song. Are
   you at peace with each one or do you need to come to
   terms with one or two? Be completely honest before the
   Lord. Hold nothing back.

3. Do you know of someone right now who is enduring the
   grind of mistreatment? If so, why not write a note of encouragement? You might even share a couple of thoughts
   from your reflections this week. Go easy. Remember the
   importance of tact. People being mistreated can be pretty
   fragile souls.

Psalm

A Psalm of David.

The Lord is my light and my
salvation;
Whom shall I fear?
The Lord is the defense of my
life;
Whom shall I dread?
When evildoers came upon me to devour
my flesh,
My adversaries and my enemies, they
stumbled and fell.
Though a host encamp against me,
My heart will not fear;
Though war arise against me,
In spite of this I shall be confident.

One thing I have asked from the Lord,
that I shall seek:
That I may dwell in the house of the Lord
all the days of my life,
To behold the beauty of the Lord,
And to meditate in His temple.
For in the day of trouble He will conceal
me in His tabernacle;
In the secret place of His tent He will
hide me;
He will lift me up on a rock.
And now my head will be lifted up
above my enemies around me;
And I will offer in His tent sacrifices
with shouts of joy;
I will sing, yes, I will sing praises to the
Lord.

Hear, O Lord, when I cry with my voice,
And be gracious to me and answer me.
When Thou didst say, "Seek My face," my
heart said to Thee,
"Thy face, O Lord, I shall seek."
Do not hide Thy face from me,
Do not turn Thy servant away in anger;
Thou hast been my help;
Do not abandon me nor forsake me,
O God of my salvation!
For my father and my mother have
forsaken me,
But the Lord will take me up.

Teach me Thy way, O Lord,
And lead me in a level path,
Because of my foes.
Do not deliver me over to the desire of
my adversaries;
For false witnesses have risen against me,
And such as breathe out violence.
I would have despaired unless I had
believed that I would see the goodness
of the Lord
In the land of the living.
Wait for the Lord;
Be strong, and let your heart take
courage;
Yes, wait for the Lord. [27:1–14]

THE GRIND OF
FEAR

One of the most paralyzing problems in all of life is fear. Our fears are directed in so many areas: fear of the unknown, fear of calamity, fear of sickness, disease, and death, fear of people, fear of losing our jobs, fear of enemy attacks, fear of being misunderstood . . . or rejected . . . or criticized . . . or forgotten . . . or (as we just considered) being mistreated. What makes matters worse is that at times the very thing we feared occurs. Sometimes it is worse than we anticipated! I've known times when I felt virtually paralyzed with feelings of panic. As fear gets a firm grip on us, we become its victim.

This reminds me of a college friend of mine who worked several summers ago on a construction crew, building a hospital in Texas. He was assigned to the twelfth story and was given the job of helping a welder who was welding the flooring structure made of huge, steel beams. So scared of falling, my friend literally shook with fear every day, though he admitted it to no one. One hot afternoon the welder looked up and noticed the man shaking in his boots. He yelled, "Are you scared, son?" The student stuttered "—s-s-s-scared! I've been t-t-t-trying to tell you for t-t-t-two weeks that I q-q-q-quit!"

Frozen with fear!

If fear has become your daily grind, Psalm 27 should prove very important—for it is a song designed to take the pain out of that dreadful grind.

♫

OUTLINE

Go back and read the fourteen verses of Psalm 27 once again . . . this time much more slowly and thoughtfully, as if for the first time in your life.

Did you notice a contrast? I'm referring to the great difference between the beginning of the song (vv. 1–6) and its ending (vv. 7–14).

The first half is filled with praise, confidence, victory, and even singing. But the last half is filled with needs—actually it is a grocery list of requests. Look at the expressions David uses in his composition:

Verse 7: "Hear, O Lord . . . and answer me."

Verse 8: "Thy face, O Lord, I shall seek."

Verse 9: "Do not hide . . . Do not turn . . . Do not abandon me nor forsake me."

Verse 11: "Teach me . . . O Lord."

There is a tone of utter dependence in those ancient lyrics.

This gives us the overall layout and helps us come up with an outline.

    I. Declaration of Praise (vv. 1– 6)
   II. Petition for Needs (vv. 7–13)
  III. Exhortation to Wait (v. 14)

What do you do when fear increases and you want to hold up under it? How do you handle such trials? We would do well to follow David's example. He first declared what he knew (vv. 1–6). He then expressed what he needed (vv. 7–13). And finally . . . he encouraged himself to wait (v. 14). Let's examine the song from that threefold perspective.

DECLARATION OF PRAISE

The key to the entire song is verse 1. It consists of two similar sentences, each ending with questions having obvious answers:

"The Lord is my light . . . my salvation . . . the defense of my life." Interestingly, David says Jehovah *is* all of this. He doesn't simply *give* these things. In other words, the psalmist laid claim upon God Himself rather than His works. David knew Jehovah personally. To him, the Lord was a very personal, ever-present Friend and Helper. God was not some distant Deity—an impersonal, abstract, theological Being who hid Himself above the clouds. No, He was David's intimate Companion.

Because of the Lord's presence (which meant more to David than anything else), the songwriter asks: "Whom shall I fear . . . whom shall I dread?"

Here the Hebrew term for *fear* is a common one: *yah-rah.* But the term for *dread* (*phah-chad*) meaning "to be in awe, to be filled with dread" is less common. The Lord God was so significant, so impressive, so overwhelmingly important to David that no other one and no other thing made him stand in awe.

I find it encouraging that Psalm 23 declares, "I shall not want" and Psalm 26 states, "I shall not slide" (KJV). And now Psalm 27 says, I "will not fear." In each case it is because of the personal presence and provisions of Jehovah-God. And by the way, how personal is your Lord? If He is distant, if you feel He is removed, I can assure you that fear is fast becoming a daily grind.

Let's look now at verses 2–3:

> When evildoers came upon me to devour my flesh,
> My adversaries and my enemies, they stumbled and fell.
> Though a host encamp against me,
> My heart will not fear;
> Though war arise against me,
> In spite of this I shall be confident.

As the writer moves on into the song, he enumerates the specific occasions of potential fear: "*evildoers . . . adversaries . . . enemies . . . a host . . . war.*"

Dark scene! And you'll notice that these things weren't mere possibilities; they were realities. He says, "when" not "if."

I hope you are realistic enough to remember that conflicts, criticisms, trials, and afflictions are not the exception but the norm. It is not correct for us to think, *if Satan attacks . . .* but rather *when he attacks. . . .* Christians should be the most realistic, well-informed people on earth. David exemplifies this as he says, "When evildoers came upon me. . . ."

Before leaving the second and third verses, let's take note of two other observations. First, look at the intensity of the conflict: The evildoers came "to devour"; the host (v. 3) had come to "encamp against me"; war had risen "against me." This was no slight affliction. Second, look at the last phrase of verse 3. ". . . In spite of this I shall be confident." The Hebrew says, literally, "I *am* confident!" Danger was imminent. Pressure was mounting. Severe days were ahead. He had every reason to be shaking in his sandals like my friend on the twelfth floor. But he was standing firm!

The Hebrew term used by David and translated "confident" does not mean self-reliant nor brave, humanly speaking. In Hebrew it means "to trust, to be secure, to have assurance." Its Arabic counterpart is picturesque: "to throw oneself down upon one's face, to lie upon the ground." The point I want to get across is that the source of David's confidence and stability was not his own strength—but God. His Lord was his only foundation for rocklike stability. What an unshakable foundation!

When pressure mounts, when a groundswell of fear invites panic, to whom do you turn? In whom do you trust? This song offers abundant reassurance. Pressure and potential fear are reminders to fall back on our Lord. "The arm of flesh will fail you, ye dare not trust your own," says the grand old hymn ("Stand Up, Stand Up for Jesus") by George Duffield.

While living under intense pressure and difficulty, the missionary to inland China, Hudson Taylor, once wrote:

> It does not matter how great the pressure is. What really matters is where the pressure lies—whether it comes between you and God, or whether it presses you nearer His heart.[10]

Verses 4–6 revolve around the idea of David's desire to maintain constant, intimate fellowship with his Lord:

One thing I have asked from the Lord, that I shall seek:
That I may dwell in the house of the Lord all the days of my life,
To behold the beauty of the Lord,
And to meditate in His temple.
For in the day of trouble He will conceal me in His tabernacle;
In the secret place of His tent He will hide me;
He will lift me up on a rock.
And now my head will be lifted up above my enemies around
    me;
And I will offer in His tent sacrifices with shouts of joy;
I will sing, yes, I will sing praises to the Lord.

Observe the repeated references to Jehovah's house, His temple, tabernacle, and tent. These are poetic expressions of being in the place of contact with the Lord. The results of maintaining this fellowship are spelled out:

. . . He will conceal me . . . He will hide me . . . He will lift me up . . . I will offer . . . sacrifices . . . I will sing praises to the Lord.

Did you notice that the first-person-singular pronoun is frequently used? It is woven through these verses—I, me, my. This is the testimony of David *alone*. This is a diary, as it were, of a man's private life, his personal struggles with life's daily grinds. This is not David on display, it is David all alone. We are what we are when we are alone. As has often been said, "Character is what we are when no one is looking."

I also observe that David says: "I will sing, yes, I will sing praises." This is the result of maintaining a close walk with the Lord. Turn to Ephesians 5. Verse 18 is a command ". . . be filled with the Spirit." In other words, allow the Holy Spirit to control your life—your thinking, motives, attitudes, activity. This is vertical fellowship at its best! And then Ephesians 5 goes on to describe the horizontal results of being Spirit-controlled:

Verse 19: a melodious heart—singing!

Verse 20: a thankful attitude—giving thanks!

Verse 21: a submissive spirit—be subject to one another!

When was the last time you burst forth all alone in song? I think it is sad that the Christian's song is seldom heard outside the church building. Living in fellowship with the Lord should bring forth spontaneous melodies throughout the day and night. Let's *sing* our faith!

PETITION FOR NEEDS

Hear, O Lord, when I cry with my voice,
And be gracious to me and answer me.
When Thou didst say, "Seek My face," my heart said to Thee,
"Thy face, O Lord, I shall seek."
Do not hide Thy face from me,
Do not turn Thy servant away in anger;
Thou hast been my help;
Do not abandon me nor forsake me,
O God of my salvation!
For my father and my mother have forsaken me,
But the Lord will take me up.

Teach me Thy way, O Lord,
And lead me in a level path,
Because of my foes,
Do not deliver me over to the desire of my adversaries;
For false witnesses have risen against me,
And such as breathe out violence. [vv. 7–12]

Rather than digging into these verses one by one, let's view them altogether. I want you to take special note of the strong imperatives (the commands) in these verses.

Verse 7: "Hear . . . be gracious . . . answer me!"

Verse 9: "Do not hide thy face . . . Do not turn . . . Do not abandon . . . nor forsake me!"

Verse 11: "Teach me . . . lead me!"

Verse 12: "Do not deliver me over to . . . my adversaries!"

I do not find David kicking back, yawning, and uttering a half-hearted request. I read boldness here, a determined, positive approach to God. Here is a respectful series of commands. With unguarded, unrestrained fervency, the songwriter declares his requests. It is this kind of prayer that is needed today.

Listen to three other verses on the same subject:

Let us therefore draw near with confidence to the throne of grace, that we may receive mercy and may find grace to help in time of need. [Heb. 4:16]

The effective prayer of a righteous man can accomplish much. [James 5:16]

Be anxious for nothing, but in everything by prayer and supplication with thanksgiving let your requests be made known to God. [Phil. 4:6]

As I read such statements, I am reminded of the hesitancy, the lack of fervency and confident boldness in our prayers. Christian friend—ask as though you mean it! Our Lord is pleased when we ask without doubting.

Before turning to the final stanza of David's song, let me ask you to glance back at verse 10. "For my father and my mother have forsaken me, / But the Lord will take me up."

Sandwiched within the commands we just considered is a brief, private admission from David's heart. His parents, for some unrevealed reason, had "forsaken" him. The original Hebrew term means "to leave, desert, abandon." It is this same term that is used in Psalm 22:1, a prophetic statement from the Messiah's lips yet to be uttered from His cross: "My God, my God, why hast Thou forsaken me?" I find it intriguing that David's own parents had turned their backs on their son, even though he was a godly man. Equally interesting is David's security as he declares, "But the Lord will take me up."

Have you ever read Isaiah 49:15–16? What hope it offers!

Can a woman forget her nursing child,
And have no compassion on the son of her womb?
Even these may forget, but I will not forget you.
Behold, I have inscribed you on the palms of My hands.

God says that mothers may forget their infant babies, but the Lord does not forget one of His.

Have you been forsaken? Have your parents turned against you even though you have tried to maintain a healthy relationship with them? Do they misread your messages? Are they on a different wavelength? Try not to become bitter. Claim the security your Lord promises you. You have nothing to fear because you have Him who has conquered fear. His care is more consistent than that of your parents.

EXHORTATION TO WAIT

"Wait for the Lord; / Be strong, and let your heart take courage; / Yes, wait for the Lord" (v. 14). What a fitting conclusion! David levels an exhortation to himself—wait! He realizes that the pressure would not suddenly leave, nor his enemies do an about-face and run immediately after he rose from his knees. He is realistic enough to know that anything worth having is worth waiting for. So he tells himself to relax . . . to enter into God's rest . . . to cease from his own works (stop and read Hebrews 4:9–11). Strength and courage are developed during a trial, not after it is over.

Look at this term *wait*. It is from the Hebrew verb *kah-wah*, meaning "to twist, stretch." The noun form means "line, cord, thread." A vivid picture emerges. It is a verb describing the making of a strong, powerful rope or cord by twisting and weaving ourselves so tightly around the Lord that our weaknesses and frail characteristics are replaced by His power and unparalleled strength. It describes very literally the truth of what has been termed the "exchanged life." As we wait, our weakness is exchanged for His strength.

Isaiah 40:31 uses this same term: "Yet those who wait for the Lord will gain new strength. . . ."

Philippians 4:13 now takes on new meaning: "I can do all things through Him [literally 'in Him'] who strengthens me."

If you are waiting for God to work this week, keep on waiting! In the wait there will come strength and courage. I urge you to read and review the truths in Psalm 27 each time you are tempted to be afraid. Don't become paralyzed and ineffective. Out with the grind of fear! Look upon each threatening circumstance as an opportunity to grow in your faith, rather than to retreat.

First: Declare what you know . . . claim it!

Second: Express what you need . . . boldly!

Third: Wait . . . twist yourself around the strands of His strength . . . and relax!

How can you? By remembering that He cares for you.

R EFLECTIONS ON FEAR

1. For the next few minutes, focus on the thought of *fear*. What, exactly, is it? Is it ever healthy? When? Are you often fearful? Why? Does fear ever lead to dread? How?

2. I wrote about pressures when we were examining the third verse in David's Twenty-seventh Psalm. Take an extremely honest look at your life. Do you live most of your days under pressure? During this week, work on a plan that will help decrease your intensity. Be specific. Spell out ways to keep yourself out of that trap.

3. Waiting, which calls for patience, is not a quick-'n'-easy discipline, is it? Focus your attention on something you cannot "fix"—something you are forced to wait for God to work out. Use the space below and write it down:

_____

_____

Look at what you wrote down. Think about it. Visualize it. Is the Lord able to handle it? Several days this week, connect with Him in prayer. Ask Him to calm your motor as you wait for Him to work. Promise Him you'll stay out of it! Wrap your weakness in His cords of strength . . . and wait for Him to work on your behalf.

When He does, give Him all the glory!

Psalm

A Psalm of David. A Maskil.

How blessed is he whose
transgression is forgiven,
Whose sin is covered!
How blessed is the man to
whom the Lord does not
impute iniquity,
And in whose spirit there is no deceit!

When I kept silent about my sin, my
body wasted away
Through my groaning all day long.
For day and night Thy hand was heavy
upon me;
My vitality was drained away as with the
fever-heat of summer.   [Selah.
I acknowledged my sin to Thee,
And my iniquity I did not hide;
I said, "I will confess my transgressions
to the Lord";
And Thou didst forgive the guilt of my
sin.   [Selah.
Therefore, let everyone who is godly pray
to Thee in a time when Thou mayest
be found;

Surely in a flood of great waters they
    shall not reach him.
Thou art my hiding place; Thou dost
    preserve me from trouble;
Thou dost surround me with songs of
    deliverance.   [Selah.

I will instruct you and teach you in the
    way which you should go;
I will counsel you with My eye upon you.
Do not be as the horse or as the mule
    which have no understanding,
Whose trappings include bit and bridle to
    hold them in check,
Otherwise they will not come near to
    you.
Many are the sorrows of the wicked;
But he who trusts in the Lord,
    lovingkindness shall surround him.
Be glad in the Lord and rejoice you
    righteous ones,
And shout for joy all you who are upright
    in heart. [32:1–11]

THE GRIND OF
AN UNFORGIVEN
CONSCIENCE

The conscience may be invisible but it is certainly not inactive! Who hasn't been kept awake by its pleadings? With incredible regularity, an unforgiven conscience can rob us of an appetite as well as drive us to distraction.

Do you remember Edgar Allan Poe's searching story, "The Tell-Tale Heart"? The main character has committed murder. Unable to escape the haunting guilt of his deed, he begins to hear the heartbeat of the victim he has buried in his basement. A cold sweat covers him as the beat-beat-beat goes on, relentlessly. Ultimately, it becomes clear that the pounding which drove the man mad was not in the grave down below but in his own chest. So it is with an unforgiven conscience.

The ancient songwriter David was no stranger to this maddening malady. As we shall soon discover, he became increasingly more physically ill and emotionally distraught the longer he refused to come to terms with the enormity of his grinding guilt. Only forgiveness can take the grind away.

As we begin to read through this song, two things catch the eye even before we get to verse one. First, we notice this is a Psalm of David. It is a song the man David was led to write . . . under the inspiration of the Spirit of God. So, at the outset let's remember that the song he writes is somehow descriptive of David's personal experience. Second, we notice this is a *Maskil*, a term that is unfamiliar to us. *Maskil* is a transliterated Hebrew word that appears before thirteen of the songs in this ancient hymnbook of the Hebrews. Most likely it is from *sah-kaal*, a Hebrew verb meaning "to be prudent, circumspect, wise—to have insight." According to my English dictionary *insight* means "the act or power to see into a situation." Putting all this together we understand that the Thirty-second Psalm is designed to give its readers wisdom and insight when dealing with certain situations.

The situation in this case is the grind that accompanies a conscience that lacks forgiveness. Psalm 51 should be tied in with Psalm 32. Both were written after David's adultery with Bathsheba and his attempt to cover up his sin by having her husband Uriah set up to lose his life on the battlefield. Of the two, Psalm 51 was probably written first, *during* the anguish of guilt under which David suffered so severely. Psalm 32 was written *after* the anguish, after his forgiveness had been secured and his peace of mind had been restored. So, the theme of Psalm 32 could be "The Blessedness of Forgiveness," and how it can be achieved. We learn right away that this song is very relevant . . . for we live in a world filled with people living under self-imposed guilt who are deeply in need of forgiveness.

OUTLINE

Read the eleven verses once again, only this time a little more slowly. Try to enter into the feelings of David. It is obvious that he is joyful at the outset, rejoicing in his present state of forgiveness (vv. 1–2). He then falls into a reflective mood as he thinks back to days past (vv. 3–5). Twice during this section of the song, he adds the word *Selah*, a musical notation meaning "pause." When we come across this marking, it is best to pause and read the section again, slowly and thoughtfully. The next three verses (vv. 6–8) look ahead to the future. They are actually directed to anyone who may read these words. Finally (vv. 9–11), he exhorts the readers to live in an upright manner.

I. Expression of Present Joy (vv. 1–2)
    "How blessed is he . . . how blessed is the man. . . ."

II. Reflection on Past Sins (vv. 3–5)
   A. Reluctance to confess (vv. 3–4)
   B. Willingness to confess (v. 5)
III. Provision for Future Needs (vv. 6–8)
   A. Invitation (v. 6)
   B. Protection (v. 7)
   C. Guidance (v. 8)
IV. Application to Every Believer (vv. 9–11)
   A. Don't be stubborn! (v. 9)
   B. Take your choice! (v. 10)
   C. Remain upright! (v. 11)

EXPRESSION OF PRESENT JOY

How blessed is he whose transgression is forgiven,
Whose sin is covered!
How blessed is the man to whom the Lord does not impute
   iniquity,
And in whose spirit there is no deceit! [vv. 1–2]

In these two verses David is overjoyed . . . unrestrained
and exuberant in his expressions of gratitude to God. The two
sentences begin just like Psalm 1 (in Hebrew, that is): "Oh, the
happiness many times over!" The idea is that of multiplied,
numberless blessings. He is rejoicing over the removal of sins
that once pinned him to the mat.

If you look closely, you'll find *four specific terms* for wrongdoing in the first two verses. They describe the downward steps
that lead a man to the same condition in which David lived
before he finally confessed his wrong.

1. Transgression. The word is from the Hebrew term *phah-
shaa* meaning "to rebel, revolt." It describes a willful act of disobedience.

2. Sin. This word is from the most common Hebrew term
for wrongdoing—*chah-tah*: "to miss the mark, to miss the way,
go wrong." It has to do with deviating from the path which
pleases God.

3. Iniquity. This term from the Hebrew *ah-wah* goes deeply into our experience after sin has occurred. It means "guilt, punishment of iniquity."

4. Deceit. *Re-mee-ah* is the original Hebrew term, meaning "treachery, deception (and in some cases—as here), self-deception."

Clearly, the songwriter traces the downward spiral of wrongdoing. It is a notorious tailspin with which most of us are familiar. First, we rebel or revolt against God's revealed will. Next, we miss the way He marked out for us—the path of righteousness. Then, guilt grabs us and we go through the inner torment of severe uncomfortable feelings. Without relief, the daily grind of an unforgiven conscience can drive a person mad.

During Billy Graham's crusade in England many years ago, a London psychiatrist told the evangelist that, in his opinion, 70 percent of those in mental institutions could be released immediately if they could find forgiveness—release from their tormenting guilt!

Finally, self-deception sets in, as it did in David when he refused to deal with his wrong. And it can do the same in us.

I remember the words of F. B. Meyer when he wrote concerning a great biblical character's compromise with sin: "No man suddenly becomes base."

Because it happens slowly, many try to tolerate sin's consequences—those inner churnings and grinding turmoil. (We'll look at the daily grind of inner turmoil next week.) If you have fallen into the torments of a guilty conscience through sin and you realize that self-deception is beginning to take over . . . I urge you to stop. Stop your downward plunge and confess your wrong to your Lord. Go to whatever length is necessary to clean up the whole mess. Read these next two statements from Scripture with great care:

He who conceals his transgressions will not prosper,
But he who confesses and forsakes them will find compassion.
   [Prov. 28:13]

If we confess our sins, He is faithful and righteous to forgive us our sins and to cleanse us from all unrighteousness. [1 John 1:9]

REFLECTION ON PAST SINS

When I kept silent about my sin, my body wasted away
Through my groaning all day long.
For day and night Thy hand was heavy upon me;
My vitality was drained away as with the fever-heat of
    summer.   [Selah.

I acknowledged my sin to Thee, and my iniquity I did not hide;
I said, "I will confess my transgressions to the Lord";
And Thou didst forgive the guilt of my sin.   [Selah.
[v. 3–5]

David takes us back to those tragic days when he refused to acknowledge his wrong (vv. 3–4). These are amazing lyrics in a song that describes what went on inside himself during his tormenting days of unconfessed sin.

He admits when he "kept silent" regarding his sin, he paid a bitter price. The inner conflict brought about what is known as psychosomatic illness . . . the presence of actual physical pain resulting from mental or emotional conflicts—in this case, the refusal to deal completely and honestly with sin. What happened?

   —His "body wasted away."
   —He groaned "all day long."
   —He endured this "day and night."
   —His "vitality [literally 'sap, juices'] drained away."
   —He had a "fever-heat" like the hot summer.

Abruptly, he adds *Selah*—pause and consider!

Obviously, God's hand was heavy upon him. In the words of Proverbs 13:15: "The way . . . [was] hard." Like a tree trying to survive without water from refreshing rains, David was utterly miserable in this sinful state.

The Modern Language Bible (MLB), a revision of the Berkeley Version in Modern English, renders Proverbs 14:30 as follows: "A relaxed mind makes for physical health, but passion is bitterness to the bones."

Finally, David confessed (Ps. 32:5). Without restraint he poured out his sinful condition. Don't miss the progression:

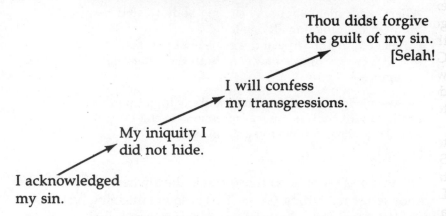

Thou didst forgive
the guilt of my sin.
[Selah!

I will confess
my transgressions.

My iniquity I
did not hide.

I acknowledged
my sin.

Like a cool, cleansing shower on a hot, sweaty day, God's forgiveness washed away not only the sins but the tormenting guilt. The Lord went far into the depths of David's inner being and provided that magnificent relief only He can bring: PEACE. God forgave completely because David confessed completely.

If you are harboring some sin—if you are keeping hidden a few secret regions of wrong—don't expect to enjoy freedom from guilt, child of God. There is an unspoken axiom threaded through Scripture: secret sin cannot coexist with inner peace. Peace returns only when our sins are fully confessed and forsaken. Few grinds are more galling than the grind of an unforgiven conscience. It's awful! And few joys are more relieving than having our sins forgiven. It's wonderful!

PROVISION FOR FUTURE NEEDS

Therefore, let everyone who is godly pray to Thee in a time
    when Thou mayest be found;
Surely in a flood of great waters they shall not reach him.
Thou art my hiding place; Thou dost preserve me from trouble;
Thou dost surround me with songs of deliverance.   [Selah.
I will instruct you and teach you in the way which you should go;
I will counsel you with My eye upon you. [vv. 6–8]

Remember, the theme of this psalm is *forgiveness*. David wants to make it clear that he doesn't have a corner on this blessed experience. He therefore issues an invitation to "everyone who is godly." This means "every believer"—every person who knows the Lord, having received Jesus Christ by faith. David urges all God's people to pray—even in the midst of "a flood of great waters" when all seems hopeless. He promises that when this is done, God will provide the same deliverance to us He brought to David.

Verse 7 places full attention on God. He is the One who protects us, preserves us, surrounds us, and even gives us a song. Selah (again, pause and consider)! Long enough has the mistaken concept of God been proclaimed—that He is a peeved Deity, some kind of heavenly brute who delights in whipping and buffeting His creatures. No . . . look again at verse 7. David breaks out into songs of deliverance! "Thou art my hiding place; Thou dost preserve me from trouble; / Thou dost surround me with songs of deliverance. [Selah."

What a comforting picture, especially to those who have been in deep sin and seek forgiveness!

The next statement is God's answer to David's invitation to all God's people. In it the Lord promises His guidance and counsel. Literally, the eighth verse concludes: "I will give counsel, keeping my eyes on you. . . ."

Do you have the feeling that God is gone? That God doesn't care? Trust me today; He *does* care. He cares personally about you (1 Pet. 5:7). He has His eyes on you. He may seem to you to be removed and distant . . . but He is near. Christians love to sing the old hymn "How Firm a Foundation":

"Fear not, I am with thee, O be not dismayed,
For I am thy God, I will still give thee aid;
I'll strengthen thee, help thee, and cause thee to stand,
Upheld by My gracious, omnipotent hand.

"When through the deep waters I call thee to go,
The rivers of sorrow shall not overflow,
For I will be with thee, thy trials to bless,
And sanctify to thee thy deepest distress.

"The soul that on Jesus hath leaned for repose,
I will not, I will not desert to his foes;
That soul, though all hell should endeavor to shake,
I'll never, no never, no never forsake!"[11]

It is time for us to start believing what we enjoy singing.

APPLICATION TO EVERY BELIEVER

Do not be as the horse or as the mule which have no
    understanding,
Whose trappings include bit and bridle to hold them in check,
Otherwise they will not come near to you.
Many are the sorrows of the wicked;
But he who trusts in the Lord, lovingkindness shall surround
    him.
Be glad in the Lord and rejoice, you righteous ones,
And shout for joy all you who are upright in heart. [vv. 9–11]

David summarizes all the lessons he wants to leave with us
into three strong statements of exhortation:
First: Don't be stubborn! (v. 9).
When it comes to dealing with sin, don't be like a mule or
any other hardheaded beast! Give in . . . and keep an open
account before the Lord. Don't let wrongdoing build up. Don't
try to maintain a standoff any longer.
Second: Take your choice! (v. 10).
In reading over these concluding words, you'll notice two and
only two paths: the path of the wicked (which brings "many sorrows") and the path of trust (which brings "lovingkindness").
Take your choice (says the songwriter), but remember the inevitable outcome.
Third: Remain Upright! (v. 11).
If you're looking for green pastures, you'll find them only in
fellowship with your Lord. So don't be a fool! Remain upright.
Stop the downward plunge into deep, involved sin by maintain-
ing an upright walk.
God is so gracious! He has planned a life for His children

that results in inner peace, outer strength, and optimism. But we are sinful and frequently choose to walk our *own* way. In the words of the prince of the prophets: "All of us like sheep have gone astray, / Each of us has turned to his own way. . . ." (Isa. 53:6).

But again, He is so gracious! Though He prefers that we not sin, He is willing to forgive and stay near us during our recovery period. He will completely forgive and restore us if we will completely repent, that is, confess and seek His cleansing.

REFLECTIONS ON AN UNFORGIVEN CONSCIENCE

1. Everyone has known the misery of living with a guilty conscience. Perhaps it was the result of using harsh angry words, or setting out to make another person miserable, or overlooking a child's needs, or taking something that didn't belong to you, or breaking a promise, or being unfaithful to your spouse. The possibilities are endless. Read verses 3–4 once again. Call to mind a time when you experienced what those words describe. Now read verse 5—what a magnificent relief! Pay special attention to the promise of being freed not only from the sin but from the guilt as well. Think about the difference between the two. Thank God for *both*.

2. According to Psalm 32:7, David portrays the Lord as (1) our "hiding place," as (2) One who preserves us from trouble, and (3) One who surrounds us with "songs of deliverance."

   During the balance of this week, fix your mind on those three comforting concepts. Instead of envisioning your Lord as an angry Judge ready to bring down the gavel, recall the safety of His presence, the security of His preservation, and His peaceful "songs of deliverance."

3. Look at the final verse of David's song. We are instructed—in fact, commanded!—to be glad . . . to rejoice . . . to shout for joy. Do you? Are you a person of contagious joy? If not, ask the Lord to bring back the pleasant spirit of happiness you once had. You have been forgiven! You are safe! Few things communicate that better than a smile that is genuine . . . one that emerges from a clear, forgiven conscience.

Psalms

BOOK 2

For the choir director.
A Maskil of the sons of Korah.

As the deer pants for the water
    brooks,
    So my soul pants for Thee, O
    God.
My soul thirsts for God, for the living
    God;
When shall I come and appear before
    God?
My tears have been my food day and
    night,
While they say to me all day long,
    "Where is your God?"
These things I remember, and I pour out
    my soul within me.
For I used to go along with the throng
    and lead them in procession to the
    house of God,
With the voice of joy and thanksgiving, a
    multitude keeping festival.

Why are you in despair, O my soul?
And why have you become disturbed
    within me?
Hope in God, for I shall again praise
    Him
For the help of His presence.

O my God, my soul is in despair within
    me;
Therefore I remember Thee from the land
    of the Jordan,
And the peaks of Hermon, from Mount
    Mizar.
Deep calls to deep at the sound of Thy
    waterfalls;
All Thy breakers and Thy waves have
    rolled over me.
The Lord will command His
    lovingkindness in the daytime;
And His song will be with me in the
    night,

A prayer to the God of my life.

I will say to God my rock, "Why hast
    Thou forgotten me?
Why do I go mourning because of the
    oppression of the enemy?"
As a shattering of my bones, my
    adversaries revile me,
While they say to me all day long,
    "Where is your God?"
Why are you in despair, O my soul?
And why have you become disturbed
    within me?
Hope in God, for I shall yet praise Him,
The help of my countenance, and my
    God. [42:1–11]

———————

Vindicate me, O God, and plead my case
    against an ungodly nation;
O deliver me from the deceitful and
    unjust man!
For Thou art the God of my strength;
    why hast Thou rejected me?
Why do I go mourning because of the
    oppression of the enemy?

O send out Thy light and Thy truth, let
    them lead me;
Let them bring me to Thy holy hill,
And to Thy dwelling places.
Then I will go to the altar of God,
To God my exceeding joy;
And upon the lyre I shall praise Thee, O
    God, my God.

Why are you in despair, O my soul?
And why are you disturbed within me?
Hope in God, for I shall again praise
    Him,
The help of my countenance, and my
    God. [43:1–5]

THE GRIND OF
INNER TURMOIL

I have a "churning place." It's in my stomach . . . on the upper, left side, just below the rib cage. When disturbing things happen, when troubling words are said, when certain letters that contain ugly words or extremely critical comments are read, the churning starts. Do you have a similar thing happen?

One friend of mine says his spot is in his head, specifically his forehead. Another fellow told me his was at the back of his neck. Most folks I know have a particular region that starts to grind within. Any number of things can trigger this feeling. They are common to all of us:

- Bad news
- Strong fears
- Strained relations
- Car accidents
- Almost running out of gas
- Dental work
- Late-night phone calls
- Earthquakes

I find it rather comforting that God's inspired hymnal does not omit the grind of inner turmoil. Since it is so common, I would think it strange if such a topic were not addressed. But before we uncover a few of the more practical remarks, let's take a look at some background information about Psalms 42 and 43.

Immediately, we are surprised to discover that Psalm 42 occupies first place in *Book 2*. Actually, the ancient psalms fall into five divisions or "books." Take the time to thumb through the entire hymnbook of The Psalms for a moment. Note the breakdown:

Book 1: Psalms 1–41
Book 2: Psalms 42–72
Book 3: Psalms 73–89
Book 4: Psalms 90–106
Book 5: Psalms 107–150

A look at the closing of each book shows that each concluding song ends with "Amen" or some other form of doxology. The last one (Psalm 150) is, in fact, one great doxology climaxing in praise—a fitting conclusion to the entire Book of Psalms.

All sorts of suggestions have been given to explain why these ancient songs are divided into five books. Jewish tradition explains this arrangement as a conscious reflection of the Pentateuch (Genesis through Deuteronomy). A Midrash (a Jewish commentary) from the Talmudic period on Psalm 1 states: ". . . as Moses gave five books of laws to Israel, so David gave five books of Psalms to Israel."

No one knows for sure why the psalms are so divided. But there is something of significant importance when we look at this first song in Book 2. I want to suggest that Psalm 42 and Psalm 43 should be taken together as a unit. Two observations lead me to make that suggestion:

1. Psalm 43 has no superscription. Nothing by way of introduction appears before verse 1. This is the only psalm in Book 2 without a superscription. I believe, therefore, it flows quite naturally from the previous song. (Remember, the chapter breaks, like the punctuation markings, have been added to the text of Scripture in later centuries. God's Word is inspired . . . but not the punctuations or various paragraph breakdowns.)

2. The phrase repeated twice in Psalm 42 also appears in identical form in Psalm 43. Notice 42:5, 11, and 43:5:

Why are you in despair, O my soul?
And why have you become disturbed within me?
Hope in God, for I shall again praise Him. . . .

These three identical phrases lead me to believe that these two songs form a natural unit, revolving around a single theme.

Look next at the superscription before verse 1 in Psalm 42: *"For the choir director. A Maskil of the sons of Korah."* Do you remember what we learned about *Maskil* last week? We found that this Hebrew title meant that the song was designed to give insight and wisdom when dealing with certain situations. In Psalm 32, the situation was the need for forgiveness.

What is the situation here in these two songs? Going back to the thrice-repeated statement mentioned above, we see clearly that the situation is inner despair and disturbance. In other words, these two songs have been preserved to provide the reader with wisdom and insight in handling those "blue days," that age-old grind of inner turmoil.

Let's look closely at the term *despair.* The Hebrew word *shah-kak* means "to crouch, bow down." It is used in Job 38:40 to describe a lion in a crouched position, lying in wait for its prey. This song talks about those days when we feel like curling up in the fetal position and quitting! It talks about how we can conquer those feelings rather than succumb to them. Christians frequently have such feelings, give in to them, and make others miserable as they grind their way through the process. The two songs are designed to help us overcome feelings of inner turmoil rather than "churn" our way through life.

As I mentioned earlier, having those disturbing feelings on occasion is quite normal. We do a real disservice to a new Christian by telling him that it is abnormal or sinful to be disturbed at any time. How unrealistic and unbiblical! David wrote many psalms while he was churning within. Of course, it is not normal for a Christian to linger for months in the pit of depression, but all of us should be transparent enough to admit we have days like that. I am comforted that even Jesus Himself on occasion was inwardly troubled (John 11:33; 12:27; 13:21).

Dr. John Henry Jowett, an outstanding preacher of yesteryear, was honest enough to admit in a letter to a friend:

> I wish you wouldn't think I'm such a saint. You seem to imagine that I have no ups and downs, but just a level and lofty

stretch of spiritual attainment with unbroken joy and equanim-
ity. By no means! I am often perfectly wretched and everything
appears most murky. I often feel as though my religious life had
only just begun, and that I am in the kindergarten stage. But I
can usually trace these miserable seasons to some personal
cause, and the first thing to do is to attend to that cause, and get
into the sunshine again.[12]

I appreciate such vulnerability. The good news is that these
two songs help us know how to "get into the sunshine again."
   The songwriter begins his Forty-second Song with the familiar words:

> As the deer pants for the water brooks,
> So my soul pants for Thee, O God.
> My soul thirsts for God, for the living God;
> When shall I come and appear before God? [vv. 1–2]

David longs for God—like a thirsty deer in a barren wilderness
longs for a cool stream. He says he "pants" for the Lord. In
Psalm 119:131 he expresses a similar thought: "I opened my
mouth wide and panted, / For I longed for Thy commandments."
   God, who was considered by biblical saints as "the fountain
of living waters" (Jer. 2:13; 17:13), was sought by the churning
singer. Being a man after God's own heart, David passionately
yearned for His presence. "My tears have been my food day
and night, / While they say to me all day long, 'Where is your
God?'" (v. 3).
   In his turmoil David misses that inner assurance of God's
presence. God has certainly not forsaken His child, but at low,
blue moments all of us could testify that there are times when it
seems like He has! What do we do to become reassured? How
can God become real again when we are feeling low . . . when
we are in the grind of such inner turmoil?

> These things I remember, and I pour out my soul within me.
> For I used to go along with the throng and lead them in
>   procession to the house of God,
> With the voice of joy and thanksgiving, a multitude keeping
>   festival. [v. 4]

A more exact rendering of the beginning of this verse would be: "These things I *will* remember. . . ." or, "These things I *would* remember. . . ." David is talking to himself. Sometimes that is great therapy. He is saying that when he is blue, he will call to remembrance past days of victory when God was very real, very present. He says, in effect, "Those were the days, my friend! Those were days of blessing, joy, and thanksgiving!"

After calling to mind such days, he asks:

> Why are you in despair, O my soul?
> And why have you become disturbed within me?
> Hope in God, for I shall again praise Him
> For the help of His presence. [v. 5]

"Why," he asks, "should I feel sad and blue with memories like that?" He admits that such vivid memories of past victory should really encourage him.

When you are "crouched" in turmoil, it helps to think back to previous victories and call to mind specific things God did for you. Remember the same Lord is your Lord right now.

I remember my first year at Dallas Seminary. Cynthia and I lived in a *un*-air-conditioned apartment on campus. It stayed hot during the early fall of the year. Knowing that summer would surely come, we began to pray for a window air conditioner. In fact, we prayed through the winter and spring months for it. We told no one; we just prayed. Nothing happened for months—zero response. Late that spring we made a trip home to Houston during Easter vacation. Summer was coming—still no air conditioner. Dallas would soon be an oven! Our trip home was unannounced. Except for our family, no one knew we were coming. We had not been home visiting Cynthia's folks for even an hour before the phone rang. On the other end of the line was a man from our home church.

Surprised, he said, "Chuck, is that you?"

I answered, "Yes."

His next words were: "Do you and Cynthia need a window air conditioner? We just installed a new central unit and my wife and I thought you two could use the one we've replaced."

What a great God we have!

Similar things have occurred since that happened, but to this day when I get low and blue regarding needs, I call to mind that marvelous day back in the spring of 1960 when He provided for our specific need.

But let's face it, sometimes that doesn't do the job. We get so low that no memory will jar us loose from our turmoil. In verses 6–8, a second technique is suggested:

> O my God, my soul is in despair within me;
> Therefore, I remember Thee from the land of the Jordan,
> And the peaks of Hermon, from Mount Mizar.
> Deep calls to deep at the sound of Thy waterfalls;
> All Thy breakers and Thy waves have rolled over me.
> The Lord will command His lovingkindness in the daytime;
> And His song will be with me in the night,
> A prayer to the God of my life.

Look at that unusual expression: "Deep calls to deep." The songwriter pictures himself on the peaks of Mount Hermon, looking toward Mount Mizar. In his mind he thinks of those awesome sounds and scenes surrounding him—as "deep calls to deep," as God communicates with nature and the unchanging, immutable relationship is enacted. In this case, the snow melts high upon Mount Hermon's peaks, causing the thunderous waterfalls, the rapids in streams below. All this display reinforces his point: "Deep calls to deep."

That which is "deep" in God communicates to that which is "deep" in nature—and suddenly change occurs. It happens all around us:

The "deep" in God calls to the "deep" in trees in the fall . . . and inevitably their leaves turn to beautiful orange, red, and yellow . . . ultimately, they fall and the tree is again barren.

The "deep" in God calls to the "deep" in the salmon . . . and millions travel back over many miles to spawn.

But wait—the psalmist is not talking about trees and fish . . . but rather about himself! As the breakers and waves of inner turmoil "rolled over me"—You speak to me, Lord! Your "deep" calls unto my "deep," and You remind me of that unchanging relationship of love and joy that exists between us! And again David asks in verse 11:

> Why are you in despair, O my soul?
> And why have you become disturbed within me?
> Hope in God, for I shall yet praise Him,
> The help of my countenance, and my God.

APPLICATION

What an application this suggests! Between God and His children, there exists an eternal, immutable relationship. The hymns we sing refer to it:

> O love that wilt not let me go;
> I rest my weary soul in Thee. . . .[13]

and

> Loved with everlasting love,
> Led by grace that love to know;
> Gracious Spirit from above,
> Thou hast taught me it is so!
> Oh, this full and perfect peace!
> Oh, this transport all divine!
> In a love which cannot cease,
> I am His, and He is mine.[14]

The next time the feelings of despair bend you low, let His "deep" call to your "deep" and be reminded of that eternal love relationship that is not subject to change. God's Spirit communicates with our spirit—and encourages us at such times.

There is yet another solution to feeling the "blahs." In Psalm 43:1–2 David is back under attack. People problems were upon him . . . and we all know how devestating *they* can be! After pleading for God to intervene, David prays (Ps. 43:3–4):

> O send out Thy light and Thy truth, let them lead me;
> Let them bring me to Thy holy hill,

> And to Thy dwelling places.
> Then I will go to the altar of God,
> To God my exceeding joy;
> And upon the lyre I shall praise Thee, O God, my God.

He asks for two specific things: Thy Light and Thy truth.

He wanted the Lord to give him His Word (truth) and an understanding of it (light). Perhaps he sought for a specific statement from Scripture that would be fitting and appropriate for his situation and, equally important, he sought for insight into it. This would bring joy and praise. When this occurred, he asked again (Ps. 43:5):

> Why are you in despair, O my soul?
> And why are you disturbed within me?
> Hope in God, for I shall again praise Him,
> The help of my countenance, and my God.

Every believer in Jesus Christ must ultimately come to the place where he is going to trust God's Word completely before he can experience consistent victory. His Book is our single source of tangible truth. We try every other crutch—we lean on self . . . on others . . . on feelings . . . on bank accounts . . . on good works . . . on logic and reason . . . on human perspective—and we continually end up with the short straw and churning. God has given His written Word and the promise of His light to all His children. WHEN WILL WE EVER LEARN TO BELIEVE IT AND LIVE IN IT AND USE IT AND CLAIM IT? I often wonder how many of His personal promises to His people exist in His Book unclaimed and ignored.

The grind of inner turmoil will not depart forever . . . but its immobilizing presence can be overcome. I hope these two ancient songs will help make that happen in your life this week.

R EFLECTIONS ON INNER TURMOIL

1. Perhaps you have recently been entertaining a low-grade depression . . . feelings of inner unrest or even despair. We just read where the psalmist asked himself, *"Why are you in despair, O my soul?"* (42:5). It's a good time for you to do that. Ask yourself why? It is a great help to pinpoint the reason(s) behind inner turmoil. Once you put your finger on the nerve, talk to God about it. Request His assistance. Express your desire to Him. Ask for relief.

2. Let's look again at 42:8. *The Living Bible* paraphrases it:

   > Yet day by day the Lord also pours out his steadfast love upon me, and through the night I sing his songs and pray to God who gives me life.

   What a thought! All day long: steadfast love poured out . . . all through the night: songs and prayers. Try that the next time the grind of inner turmoil tries to steal your daytime joy or your night's rest. Remind yourself, "I am the recipient of my Lord's steadfast love," or recall the words of a favorite hymn. It works! I know; I did it last night.

3. Here is a surprise suggestion: Break your predictable mold this next weekend. Do something totally different. Go on a picnic. Or fly a kite . . . or both! If you prefer, take a long walk through the woods or a local park. A change in scenery does wonders for getting rid of inner churnings!

Psalm

For the choir director.
A Psalm of the sons of Korah, set to Alamoth.
A Song.

God is our refuge and strength,
   A very present help in trouble.
Therefore we will not fear,
   though the earth should
   change,
And though the mountains slip into the
   heart of the sea;
Though its waters roar and foam,
Though the mountains quake at its
   swelling pride.   [Selah.

There is a river whose streams make glad
   the city of God,
The holy dwelling places of the Most
   High.
God is in the midst of her, she will not
   be moved;
God will help her when morning dawns.
The nations made an uproar, the
   kingdoms tottered;
He raised His voice, the earth melted.

The Lord of hosts is with us;
The God of Jacob is our
    stronghold.   [Selah.

Come, behold the works of the Lord,
Who has wrought desolations in the
    earth.
He makes wars to cease to the end of the
    earth;
He breaks the bow and cuts the spear in
    two;
He burns the chariots with fire.
"Cease striving and know that I am God;
I will be exalted among the nations, I will
    be exalted in the earth."
The Lord of hosts is with us;
The God of Jacob is our
    stronghold.   [Selah.
[46:1–11]

THE GRIND OF PERSONAL WEAKNESS

We deny it. We fake it. We mask it. We try to ignore it. But the truth stubbornly persists—we are *weak* creatures! Being sinful, we fail. Being prone to sickness, we hurt. Being mortal, we ultimately die. Pressure wears on us. Anxiety gives us ulcers. People intimidate us. Criticism offends us. Disease scares us. Death haunts us. This explains why the apostle Paul writes: ". . . we ourselves groan within ourselves, waiting eagerly for our adoption as sons, the redemption of our body" (Rom. 8:23).

How can we continue to grow in this bag of bones, covered with weaknesses too numerous to mention? We need a big dose of Psalm 46. What hope for those struggling through the grind of personal weakness!

A great historic hymn of Protestant Christianity found its origin in Psalm 46. Read verse 1 and see if you can determine which hymn I have in mind: "God is our refuge and strength, / A very present help in trouble."

It is, of course, Martin Luther's immortal "A Mighty Fortress Is Our God." Remember the first stanza?

> A mighty fortress is our God,
> A bulwark never failing;
> Our helper He, amid the flood
> Of mortal ills prevailing. . . .[15]

You may not have noticed that the psalm is to be "set to Alamoth." These words are addressed to the choir director. The word *Alamoth* is derived from *Almah*, a Hebrew term meaning "maiden, young woman." Some say, therefore, that this means the song was to be sung by a choir of women—but the place of worship back in the days of the psalms had no such choir. We are given a hint from a reference in 1 Chronicles 15:20, where we read that harps were to be tuned ". . . to Alamoth." The marginal reference in the New American Standard Bible says: "harps of maidenlike tone." Quite likely, this song was to be played on soprano-like instruments, on highly pitched instruments of music. Perhaps this was to make the psalm unique and easily remembered—much like certain lilting strains of Handel's *Messiah* ("For unto us a child is born" or "O Thou, that tellest good tidings to Zion"). This song was to be perpetually remembered.

As you were reading the lyrics, did you notice anything that is repeated? It is true that verses 7 and 11 are identical . . . but look at the thrice-repeated "Selah." As we have pointed out in our previous weekly studies, this is most likely a musical marking that denotes a pause. In Hebrew poetry it suggests our pausing and thinking about what we have just read before proceeding.

The three pause markings assist us in understanding this song. They are built-in hints the reader should not overlook. As in many of the psalms, verse 1 states the theme, which we might render: "God is an immediate source of help (strength), / When we are in a tight squeeze!"

The term translated "trouble" in most versions of the Bible is from a Hebrew verb meaning "to be restricted, to tie up, to be narrow, cramped." It reminds me of an expression we sometimes use to describe the idea of being in a jam: "between a rock and a hard place." It means to be in a pinch or tight squeeze. The psalmist declares that God is immediately available, instantly present in any situation . . . certainly at those times when we are weak!

In the remaining verses he develops this great theme by

describing three very serious situations and his corresponding reaction to each. Let me explain:

Situation 1:   Nature . . . in upheaval
Reaction: I will not fear (vv. 2–3)
               Selah!

Situation 2:   Jerusalem . . . under attack
Reaction: I will not be moved (vv. 4–7)
               Selah!

Situation 3:   Battlefield . . . after war
Reaction: I will not strive (vv. 8–11)
               Selah!

I WILL NOT FEAR

In the second and third verses the psalmist introduces some of the most terrifying scenes in all of life. Each traumatic situation is introduced with the word "though." Count them . . . four in all:

. . . though the earth should change
. . . though the mountains slip into . . . the sea
. . . though its waters roar and foam
. . . though the mountains quake

The picture is familiar to all who live in Southern California, the great land of mud slides, earthquakes, and tremors! The scene is filled with havoc, the situation is awesome, a wild uproar sweeps across the psalmist's life. He feels weak . . . totally helpless. As the earth beneath him shifts, rolls, and slides, his belongings instantly become insignificant and life seems insecure, but even so the songwriter declares, "I will not fear."

Why? How could anyone in such a threatening situation say that? Back to verse 1 for the answer: Because God, our heavenly Father, is our immediate helper, our immutable, ever-present source of strength, our bridge over troubled waters!

When personal weakness begins to plague us, that is a marvelous reminder. God is our "very present help," *our strength.* Selah!

I WILL NOT BE MOVED

The scene changes in verses 4–7:

> There is a river whose streams make glad the city of God,
> The holy dwelling places of the Most High.
> God is in the midst of her, she will not be moved;
> God will help her when morning dawns.
> The nations made an uproar, the kingdoms tottered;
> He raised His voice, the earth melted.
> The Lord of hosts is with us;
> The God of Jacob is our stronghold.   [Selah.

The subject? "The city of God" (v. 4). This is a reference to the Jews' beloved Jerusalem. As you read over these inspired stanzas, you quickly discover that the city is under attack. Nations and kingdoms have risen up against her . . . yet "she will not be moved." The reason is clearly stated in the first part of verse 5: "God is in the midst of her."

And it is ratified in verse 7: "The Lord of hosts is with us; / The God of Jacob is our stronghold."

What is it that gave Jerusalem her safety? Quite simply, it was the indwelling, omnipotent presence of Jehovah God!

Do you remember that account in Mark's Gospel (4:35–41, KJV) of the trip Jesus and His disciples made across the Sea of Galilee? It has been made famous by a song believers sing entitled "Peace, Be Still!" The trip was a stormy one and the disciples greatly feared for their lives. Gripped with thoughts of their own personal weakness, they woke Jesus and questioned how He could sleep at a time like that. After calming the wind and the sea, Jesus rebuked the disciples for their lack of faith. How could they ever sink? Why would they fear? They had God in the boat with them! The boat would never sink as long as God was in it. They should not have been moved, for the

Lord Himself was in their midst. I'd call that a perfect illustration of Psalm 46:5 in action.

Look also at the term *moved* in verse 5. It literally means "to totter or shake." We have the descriptive slang expression "all shook up." I suppose it would fit here in verse 5. Because God is in me, I really have no reason to get "shook up." Do you realize, Christian friend, that from the moment the Lord Jesus Christ became the Lord and Savior of your life, He has been living *in you?* In fact, Christ is called "your life" in Colossians 3:4. Furthermore, the hope of glory is "Christ in you." You, child of God, have the Lord God *within you*. In your midst! Therefore, with Him present, there is no reason to totter. God is not going to totter and shake, nor is His dwelling place. So, the next time you are tempted to panic, call to mind that God is literally in your midst.

Selah!

I WILL NOT STRIVE

The last four verses (vv. 8–11) are nothing short of magnificent. Read them over once again.

> Come, behold the works of the Lord,
> Who has wrought desolations in the earth.
> He makes wars to cease to the end of the earth;
> He breaks the bow and cuts the spear in two;
> He burns the chariots with fire.
> "Cease striving and know that I am God;
> I will be exalted among the nations, I will be exalted in the
>   earth."
> The Lord of hosts is with us;
> The God of Jacob is our stronghold.   [Selah.

The scene has changed to a battlefield. The psalmist invites us to view the mute reminders of war. The terrain is strewn with the litter of a battlefield aftermath. The chariots are overturned, burned, and rusty. Bows, spears, and other destroyed implements of warfare are covered with dust and debris. It is a sight to behold! This imaginary tour reminds us of the scenes after World War II . . . the beaches of Normandy, the cities of Berlin, Hiroshima, London, the islands of Iwo Jima, Okinawa. When you look at the remains, it is a moving experience. Rusty tanks. Sunken boats covered with barnacles. Concrete bunkers. A silence pervades. Quietness is fitting. It is as though our God has said, "That is enough!" God's work is a thorough thing.

At this point (v. 10), the writer commands:

"Cease striving and know that I am God;
I will be exalted among the nations, I will be exalted in the
  earth."

Look at the word *cease*. The Hebrew term means "relax, do nothing, be quiet!" And the stem of this verb is the causative stem, suggesting that *you* do it! You stop striving, quit racing around . . . relax. Or to use a common expression, "Don't sweat it!" The point is that God is in full control, so let Him handle your situation. As He does, we are to "cause ourselves to relax!" He will be exalted; He is with us.

So much for the ancient songwriter. How about you? Do you live in strife and panic? Is there a fretful spirit about you? Did you realize that God has designed and reserved a spirit of rest for you? Hebrews 4:9 promises: "There remains therefore a Sabbath rest for the people of God."

Does this mean I slip everything into neutral and do nothing? Hardly. It means I first enter that rest He has provided (Heb. 4:11—please read), and then face the situation without panic or strife. If He wants me involved, He will show me clearly and there will be no doubt. My responsibility, however, is to enter deliberately into His invisible sanctuary of rest . . . to trust Him completely for safety. That is my best preparation for battle—to be armed with His Sabbath rest. It is amazing what that does to stop the grind of personal weakness. Listen to what Proverbs 21:31 says: "The horse is prepared for the day of battle, / But victory belongs to the Lord."

In the final analysis, it is the Lord's job to provide the victory over every one of our weaknesses. He can handle whatever is needed. Our striving will never do it.

Selah!

R EFLECTIONS ON PERSONAL WEAKNESS

1. Pause (Selah) and consider this. Are you fearful? Are you trapped in your prison of fears, wrapped tightly and squeezed in by worry and pessimism and agitation? These are the signs of a person preoccupied with his or her own weaknesses. God longs to prove Himself as your source of victory, power, and stability. Let me give you some "victory verses." Please read each one.

Genesis 15:1	Hebrews 13:5–6
Joshua 1:9	2 Timothy 1:7
Proverbs 3:5–6	1 Corinthians 15:57–58
Isaiah 40:31; 41:10	Ephesians 6:10–18
Psalm 27:1; 91:1–2, 5–10	1 Peter 5:6–8
Matthew 11:28–30	

   Take your fears, wrap them into a neat mental bundle, and toss them out the window as you read those verses, one by one. Ask the Lord to take each specific fear and replace it with His calm, victorious presence.

2. Find a hymnal and read each stanza of Martin Luther's "A Mighty Fortress Is Our God." Meditate on the vivid word pictures he uses. Hum it to yourself each time you shower this week.

3. Most of us—though weak—continue to strive, don't we? We "sweat the small stuff." We say we're not going to but

we do! This is the week to start breaking that habit. Take the next eight words, "Cease striving and know that I am God," and (1) commit them to memory, (2) say them to yourself each morning this week before you roll out of bed, (3) share them with at least one other person each day this week, and (4) every time you feel the sparks flying off the daily grind of some weakness in your life, say them aloud . . . quietly but aloud. Ask the Lord to take charge as you relax. And I mean really relax.

Selah!

Psalm

For the choir director; on stringed instruments.
A Maskil of David, when the Ziphites
came and said to Saul,
"Is not David hiding himself among us?"

Save me, O God, by Thy name,
And vindicate me by Thy power.
Hear my prayer, O God;
Give ear to the words of my
mouth.
For strangers have risen against me,
And violent men have sought my life;
They have not set God before
them. [Selah.

Behold, God is my helper;
The Lord is the sustainer of my soul.
He will recompense the evil to my foes;
Destroy them in Thy faithfulness.

Willingly I will sacrifice to Thee;
I will give thanks to Thy name, O Lord,
for it is good.
For He has delivered me from all trouble;
And my eye has looked with satisfaction
upon my enemies. [54:1–7]

THE GRIND OF
DIFFICULT
PEOPLE

The cartoon scene created by Charles Schulz is familiar to most American homes. Charlie Brown and Lucy are engaged in conversation. Lucy's back is turned, her arms are folded and a look of disgust appears on her face. Charlie is pleading, as usual, for her to be tolerant and understanding. With outstretched arms he says:

> "Lucy, you *must* be loving. This world really needs love. You have to let yourself love to make this world a better place in which to live!"

Lucy whirls around and screams (as Charlie does his famous back flip):

> "Look, blockhead—the *world* I love. It's *people* I can't stand!"[16]

We smile, not because it is an unrealistic cartoon but because it is so very true. There are no problems quite like *people problems*, are there? You can have a job that demands long hours and great physical effort, but neither the hours nor the energy drain gives you the problems difficult people do. You can have financial difficulties, physical pain, a tight schedule, and miles of driving, but these things are not the cause of our major battles. It's *people*, as Lucy said. The grind of difficult people is quite an assignment!

The song we're looking at this week talks about living beyond people problems. It gives us some very practical advice on how to respond to *people* anxieties, problems brought into our lives because of other members of the human race who are just as ornery as we are!

BACKGROUND

If you will take a moment to look at the superscription, you'll find it worth your while. By the way, I hope you are learning to do that when studying the ancient songs in the Bible. The words that appear before the first verse of each psalm are part of the original text, giving the reader some helpful hints about the song. Most folks don't realize that.

In the Fifty-fourth Psalm the superscription reads:

For the choir director; on stringed instruments. A Maskil of David, when the Ziphites came and said to Saul, "Is not David hiding himself among us?"

This is a very lengthy and helpful superscription. From it we learn that David wrote the song. We also learn that it is a *Maskil*. By now we should be getting familiar with the term. We've seen it at other times in our previous weeks' studies. It means "instruction, insight." All Maskil songs are designed to give instruction and insight when dealing with certain situations. In this case, the situation is problems with people, as we've already stated, so we don't have to guess and wonder what prompted David to write it. The historical setting appears here at the beginning . . . an event that is recorded in 1 Samuel 23:14–26.

David is being hunted by jealous King Saul. The singer's hiding place is bleak and rugged. His life is in danger, so he tries to find a place of safety. Everything backfires. He gets to a spot called the *hill of Hachilah* and thinks he is safe. It is Ziphite territory, and so far as he can tell, he has found neutral ground, a place to rest and sleep. But no rest is possible. The Ziphites turn against him and report his whereabouts to Saul. The chase is on again! David then goes to *the wilderness of Maon* but finds himself surrounded by Ziphites and Saul's soldiers. I can just picture David. He is dirty, sweaty, hungry, thirsty, exhausted, and no doubt discouraged. He slumps down beside a leafy bush or beneath the shadow of a rock to escape the searing rays of that Palestinian sun, and he begins to write his feelings in poetic form. He has been attacked and let down by people. Now he is led by the Holy Spirit to record his feelings. Those expressions are what we have today preserved in the lyrics of this song, Psalm 54.

The first three verses are a prayer with emphasis on the enemy. The spotlight then turns to the defender as the next two verses form a picture. The last two verses are words of praise as the defended, David himself, becomes the subject of interest.

THE ENEMY—A PRAYER

> Save me, O God, by Thy name,
> And vindicate me by Thy power.
> Hear my prayer, O God;
> Give ear to the words of my mouth.
> For strangers have risen against me,
> And violent men have sought my life;
> They have not set God before them.   [Selah.
> [vv. 1–3]

Verses 1 and 2 in the Hebrew Bible begin differently than in our English version. Literally, they read: "O God, save me . . . vindicate me. . . ! O God, hear my prayer. . . !"

Normally, the verb appears first in the Hebrew sentence, but in this case it is, "O God . . . O God. . . ." By rearranging the normal word order, great emphasis is placed on God. The emphasis is strengthened by the repetition of His name, "O God . . . O God!"

What we discover immediately is that David gives us a perfect example of what to do when we find ourselves under attack by people. Pray first! Don't wait! Ask for His strength and stability! Normally, we pray last, don't we?

We usually fight back first. We retaliate or develop a resentment for the one who makes life miserable for us.

I read some time ago of an animal, a gnu. It has a curious habit when it is being hunted or when it is cornered. It kneels on it forelegs and remains completely silent, as if in prayer. David was a human gnu and so we should be!

Observe that David requests deliverance and vindication on the basis of two things: God's name and God's power.

> Save me, O God, by Thy name,
> And vindicate me by Thy power.
> Hear my prayer, O God;
> Give ear to the words of my mouth.

Throughout the Old Testament God is called at least twelve different names. Each name signifies a particular aspect of His character. David called to mind God's attributes. He also called upon His power, His omnipotence. We all know our need for strength when people have disappointed us, don't we? God's presence and God's strength are two things we cannot do without when enduring people-related conflicts.

In verse 3, David specifies his problem:

> For strangers have risen against me,
> And violent men have sought my life;
> They have not set God before them.   [Selah.

The enemies are given two descriptive names: "strangers" and "violent men." The first name refers to the Ziphites. The other no doubt refers to Saul and his soldiers.

The term *strangers* comes from a term that means "to scatter, disperse" and is used in the Old Testament for investigating a matter, searching out or tracing something—like spies would do. The Ziphites had become spies for Saul. They were dispersed throughout the land, searching for David.

I mention this because I may be writing to someone as innocent as David was, but perhaps you, too, are being "spied upon;" you're being investigated. It is a frightening thing to be falsely accused, especially when the accusations lead to suspicious actions against you. And it is worse when the enemy is one whom you once trusted as your friend! Like Judas, who turned against the Savior, one who was your friend may have now turned against you. If so, you have One who fully understands your experiences. In fact, He sympathizes with your feelings.

> Since then we have a great high priest who has passed through the heavens, Jesus the Son of God, let us hold fast our confession. For we do not have a high priest who cannot sympathize with our weaknesses, but one who has been tempted in all things as we are, yet without sin. Let us therefore draw near with confidence to the throne of grace, that we may receive mercy and may find grace to help in time of need. [Heb. 4:14–16]

David states that they did not have God set before them. God was not in their thinking. He was not the One responsible for their actions. Their insidious suspicions were not prompted by the Lord, which brings up a very practical point. When people turn against you and you are in the right, it is somewhat like being kicked by a mule; it's best to consider the source! You were kicked by a creature whose nature it is to kick. "Why do the heathen rage?" asks the psalmist. A simple answer could be because *they're heathen!* So, when you're wrongly treated, consider the source. They have not set the Lord before them. He doesn't energize their actions. That means, by the way, that He is on your side, not theirs; so (as we learned in Psalm 46) *relax!*

Before moving on, notice that verse 3 concludes with *Selah,* that musical sign meaning "pause." Do that right now; pause and consider your life for a moment. Think through these verses by making them personal to you.

THE DEFENDER—PICTURE

> Behold, God is my helper;
> The Lord is the sustainer of my soul.
> He will recompense the evil to my foes;
> Destroy them in Thy faithfulness. [vv. 4–5]

The first part of these verses sounds like Psalm 46:1, where we are told that God is ". . . a very present help in trouble." An archaic English term for help is *succor.* It means "to furnish relief." Our Defender does just that. The passage goes on to say He is our "sustainer." He comprises in Himself the highest degree or class of helpers. David says, "If I were to call together all who have helped me, underneath would be the sustaining arms of my Lord." Moses mentioned this same thought in Deuteronomy 33:27:

> The eternal God is a dwelling place,
> And underneath are the everlasting arms;
> And He drove out the enemy from before you,
> And said, "Destroy!"

The fifth verse promises the evil that is planned against David would return upon those who planned it. Their wrong would backfire and God would see to it that David's integrity would win the day.

To picture this, it would help if you would call to mind "The Roadrunner," a familiar Saturday TV cartoon for children (and a host of adults!). The entire program revolves around a victorious roadrunner and a frustrated coyote who tries in vain to capture or kill that speedy little bird. Every ingenious plan backfires against the coyote as the roadrunner inevitably enjoys the last laugh! Without exception, the evil planned against the roadrunner ultimately returns to the coyote.

So it is with the *believer* who maintains his integrity while under the attack of difficult people! The evil planned against us will return upon the attacker, thanks to our Defender! Thanks to His faithfulness, the attack will be foiled. Psalm 91:5–10 (TEV) expresses this same idea:

> You need not fear any dangers at night
>   or sudden attacks during the day
>   or the plagues that strike in the dark
>   or the evils that kill in daylight.
>
> A thousand may fall dead beside you,
>   ten thousand all around you,
>   but you will not be harmed.

> You will look and see
>> how the wicked are punished.
>
> You have made the Lord your defender,
>> the Most High your protector,
> and so no disaster will strike you,
>> no violence will come near your home.

We'll look into that song in much greater depth in the second volume of this book.

As I first read verse 5 of Psalm 54, it seemed awfully severe. *Surely it doesn't mean what it says*, I thought. *Surely God won't actually destroy the enemy*, I said to myself. How wrong I was! I looked up the term *destroy* in the Hebrew text. Do you know what it actually means? It is taken from the Hebrew verb *tzah-math*, which means "to exterminate"! In fact, the verb appears in this verse in the *hiphil* stem (causative stem) meaning, literally, "to cause to annihilate"! What I am pointing out is that David is actually declaring, by faith, that God will cause those who have become his enemies to be totally, completely, thoroughly removed! But I remind you that David doesn't do the removing; *God* does.

It is so easy, under pressure, to play God, isn't it? We have thought about the temptation to take our own vengeance before. Romans 12:17–19 warns us against doing that:

> Never pay back evil for evil to anyone. Respect what is right in the sight of all men. If possible, so far as it depends on you, be at peace with all men. Never take your own revenge, beloved, but leave room for the wrath of God, for it is written, "Vengeance is Mine, I will repay," says the Lord.

Living beyond the daily grind of difficult people requires our leaving the vengeance to the One who can handle it best.

THE DEFENDER—PRAISE

The attention shifts again. It is now on the psalmist himself. "Willingly I will sacrifice to Thee; / I will give thanks to Thy name, O Lord, for it is good" (Ps. 54:6).

A major step in dealing with difficult people is taken when we can say, "Thank you, Lord, for this painful experience of being misused, misunderstood, and spied upon." David finally reached this point. He not only gave thanks, but he said, "It is good." Something marvelous suddenly happened.

Let me point out what I think took place between verses 6 and 7. I want you to read 1 Samuel 23:26–29 right now.

> And Saul went on one side of the mountain, and David and his men on the other side of the mountain; and David was hurrying to get away from Saul, for Saul and his men were surrounding David and his men to seize them. But a messenger came to Saul, saying, "Hurry and come, for the Philistines have made a raid on the land." So Saul returned from pursuing David, and went to meet the Philistines; therefore they called that place the Rock of Escape. And David went up from there and stayed in the strongholds of Engedi.

Do you see? *The enemy actually left.* Suddenly, perhaps as soon as David said, "I will give thanks to Thy name, O Lord, for it is good," the enemy retreated. Then David said: "For He has delivered me from all trouble; / And my eye has looked with satisfaction upon my enemies" (Ps. 54:7).

The enemy had actually turned back, removing the threat of immediate danger. Furthermore, David said his eye could now "look upon my enemies." This is a beautiful expression that describes a man without bitterness. He could look his enemy squarely in the eye.

By the way, that is a fairly good way to tell whom you consider your enemies to be—those you cannot look at eyeball-to-eyeball. If you hold hard resentment, unforgiveness, and hatred for someone, you will find it nearly impossible to look directly into his eyes for a sustained period of time. Haven't you heard the expression, "She dislikes me so much, she won't even *look* at me anymore."

David found no place in his heart for bitterness toward his enemies. That is the way it ought to be. When that is true, our *people problems* have a way of diminishing!

CONCLUSION

I read a little poem many years ago that sounds amusing but isn't so funny when we experience it:

> To dwell above with saints we love,
>   Oh, that will be glory!
> But to dwell below with saints we know,
>   Well . . . that's another story!

It seems strange to me that we all talk of the glory and delight of heaven where we will be surrounded by the very saints we couldn't look at or get along with on earth! Let me urge you to set your house in order, especially the room where you spend time with people. Review this Fifty-fourth Psalm frequently until its principles become second nature to you.

Let's declare war on those ugly habits we cultivate against others—negative feelings, unforgiveness, resentment, competitiveness, grudges, jealousy, revenge, hatred, retaliation, gossip, criticism, and suspicion. Let's leave this rugged, well-worn road forever!

The only other route to take is *love*. The longer I live and the more time I spend with the Lord (and with others), the more I am driven back to the answer to most people's problems: sincere, Spirit-empowered, undeserved love.

How beautifully Amy Carmichael reminds us of this in her small but penetrating book *If*.

> If I belittle those whom I am called to serve, talk of their weak points in contrast perhaps with what I think of as my strong points; if I adopt a superior attitude, forgetting "Who made thee to differ? and what hast thou that thou hast not received?" then I know nothing of Calvary love. . . . [p. 13]

> If I take offense easily, if I am content to continue in a cool unfriendliness, though friendship be possible, then I know nothing of Calvary love. . . . [p. 44]

> If I feel bitterly towards those who condemn me, as it seems to me, unjustly, forgetting that if they knew me as I know myself they would condemn me much more, then I know nothing of Calvary love. [p. 47][17]

REFLECTIONS ON DIFFICULT PEOPLE

1. Difficult people constitute a big slice of everyone's life, don't they? If we allow it to happen, they will dominate our thinking and drain our energy. This week is an excellent time to stop all that nonsense! Right now, make a mental list of those who give you grief. One by one . . . pray. Pray for relief from the grind of their presence. Pray that God will change their hearts (remember, *you* can't). And pray that you will see the day when enmity is replaced with amity. Pray all this week for those three things.

2. In the song we just looked at, we saw the Lord as "my helper" and also "the sustainer of my soul" (v. 4). I suggested the word "Defender." Look up these three words in the dictionary and write the definition of each:

   Helper: _____

   Sustainer: _____

   Defender: _____

   Starting to feel a little more relieved?

3. Here is a gutsy idea. I hope you are game for it. This week, with the right motive, do something thoughtful for someone who has made life difficult for you. Yes, you read that correctly. You may want to write a brief note or send some flowers. <u>Decide on some way to demonstrate love</u> . . . then *do* it. Whatever, extend the love of God and watch Him work!

Now that we have reached the end of the first thirteen weeks of our year together, it is a good time to change gears. I hope the next section will help relieve even more of the grind!

We are one-fourth of our way through the year, a natural turning point and a good place to switch our emphasis from the songs of Scripture to some of the sayings.

For many years I have taught that the Psalms give us a vertical perspective and the Proverbs a horizontal one. The Psalms help us know how to relate to our God, while the Proverbs help us know how to relate to our fellow human beings. The Psalms assist us in our praise and adoration of the Lord. The Proverbs offer us counsel and wisdom in dealing with other people. We need them both in order to maintain our balance.

So then . . . for the next thirteen weeks, let's focus on some of the insightful words Solomon wrote centuries ago. To this day they remain as true as they are timeless. If you're like me, you'll have a tough time deciding which you appreciate the most!

THE SAYINGS IN SCRIPTURE

WEEK 14
THROUGH
WEEK 26

Probverbs

The proverbs of Solomon the son
of David, king of Israel:
To know wisdom and instruction,
To discern the sayings of
understanding,
To receive instruction in wise behavior,
Righteousness, justice and equity;
To give prudence to the naive,
To the youth knowledge and discretion,
A wise man will hear and increase in
learning,
And a man of understanding will acquire
wise counsel,
To understand a proverb and a figure,
The words of the wise and their riddles.

The fear of the Lord is the beginning of
knowledge;
Fools despise wisdom and instruction.

Hear, my son, your father's instruction,
And do not forsake your mother's
teaching;
Indeed, they are a graceful wreath to
your head,
And ornaments about your neck.   [1:1–9]

THE GRIND OF
HUMAN
VIEWPOINT

Every waking moment of our lives we operate from one of two viewpoints: human or divine. I sometimes refer to these as horizontal perspective and vertical perspective. The more popular of the two is human. We much prefer to think, maintain our attitudes, and conduct our lives independently. Human opinions influence us more than God's commands and principles. Horizontal solutions give us greater security and pleasure, unfortunately, than vertical ones. For example, when under the gun of some deadline, we much prefer a tangible way out than God's telling us to trust Him to see us through. Rather than waiting on our Lord to solve our dilemma in His own time, we would normally choose the option of stepping in and manipulating a fast, painless escape.

Because the Book of Proverbs is full of divine wisdom, yet packed with practical counsel, we can anticipate vertical perspective (even though the grind of human viewpoint comes so naturally). The good news is this: The more we pore over the sayings in Scripture, the more oil we will apply to the daily grind of our horizontal perspective. But before I say more about that, let's get a good grasp on the Book of Proverbs as a whole.

Without a doubt, Solomon's sayings offer the most practical, down-to-earth instruction in all the Bible. The entire book of thirty-one chapters is filled with capsules of truth . . . short, pithy maxims that help us face and, in fact, live beyond life's daily grinds. These sayings convey specific truth in such a pointed, easily understood manner, we have little difficulty grasping the message.

The most commonly employed style of expression in Proverbs is the "couplet" . . . two ideas placed next to each other. Take Proverbs 13:10 for example:

> Through presumption comes nothing but strife,
> But with those who receive counsel is wisdom.

Interestingly, in Proverbs there are three main categories of couplets: contrastive, completive, and comparative.

In the contrastive couplet, the key term is usually *but*. One statement is set in contrast to the other statement, and *but* links the statements together; however, it separates the two ideas.

> A wise son accepts his father's discipline,
> But a scoffer does not listen to rebuke. [13:1]

> Poverty and shame will come to him who neglects discipline,
> But he who regards reproof will be honored. [13:18]

> He who spares his rod hates his son,
> But he who loves him disciplines him diligently. [13:24]

In the completive couplets, the second statement completes the first. In these couplets, the key connecting links are usually *and* or *so*.

> The heart knows its own bitterness,
> And a stranger does not share its joy. [14:10]

> Even in laughter the heart may be in pain,
> And the end of joy may be grief. [14:13]

> Commit your works to the Lord,
> And your plans will be established. [16:3]

In the comparative couplets, the one statement serves as a comparison of the other. In such cases, the keys to look for are *"better . . . than"* and *"as . . . so"* or *"like . . . so."*

> Better is a little with the fear of the Lord,
> Than great treasure and turmoil with it. [15:16]

It is better to live in a corner of the roof
Than in a house shared with a contentious woman. [25:24]

Very picturesque. Often the comparative sayings are the most graphic.

While we are getting better acquainted with the ancient sayings, I should mention that this is a book full of various kinds of people. Years ago I did an in-depth analysis of Proverbs and was surprised to discover that the book includes over 180 types of people. No wonder it is so helpful when it comes to giving wise counsel for our horizontal living!

The major question is this: Why has God preserved these sayings down through the centuries? If we go back to the opening words of the book, we'll find the answer to that question. You might want to glance back over Proverbs 1:1–9.

As I read those words, I find five reasons God gave us this book of wisdom:

1. To give reverence and obedience to the heart. "The proverbs of Solomon the son of David, king of Israel: To know wisdom and instruction" (1:1–2).

These sayings bring God into proper focus. They help us look at life from God's point of view. They assist us in knowing how to "read" God's reproofs. The Proverbs will help make our hearts obedient.

2. To provide discernment to the eye. "To discern the sayings of understanding" (1:2).

Discern is a crucial term. It means (in the original Hebrew verb) "to separate, to make distinct." The whole idea of giving insight is in Solomon's mind. Proverbs provides us with the ability to distinguish truth from error.

3. To develop alertness in the walk. "To receive instruction in wise behavior, / Righteousness, justice and equity" (1:3).

The original term translated receive carries with it the thought of mobility . . . taking something along with you, carrying something. In this case, what the student of God's sayings carries with him (or her) is "instruction in wise behavior." We glean from the proverbs an alertness in our daily walk. The sayings assist us when we are on the move. They help us "keep on truckin'!"

4. *To establish discretion and purpose in life.* "To give prudence to the naive, / To the youth knowledge and discretion" (1:4).

Isn't it interesting that the dual objects of verse 4 are the naive and the young? Those who are wide open to everything, who have little knowledge of danger—those who are gullible. Solomon assures us that these sayings will add substance and purpose to our lives.

For all those who wander aimlessly, lacking purpose and embracing merely a human viewpoint of existence, there is hope!

5. *To cultivate keenness of mind.* "To understand a proverb and a figure, / The words of the wise and their riddles" (1:6).

Finally, these sayings will help us think keenly; they will sharpen the edges of our minds. They will quicken our thoughts and enable us to understand more of life's riddles. And as that occurs, the grind of human viewpoint will slowly be replaced with the wisdom of divine perspective.

R EFLECTIONS ON HUMAN VIEWPOINT

1. It is quite possible that you have begun to endure the grind of life strictly from its human perspective: Two-dimensional. Little depth. Less and less hope. That viewpoint comes from a society that leaves God out. Everything is gauged from what can be seen, weighed, measured, and proven. We are learning that God's Book offers a broader, deeper, richer perspective. These sayings in Proverbs have the ability to change your whole outlook. Are you willing? Before going one page further, tell the Lord that you long to have *His* viewpoint . . . that you want *His* wisdom.

2. Maybe you are among the naive. You have perhaps suffered the consequences of being gullible. Look again at Proverbs 1:7. Define "fear of the Lord." What does it mean when it says that such a fear is the beginning of knowledge? Growing up is a painful, slow process . . . but it can happen. It will help you to keep a journal of the things God is teaching you these days. Start one.

3. Tell a friend about your renewed interest in Proverbs. Explain why these sayings can be of help to people. Take along this book and read the five reasons we have the Proverbs available. Ask him (or her) to pray for you as you search for greater wisdom.

Wisdom shouts in the street,
    She lifts her voice in the
        square;
    At the head of the noisy
        streets she cries out;
At the entrance of the gates in the city,
    she utters her sayings:
"How long, O naive ones, will you love
    simplicity?
And scoffers delight themselves in
    scoffing,
And fools hate knowledge?
"Turn to my reproof,
Behold, I will pour out my spirit on you;
I will make my words known to you.
Because I called, and you refused;
I stretched out my hand, and no one paid
    attention;
And you neglected all my counsel,
And did not want my reproof;
I will even laugh at your calamity;
I will mock when your dread comes,
When your dread comes like a storm,
And your calamity comes on like a
    whirlwind,

When distress and anguish come on you.
"Then they will call on me, but I will not
    answer;
They will seek me diligently, but they
    shall not find me,
Because they hated knowledge,
And did not choose the fear of the Lord.
"They would not accept my counsel,
They spurned all my reproof.
"So they shall eat of the fruit of their own
    way,
And be satiated with their own devices.
"For the waywardness of the naive shall
    kill them,
And the complacency of fools shall
    destroy them.
"But he who listens to me shall live
    securely,
And shall be at ease from the dread of
    evil."   [1:20–33]

THE GRIND OF
DISOBEDIENCE

Let's face it, we are a pretty wayward flock of sheep! It's not so much that we are ignorant, but rather that we are disobedient. More often than not we know what we ought to do. We just, plainly and simply, do not do it. And so our days are often spent having to endure the irksome and painful consequences of going our own way. The grind of disobedience is neither easy nor new. Unfortunately, it is a well-worn path.

Solomon's sayings address this tendency of ours head-on. The secret of counteracting our bent toward waywardness rests with *wisdom*. In those verses you just read (Prov. 1:20–33), wisdom is personified. She is portrayed as a courageous heroine who stands in the street (symbolic of everyday life) and shouts! She is calling for our attention. She doesn't want us to drift throughout the day without taking her along as our companion. As I read these verses, I observe three facts related to wisdom:

1. Wisdom is available (vv. 20–21).
2. Wisdom can be ignored or spurned (vv. 24–25).
3. Living without wisdom results in serious consequences (vv. 26–28, 31–32).

The deeper we dig into Solomon's sayings, the more clearly we discover what brings wisdom into our lives. The secret? Accepting God's reproofs. Jump ahead for a moment and look at a "completive couplet" with me from Proverbs 3:11–12:

> My son, do not reject the discipline of the Lord,
> Or loathe His reproof,
> For whom the Lord loves He reproves,
> Even as a father, the son in whom he delights.

And while we're at it, look at another even more serious saying in Proverbs 29:1:

> A man who hardens his neck after much reproof
> Will suddenly be broken beyond remedy.

Reproof is from a Hebrew term that means "to correct . . . to convince." I often think of reproofs as God's proddings, those unmistakable nudges, His "still small voice." They are inner promptings designed to correct our ways. They alert us to the fact that we are off course. They communicate, in effect, "My child, that's wrong; change direction!"

These God-given "reproofs" sometimes appear in Scripture. They are spelled out—one, two, three. For example, glance at Proverbs 6:23–24:

> For the commandment is a lamp, and the teaching is light;
> And reproofs for discipline are the way of life,
> To keep you from the evil woman,
> From the smooth tongue of the adulteress.

God's Book shines bright lights into dimly lit caves of immorality, shouting "Danger! Do not enter!" There are dozens of scriptures that offer similar reproofs. Such inner restraints may be silent, but they are nevertheless eloquent.

On other occasions the reproofs come verbally from those who love us. For example:

- From children: "Dad, you're sure gone a lot." Or, "Mom, you seem to be pretty impatient."

- From employers: "You're not showing the same enthusiasm you once did." Or, "You've been coming in late to work recently."

- From friends: "Is something wrong? Your attitude is negative!"

- From a wife: "I feel that you're getting pretty selfish, Hon."

- From a husband: "You don't seem very happy these days. Are you aware that your tone of voice is harsh?"

All of us have sagging character qualities that need attention. To ignore them is to open the gate that leads to disobedience. To address them is to learn and grow from God's personal reproofs. I have listed over thirty character traits in the Reflections section of this week's chapter, specifying some areas worth our attention.

A big question remains: Why? Why do we ignore life's reproofs? What does Solomon say about the reasons we refuse reproofs? As we look back at those sayings in Proverbs 1, I find four reasons reproof is refused. Hold on tight . . . they may hurt!

1. Stubbornness. "Because I called, and you refused . . ." (1:24).

See that last word—*refused?* It means literally "to directly refuse." It is used most often in the Old Testament for refusing established authority, stubbornly and openly rejecting it, as in the case of Pharaoh, who refused to let the Hebrews go. In another of Solomon's sayings, the sluggard *refuses* to get a job. A stubborn will stiff-arms reproofs.

2. Insensitivity. ". . . I stretched out my hand, and no one paid attention" (1:24).

When Solomon states that "no one paid attention," he uses a term that suggests lack of awareness. It would correspond to the New Testament concept of being "dull of hearing." If you have ever tried to pierce through the armor plate of an insensitive individual, you know how frustrating it can be. Though wisdom "stretches out her hand," there are many who completely miss her message due to a lack of awareness.

3. Indifference. "And you neglected all my counsel . . ." (1:25).

To neglect means "to let go." In other words, to keep something from making any difference. This individual says, in effect, "I really couldn't care less!" This is often evidence of low self-esteem. In Proverbs 15:31–32, Solomon writes:

> He whose ear listens to the life-giving reproof
> Will dwell among the wise.
> He who neglects discipline despises himself,
> But he who listens to reproof acquires understanding.

4. <u>Defensiveness</u>. ". . . and did not want my reproof" (1:25).

The Hebrew language is extremely vivid! The original word translated "did not want" means "to be unwilling, unyielding, one who won't consent." This individual is usually defensive and proud.

Disobedience grinds on, most often not because we don't know better but because we don't heed God's reproofs, which are a primary source of wisdom. It's initially more satisfying, quite frankly, to disobey. It can also seem far more exciting and adventurous. But in the long run, every time we fight against wisdom, we lose. A bit of "folk wisdom" comes to mind: "Never git in a spittin' match with a skunk. Even if ya out-spit him, ya come out stinkin'."

Enough said.

R EFLECTIONS ON DISOBEDIENCE

1. Take a close look at these character qualities. Circle those that would rank near the top of your personal struggle list.

Alertness	Discernment	Love	Sincerity
Appreciation	Discipline	Loyalty	Submissiveness
Compassion	Efficiency	Objectivity	Tactfulness
Confidentiality	Enthusiasm	Patience	Teachability
Consistency	Flexibility	Peacefulness	Thoroughness
Cooperativeness	Gentleness	Punctuality	Thoughtfulness
Courtesy	Honesty	Self-control	Tolerance
Creativity	Humility	Sense of humor	Understanding
Dependability	Initiative	Sensitivity	Unselfishness

2. God's reproofs don't always come directly from God's Word. He doesn't limit His warnings to specific commands or precepts found in His Book. As we discovered in this chapter, they can come through parents, friends, children, mates, employers, neighbors, a policeman, a teacher, a coach . . . any number of people. And they aren't always verbalized. A look can convey a reproof. All this week, be more sensitive to the reproofs of others.

3. We learned of four reasons most people refuse reproofs. Can you repeat them?

_____   _____

_____   _____

Choose someone you know well enough to be vulnerable with and discuss which of those four reasons represents your most consistent battleground. Probe to find out why. Ask the Lord to help you break the bad habit(s) so you can begin to get a handle on disobedience.

My son, if you will receive my
sayings,
And treasure my
commandments within
you,
Make your ear attentive to wisdom,
Incline your heart to understanding;
For if you cry for discernment,
Lift your voice for understanding;
If you seek her as silver,
And search for her as for hidden
treasures;
Then you will discern the fear of the
Lord,
And discover the knowledge of God.
For the Lord gives wisdom;
From His mouth come knowledge and
understanding.
He stores up sound wisdom for the
upright;
He is a shield to those who walk in
integrity,
Guarding the paths of justice,
And He preserves the way of His godly
ones.
Then you will discern righteousness and
justice
And equity and every good
course.   [2:1–9]

THE GRIND OF SHALLOWNESS

In our image-conscious, hurry-up lifestyle, hitting the high spots is in vogue—doing just enough to get by. No big deal . . . it's okay to ignore depth in your life so long as you project an image that says you've "got it all together."

Nonsense! People who really make a dent in society are those who peel off the veneer of shallow superficiality and live authentic lives that have depth.

This week, let's level our gun barrels at shallowness. Let's allow the sayings we just read to cut cross-grain against our times and speak with forceful relevance. I should warn you ahead of time, this may not be easy. Solomon takes us into a mine shaft, as it were, a place of hard work, but it will lead us to a most valuable discovery.

As I look closely at these nine verses in Proverbs 2, I find that they can be divided rather neatly into three sections:

    I. The Conditions (vv. 1–4—emphasis on the worker)
       (Note: "if . . . if . . . if . . .")
   II. The Discovery (v. 5—emphasis on the treasure)
      (Note: "then . . .")
 III. The Promises (vv. 6–9—emphasis on the benefits)
     (Note: "For . . .")

Let's dig deeper.

You say you're tired of that daily grind of shallowness?

Weary of faking it? Good for you! But you must remember that breaking out of that mold is awfully hard work. Solomon writes about that when he presents *the conditions* of deepening our lives. "If we will do this . . ." "If we are committed to doing that . . ." Tough talk!

I find four realms of discipline that we must come to terms with if we hope to live beyond the grind of shallowness.

1. The discipline of the written Word of God. "My son, if you will receive my sayings, / And treasure my commandments within you" (v. 1).

It is essential that we receive God's sayings—take them in on a regular basis and allow them to find lodging in our minds. Few things are more astounding in our world than biblical ignorance. People who go beneath the surface of shallow living treasure God's truths and saturate their minds with the Scriptures.

2. The discipline of inner desire. "Make your ear attentive to wisdom, / Incline your heart to understanding" (v. 2).

If we read that correctly, we'll need to have an attentive ear to God's reproofs (remember last week's subject?) and cultivate an open heart before Him.

Are you ready for that? I mean, really motivated? If so, look at the next level.

3. The discipline of prevailing prayer. "For if you cry for discernment, / Lift your voice for understanding" (v. 3).

Perhaps the single most overlooked (and among the most difficult) discipline in the Christian life is consistent prayer. Prevailing prayer. Fervent prayer. In such prayer we "cry for discernment" and we "lift our voice for understanding." In prayer, the sincere believer puts an end to a quick tiptoe trip through the kingdom, chattering like children running through a mall. This person gets down to serious business.

4. The discipline of daily consistency. "If you seek her as silver, / And search for her as for hidden treasures" (v. 4).

We're talking diligence and effort here! The saying describes our seeking God's truths as though digging for silver and searching His mind as we would pursue hidden treasures. This is no superficial game—it's a heavy, consistent pursuit of the living God!

And the results? The discovery?

> Then you will discern the fear of the Lord,
> And discover the knowledge of God. [v. 5]

We'll find true treasure: the fear of the Lord (we'll start taking Him seriously) and the knowledge of God (we'll get to know Him intimately).

Finally, He promises us benefits—benefits from within, without, and above.

1. *From within:* wisdom, knowledge, understanding.

> For the Lord gives wisdom;
> From His mouth come knowledge and understanding. [v. 6]

2. *From without:* protection.

> He stores up sound wisdom for the upright;
> He is a shield to those who walk in integrity,
> Guarding the paths of justice,
> And He preserves the way of His godly one. [vv. 7–8]

3. *From above:* righteousness, justice, equity.

> Then you will discern righteousness and justice
> And equity and every good course. [v. 9]

Yes, "every good course" will accompany the path of those who get rid of shallowness.

Aren't you tired of trifling with sacred things? Haven't you had your fill of superficial skating? Isn't it about time to move off the barren plateau of spiritual neutrality?

This week . . . yes, *this* week, dig in. I dare you!

R EFLECTIONS ON SHALLOWNESS

1. Memorize the first five verses of Proverbs 2 this week. You said you wanted to grow deeper, didn't you? Well, here's a place to start. If you really want to get with it, memorize all *nine* verses.

2. Go back and review the four disciplines taken from Proverbs 2:1–9. Be honest . . . which one represents the biggest challenge for you? Each day this week remind yourself of the discipline, pray about it, search for ways to turn your prayer into action. Think very practically:

   - What are the obstacles?

   - Who stands in your way?

   - Why do you hesitate?

   - What can be done *now*?

3. Focus on "the fear of the Lord" and on "the knowledge of God." Record your own definitions of both:

   Fear: _____

   Knowledge: _____

   Choose a category of your life where "the fear of the Lord" could be applied. Do the same with "the knowledge of God." Be specific. Share the results with your best friend.

My son, do not forget my
    teaching,
    But let your heart keep my
    commandments;
For length of days and years of life,
And peace they will add to you.
Do not let kindness and truth leave you;
Bind them around your neck,
Write them on the tablet of your heart.
So you will find favor and good repute
In the sight of God and man.
Trust in the Lord with all your heart,
And do not lean on your own
    understanding.
In all your ways acknowledge Him,
And He will make your paths
    straight.   [3:1–6]

THE GRIND OF
WORRY

This chapter is dedicated to all of you who have worried in the past . . . all of you who are now worried . . . and all who are *making plans to worry soon!* That might sound amusing, but worry is no laughing matter. Quite frankly, it is a sin. It is, however, one of the "acceptable" sins in the Christian life. We would never smile at a Christian who staggered into his home night after night drunk and abusive. But we often smile at a Christian friend who worries. We would not joke about a brother or sister in God's family who stole someone's car, but we regularly joke about our worrying over some detail in life.

Worry is serious business. It can drain our lives of joy day after day. And there is not one of us who doesn't wrestle with the daily grind of it. In the following study we will look at Solomon's answer to this age-old habit unique to humanity.

Instead of focusing on all six verses at the beginning of Proverbs 3, let's spend some time in those last two. They may be familiar to some, but I have the feeling they have more in them than most of us ever realized.

Please glance back and re-read the final two verses of this saying once again. As you do, think about how to rid your life of that all-too-familiar grind of worry.

A primary rule in meaningful Bible study is to determine the context. These verses fall into a surrounding atmosphere of verses that "sets the stage." Let me show you:

1:8 *Hear, my son, your father's instruction* . . .
1:10 *My son* . . .
1:15 *My son* . . .
2:1 *My son* . . .
3:1 *My son* . . .
3:11 *My Son* . . .
3:21 *My son* . . .

Solomon is giving some wise "fatherly advice" to his son in this section of his book. If you should ever take the time to read the first seven chapters, you will discover they are intensely potent and practical. They contain vital information on how to live a stable, wise, well-balanced life. Proverbs 3:5–6, therefore, contains truth for everyday living—the kind of truth that will assist us toward a meaningful life free of worry.

OBSERVATIONS

There are three initial observations I want to make about Proverbs 3:5–6. Then I want to break the verses into smaller parts so that when we put the saying together it makes better sense to you.

1. There are four verbs in these two verses. Verbs are action words and therefore of special interest to all who want to live beyond the daily grind.

- trust
- lean
- acknowledge
- make straight

Three of these terms are *imperatives;* in other words, they are commands. They are directed to the child of God. They are *our* responsibility: *"Trust . . . do not lean . . . acknowledge. . . ."*

The last is the simple declaration of a *promise.* It declares God's part in the verse. It states *His* responsibility: *". . . He will make your paths straight."*

Before going to the next observation, let's understand that these four words give us a very brief outline:

I. <u>My Part</u>
   A. Trust!
   B. Do not lean!
   C. Acknowledge!

II. <u>God's Part</u>
   A. He will make straight. . . .

2. The same term is mentioned four times. Can you find it? Sure, it is the term *your*. Your responsibility in a given situation is to trust with all *your* heart . . . refuse to lean on *your* understanding . . . acknowledge Him in all *your* ways . . . so that He might make straight *your* paths.

3. The first phrase is linked with the last phrase, giving us the main idea. The two in the middle merely amplify the main idea. Let me explain.

The main idea of these verses is, <u>I am to trust in my Lord without reservation—with all my heart—so that He makes my paths straight</u>. What is involved in trusting with all my heart? Two actions: one negative, the other positive.

Negative: *I am not to lean on my own understanding.*
Positive: *I am to acknowledge Him in all my ways.*

CLARIFICATION

Without the desire to be pedantic, I want us to dig into the meaning of several terms. I believe it will help you to understand their original meaning and to see how they fit together. At the end I'll tie up all the loose ends with an amplified paraphrase.

1. <u>Trust</u>. At the root of the original Hebrew term is the idea of throwing oneself down, lying extended on the ground—casting all hopes for the present and the future upon another, finding shelter and security there.

To illustrate this, look at Proverbs 11:28:

> He who trusts in his riches will fall,
> But the righteous will flourish like the green leaf.

We are told *not* to trust in riches, for riches are not secure (see Proverbs 23:4–5). If you set your heart on getting rich, throwing yourself down upon them so as to find your security, you will be sadly disappointed. Riches fail and fade away. Riches do not deserve our trust.

Next, glance at Proverbs 3:21–23:

> My son, let them not depart from your sight;
> Keep sound wisdom and discretion,
> So they will be life to your soul,
> And adornment to your neck.
> Then you will walk in your way securely,
> And your foot will not stumble.

The word translated *securely* is the same Hebrew root word as our term *trust*. We are commanded by our Lord to cast ourselves *completely, fully, absolutely* on Him—and Him only!

2. <u>Lord</u>. This, as you may know, is the most intimate and sacred name for God in all the Bible. To this day Orthodox Jews will not even pronounce it. It is the title given Israel's covenant-keeping God . . . the One who is bound to His people by love and by promise. To us, it is applied to our Lord Jesus Christ, God's precious Son. We are to rely fully upon Him, finding our safety and security in Him. He, *unlike money*, is dependable.

3. <u>Heart</u>. This does not refer to the bodily organ in the chest that pumps blood. It is used throughout the Old Testament to refer to our "inner man," that part of us that constitutes the seat of our intellect, emotion, and will—our conscience and our personality. What is the Lord saying? He is saying we are to cast upon our Savior-God our *total* trust, not holding back in any area of our mind or will or feeling. That, my friend, is quite an assignment!

4. <u>Understanding</u>. I direct your attention to this word next because it appears first in its phrase in the Hebrew Bible.

Literally, the second part of verse 5 says: ". . . and upon your understanding, do not lean." This word *understanding* has reference to *human* understanding. It means that we are not to turn first to our own limited point of view, our own ideas or way of thinking, but to our Lord's wisdom.

5. <u>Lean</u>. This is the Hebrew *shan-ann,* meaning "to support oneself, as though leaning for assistance." It occurs in Judges 16:26 where blind Samson leaned against the huge pillars supporting the Philistine temple. It also appears in 2 Samuel 1:16 where King Saul leaned upon his spear for support. It represents the idea of resting one's weight upon something else as though leaning on a crutch. You will notice the strong negative: ". . . do not lean on your own understanding."

We have a gentleman in our church who could tell you about this much better than I. He was injured on a ski outing several years ago and as a result he was confined to crutches for many long weeks. Sometimes you would find him panting at the top of a flight of stairs. If you looked at his hands, you would notice they had gotten red and sore. The man found that leaning on crutches was *exhausting*.

So is leaning on our own understanding! If you want to spend an exhausting day, try to work out your circumstances leaning on your *human viewpoint*. Chase down all the possibilities you can think of. When you hit a dead-end street, back out, then turn down into another one. Drive fast, then slam on your brakes. Try a dash of panic, a pinch of fear, add a tablespoon of manipulation, three cups of scheming, and a handful of pills! When you are through, consider where you have been. That is an excellent recipe for "instant depression." Furthermore, you will be mentally exhausted. Peace will flee from you.

MAN says: *Why trust when you can worry?*
GOD says: *Why worry when you can trust?*

6. <u>Acknowledge</u>. This means "to recognize." Rather than leaning on the manmade crutch of our own devices, we are exhorted to recognize God's presence and His will in our plight.

By acknowledging Him we remind ourselves that we are not alone.

7. Make straight. The Hebrew term means "to make smooth, straight, right." It includes the idea of removing obstacles that are in the way. It appears in a particular stem (*Piel* stem) that suggests *intensity*. In other words, when the Lord is fully relied upon to handle a given situation, He will remove all the obstacles and smooth out our path thoroughly, not halfheartedly.

APPLICATION

Now that we have analyzed all the vital parts, let's put the verses back together in an extended paraphrase:

> Throw yourself completely upon the Lord—that is, cast all your present and future needs on Him who is your intimate Savior-God . . . finding in Him your security and safety. Do this with all your mind and feeling and will. In order to make this possible, you must refuse to support yourself upon the crutch of human ingenuity. Instead, recognize His presence and concern in each one of your circumstances. Then He (having taken full control of the situation) will smooth out and make straight your paths, removing each obstacle along the way.

From now on when you find yourself approaching the grind of worry, turn to this paraphrase and read it aloud.

R EFLECTIONS ON WORRY

1. Each remaining morning of this week read the paraphrase I have suggested. But instead of reading "that is, cast *all your present and future needs* on Him," insert the specific things that you are tempted to worry about.

2. Locate a pair of crutches. Borrow them from a friend or maybe from a local hospital. Try walking with crutches for an hour each day this week. When you are not on them, carry them in your car or prop them up by the table where you eat and by the bed where you sleep. Why? They will be a tangible, irritating reminder of how bothersome it is to the Lord for you to "support yourself on the crutch of human ingenuity."

3. All this week, think *seriously* about how sinful it is to worry. Yes, call it sin! Realize that it breaks that vital fellowship between you and God. Ponder the fact that when we carry our own burdens we are saying to God "No help needed!" As soon as you get even a fleeting thought to worry, deliberately give it to the Lord. Tell Him that you are refusing to lean any longer on your own abilities.

M y son, give attention to my
        words;
        Incline your ear to my
        sayings.
Do not let them depart from your sight;
Keep them in the midst of your heart.
For they are life to those who find them,
And health to all their whole body.
Watch over your heart with all diligence,
For from it flow the springs of
        life. [4:20–23]

THE GRIND OF
AN UNGUARDED
HEART

At first glance this may seem to be a rather remote area of concern. After all, what is an unguarded heart in comparison to something as real as worry or as troublesome as disobedience? How could anyone struggle that much with an unguarded heart? Well, you may be surprised. To unveil our hearts and put all our secrets on display is to open ourselves to enemy attack. Our Lord is pleased when we reserve an "inner vault" of our lives to hold His treasures. To "tell it all" is to traffic in a world of superficiality. Once we have done a little digging into this subject, I think you will realize how pertinent this daily grind can be.

To begin with, let's remember what I mentioned earlier, that the *heart* in Solomon's sayings is never a reference to the organ in the chest that pumps blood. We learned in last week's reading that it is a term used to describe our whole inner being . . . the center of our mind, our emotions, and our will. In fact, the Hebrew word *labe* is used over ninety times in Proverbs alone.

So when I address an "unguarded heart" this week, I have in mind the very common problem of living without inner restraint, without concern for protection from the adversary, being insensitive to God's delicate leading. Now you see why I feel this is just as great a hassle as the others we've been dealing with . . . maybe greater!

As we look at the saying of Solomon in Proverbs 4, we'll notice we are, again, in one of the "My son . . ." sections. Here is more wise counsel from a father to his family members. Observe his comment about inclining your ear to his sayings and keeping them "in the midst of your heart." Very interesting!

For the next few minutes I want us to direct our full attention to this whole idea of guarding the heart, or, as Solomon put it:

> Watch over your heart with all diligence,
> For from it flow the springs of life. [Prov. 4:23]

I notice three significant observations:

1. This is a command—"Watch over!"

2. There is an intense priority included in this command—"with *all* diligence."

3. The reason for the command is stated in the last part of the verse—"for. . . ."

KEY TERMS

As you may have noticed, there are several words that are keys toward understanding the full meaning of the statement.

Watch over, diligence, and *springs* would have to be understood before the true meaning can emerge. So, now let's dig into each one of them.

1. Rather than beginning the verse as our English version does, the Hebrew text begins with: "More than all else" or "Above all else. . . ."

In Hebrew, when something appears first in a sentence, different from the normal word order, that word is emphatic. That means these words "more than all else" are emphatic. This tells us that our God puts a premium on the matter. Actually, these beginning words are a literal translation of "with all diligence."

We have now established that the verse begins: "More than all else . . ."

2. The next part of the Hebrew verse refers to something that is to be watched closely. Actually, the word originally

comes from a noun which means "a place of confinement." It is periodically rendered *prison*, and in a broader sense it means something that is closely observed, protected, preserved, or guarded.

That gives us even more light. If we went a step further, inserting those thoughts, the verse would read: "More than all else to be closely watched and protected (as something in a confined place). . . ."

3. Now we come to the main Hebrew verb translated *watch over* in English. It is the word *nah-tzaar*, meaning "to preserve, keep." This same word occurs in Isaiah 26:3:

> "The steadfast of mind Thou *wilt keep* in perfect peace,
> Because he trusts in Thee." [Emphasis mine]

The Lord's peace preserves and keeps the believer's mind, making us "steadfast." In Solomon's saying, the words "your heart" follow that same verb:

> More than all else to be closely watched and protected (as something in a confined place), preserve your heart (your inner self, the place where God speaks to you through His Word and Spirit). . . .

We are beginning to understand why this is so essential, why it is imperative for our "heart" to be watched over and preserved, kept sensitive.

4. The word *for* could just as well be rendered *because*. Now we are told *why*.

5. The Hebrew says: ". . . because from within it. . . ." Referring to the heart, the verse declares that it is to be closely protected and kept in a state of "readiness," because it is *within* it that something extremely important occurs.

6. The Hebrew *mo-tzah* is translated "springs," but the word *source* or *direction* would be more accurate. Why is the heart to be protected and kept sensitive to the Lord? ". . . because from within it comes direction for life." Basically, then, we find this verse is dealing with the will of God—both discovering it and walking in it.

ACTUAL MEANING

Now let's put all the pieces of our research together and see what the verse actually says. A paraphrase based on the Hebrew text might read:

> More than all else to be watched over and protected (as something in a confined place), it is imperative that you preserve and keep your heart sensitive; because from within it comes divine direction for your life.

Read that over again, this time very slowly.

The verse is saying that since your inner self—your heart—is the source and basis of knowing God's will, it is more important than *any other single thing* that your heart be in a state of readiness, receptivity, and sensitivity.

If your heart is carnal, calloused, and bent on having your own way, then direction from God for life will not come through. Look at Psalm 16:11:

> Thou wilt make known to me the path of life;
> In Thy presence is fullness of joy;
> In Thy right hand there are pleasures forever.

We learn from that statement that God wants to show His children His plan for their lives.

HOW GOD DIRECTS

Look at Proverbs 4 for one final glance. Go back to the beginning of the chapter. In the first four verses God tells us how He directs us—how He speaks to our "heart."

First, verses 1–4:

> Hear, O sons, the instruction of a father,
> And give attention that you may gain understanding,
> For I give you sound teaching;
> Do not abandon my instruction.

When I was a son to my father,
Tender and the only son in the sight of my mother,
Then he taught me and said to me,
"Let your heart hold fast my words;
Keep my commandments and live."

The *Word of our Father* directs us.
Second, verses 5–7:

Acquire wisdom! Acquire understanding!
Do not forget, nor turn away from the words of my mouth.
Do not forsake her, and she will guard you;
Love her, and she will watch over you.
The beginning of wisdom is: Acquire wisdom;
And with all your acquiring, get understanding.

The practical application of our Father's Word to life's decisions helps direct us into His will. This explains why Solomon uses the words "wisdom" and "understanding" several times. The Lord desires for us to apply *practical common sense* in determining His will.

Third, verses 10–11, 20–22:

Hear, my son, and accept my sayings,
And the years of your life will be many.
I have directed you in the way of wisdom;
I have led you in upright paths. . . .

My son, give attention to my words;
Incline your ear to my sayings.
Do not let them depart from your sight;
Keep them in the midst of your heart.
For they are life to those who find them,
And health to all their whole body.

Solomon reminds us of the value of *trustworthy counselors* in these verses. Specifically, he wrote to his own child. He assures his son that the counsel of a godly parent is one of several ways God directs our hearts.

Fourth, verses 26–27:

Watch the path of your feet,
And all your ways will be established.
Do not turn to the right nor to the left;
Turn your foot from evil.

A final word regarding evaluation always helps. "Watch" means "weigh," as one would weigh baggage. Look discerningly into the matter. *Personal evaluation* (meditation) is another very important part of knowing God's will.

All these things explain why it is important to keep your heart open, sensitive, and carefully watched. Unless it is right before God, He cannot communicate divine direction. And unless we receive and walk in His will, misery and ultimate unhappiness are our constant companions.

Now, let me ask you: Is an "unguarded heart" really that important?

R EFLECTIONS ON AN UNGUARDED HEART

1. Let's see how well you understood Solomon's saying in Proverbs 4:23.

   - "Heart" would include the _____, _____, and _____.
   - "Springs" of life means _____ or _____.
   - God wants to show us His will ____ True ____ False?

   Check and see how you did.

2. From Proverbs 4, I presented some ways God directs us into His will:

   - His Word, the Bible
   - Common sense
   - Trustworthy counselors
   - Personal evaluation

   As you look over that list, which has proven the most helpful to you? Why?

3. Think of three ways you could do a better job of "guarding your heart." What has been allowed to slip in that could make it insensitive or slow to react? You may wish to confine your answers to three areas:

   My mind _____.

   My emotions _____.

   My will _____.

Then he taught me and said to me,
"Let your heart hold fast my
words;
Keep my commandments and live;
Acquire wisdom! Acquire
understanding!" [4:4]

My son, observe the commandment of
your father,
And do not forsake the teaching of your
mother;
Bind them continually on your heart;
Tie them around your neck.
When you walk about, they will guide
you;
When you sleep, they will watch over
you;
And when you awake, they will talk to
you.
For the commandment is a lamp, and the
teaching is light;
And reproofs for discipline are the way of
life. [6:20–23]

Keep my commandments and live,
And my teaching as the apple of your eye.
Bind them on your fingers;
Write them on the tablet of your
heart. [7:2–3]

Incline your ear and hear the words of the
wise,
And apply your mind to my knowledge;
For it will be pleasant if you keep them
within you,
That they may be ready on your
lips. [22:17–18]

THE GRIND OF BIBLICAL ILLITERACY

Few things are more obvious and alarming in our times than biblical illiteracy. Even though the human mind is able to absorb an enormous amount of information, mental laziness remains a scandalous and undeniable fact.

So much for the bad news—the problem; let's focus, rather, on the good news—the solution. While there is not some quick-'n'-easy cure-all that will suddenly remove the grind of biblical illiteracy, I do believe that one particular discipline (more than any other) will keep us on the right road. When I began to get serious about spiritual things, it was this discipline that helped me the most. None other has come to my rescue like this one: *memorizing Scripture.*

I can still recall more than one occasion when the memorized Word of God rescued me from sexual temptation. It was as if God drew an imaginary shade (something on the order of a Venetian blind) between the other person and me, having inscribed on the surface: "Be not deceived God is not mocked; Whatever a man sows that shall he also reap" . . . a verse I committed to memory as a young teenager. During times of great loneliness, memorized Scripture has also rescued me from the pit of depression. Verses like Isaiah 41:10 and 49:15–16, along with Psalms 27:1 and 30:5 have brought me great companionship.

Before developing that concept, let's understand that we can absorb God's Word in various ways.

First, we can *hear* it. This is the simplest, least-difficult method of learning the precepts and principles of the Bible. There are plenty of trustworthy Bible teachers and preachers in our great nation. There are churches and schools, radio and TV programs, audio and video tapes, even record albums that specialize in scriptural instruction. No one in America—except those with physical hearing impairment—has any excuse for not hearing God's Word.

Second, we can *read* it. This requires more personal involvement than simply hearing the Scriptures. Those who start getting serious about their spiritual maturity buy a copy of the Bible and begin to read it. There are numerous versions, paraphrases, and styles available. Various through-the-year Bibles can be purchased, which set forth a plan that enables an individual to read through all sixty-six books of Scripture in 365 days.

Third, we can *study* it. It is at this point people begin to really mean business for God. With pen and paper, reference works, and other tools available today, the Christian starts to dig in on his (or her) own. Some take correspondence courses, others chart their own course or prefer one of the many excellent programs offered through their local church.

Fourth, we can *meditate* on it. As Scripture is heard, read, and studied, the mind becomes a reservoir of biblical truth. Those truths need to be thought through, pondered, personalized, and applied. Through times of quiet meditation, we allow the Word to seep into our cells . . . to speak to us, reprove us, warn us, comfort us. Remember those two great verses from the Book of Hebrews?

> For the word of God is living and active and sharper than any two-edged sword, and piercing as far as the division of soul and spirit, of both joints and marrow, and able to judge the thoughts and intentions of the heart. And there is no creature hidden from His sight, but all things are open and laid bare to the eyes of Him with whom we have to do. [Heb. 4:12–13]

Fifth, we can *memorize* it. What a magnificent way to replace alien and demoralizing thoughts! In all honesty, I know of no more effective way to cultivate a biblical mind and to accelerate spiritual growth than this discipline.

SOLOMON ON SCRIPTURE MEMORY

There are several sayings worth considering as we think of placing God's Word in our hearts.
Proverbs 4:4:

> Then he taught me and said to me,
> "Let your heart hold fast my words;
> Keep my commandments and live."

You'll notice the words "hold fast." In the Hebrew, the words translated "hold fast" mean "to grasp, lay hold of, seize, hold firmly." It is the verb *tah-mack*, the same term is found in Isaiah 41:10, which says:

> Do not fear, for I am with you;
> Do not anxiously look about you, for I am your God.
> I will strengthen you, surely I will help you,
> Surely I will uphold you with My righteous right hand.

The word *uphold* is from the same verb, *tah-mack*. Scripture memory gives you a grasp, a firm grip of confidence in the Bible. As God's Word gets a grip on you, it "upholds" you!
Proverbs 6:20–23:

> My son, observe the commandment of your father,
> And do not forsake the teaching of your mother;
> Bind them continually on your heart;
> Tie them around your neck.
> When you walk about, they will guide you;
> When you sleep, they will watch over you;
> And when you awake, they will talk to you.
> For the commandment is a lamp, and the teaching is light;
> And reproofs for discipline are the way of life.

Go back and locate "bind . . . tie." Scripture memory straps the truths of God to you. The word translated "bind" really means "to tie together, to bring something in league with something else." Our word *correlate* fits. Scriptures correlate so much better when we store them up. They help us come to terms with life; things make better sense when certain Scriptures are in place in our heads.

Proverbs 7:2–3:

> Keep my commandments and live,
> And my teaching as the apple of your eye.
> Bind them on your fingers;
> Write them on the tablet of your heart.

No clearer verses encouraging scripture memory could be found than these in The Proverbs. When we write something, we don't abbreviate or confuse matters. Quite the contrary, we clarify them. The Lord says "write them on the tablet of your heart." Don't be sloppy or incomplete in your memory work. It is essential that we be exact and thorough when we memorize. Without this, confidence slips away. I often think of being thorough in Scripture memory in the same way we plan a flight. Every number is precise and important (flight number, seat number, gate number) and the time as well. Being exact is extremely important!

Proverbs 22:17–18:

> Incline your ear and hear the words of the wise,
> And apply your mind to my knowledge;
> For it will be pleasant, if you keep them within you,
> That they may be ready on your lips.

I love those two sayings. They constantly encourage me to stay at this discipline! The idea of having His Word "ready on your lips" should convince us of the importance of maintaining this discipline. I say again, nothing will chase away biblical illiteracy like memorizing Scripture.

CONCLUSION

Let's conclude with three practical suggestions that have helped me in my own Scripture-memory program.

First, it is better to learn a few verses perfectly than many poorly. Learn the place (reference) as well as the words exactly as they appear in your Bible. Do not go on to another verse until you can say everything perfectly, without a glance at the Bible.

Second, review often. There is only one major secret to memory—review. In fact, it is a greater discipline to stay current in review than to take on new verses regularly.

Third, use the verse you memorize. The purpose of Scripture memory is a practical one, not academic. Who cares if you can spout off a dozen verses on temptation if you fall victim to it on a regular basis? Use your verses in prayer, in conversations and counsel with others, in correspondence, and certainly in your teaching. Use your memorized verses with your children or mate. God will bless your life *and theirs* as you tactfully share His Word. Isaiah 55:10–11 promises:

> For as the rain and the snow come down from heaven,
> And do not return there without watering the earth,
> And making it bear and sprout,
> And furnishing seed to the sower and bread to the eater;
> So shall My word be which goes forth from My mouth;
> It shall not return to Me empty,
> Without accomplishing what I desire,
> And without succeeding in the matter for which I sent it.

Caught in the grind of biblical illiteracy? Here's a good place to begin. Trust me, you will never regret the time you invest in hiding God's Word in your heart.

R EFLECTIONS ON BIBLICAL ILLITERACY

1. Living beyond the daily grind of biblical illiteracy will not "just happen" any more than a flat tire will automatically repair itself. It will call for extra effort! To begin realistically, select six to ten verses you have come to appreciate. Perhaps you would like to use three or four from the Psalms we have looked at in Section One and several from Proverbs in this second section. Spend some time each day this week on those verses. Take them one at a time. Don't go on to the next until you have firmly committed the previous one to memory. And don't forget that the secret of Scripture memory is review.

2. As situations occur in your life where the truth of what you have memorized applies, remind yourself of it. State it aloud. Use your verse(s) also in your prayers. Share them with someone else when it is appropriate. I have found that few things bring more encouragement than the repeating of Scripture when the time is right.

3. There are Scripture-memory programs available in which you may want to enroll. One I would recommend is:

> The Navigators
> Post Office 6000
> Colorado Springs, CO 80934

Why not write today so you can get started?

D eceit is in the heart of those
who devise evil,
But counselors of peace have
joy.   [12:20]

Anxiety in the heart of a man weighs it
down,
But a good word makes it glad.   [12:25]

Even in laughter the heart may be in
pain,
And the end of joy may be grief.
The backslider in heart will have his fill
of his own ways,
But a good man will be satisfied with
his.   [14:13–14]

Everyone who is proud in heart is an
abomination to the Lord;
Assuredly, he will not be
unpunished.   [16:5]

The heart of the wise teaches his mouth,
And adds persuasiveness to his lips.
Pleasant words are a honeycomb,
Sweet to the soul and healing to the
    bones. [16:23–24]

––––––––––

Before destruction the heart of man is
    haughty,
But humility goes before honor. [18:12]

––––––––––

The foolishness of man subverts his way,
And his heart rages against the
    Lord. [19:3]

––––––––––

A plan in the heart of a man is like deep
    water,
But a man of understanding draws it
    out. [20:5]

THE GRIND OF A
TROUBLED HEART

The major cause of death in our world is still heart trouble. If I
were to reverse those two words, we would put our finger on a
daily grind most people live with: *a troubled heart.* I realize those
words are vague . . . but that's on purpose. The "troubled"
heart affects us many different ways. It comes in the form of
anxiety and low-grade depression. On other days it is inner
churning, discontentment, feelings of insecurity, instability, often doubt, unrest, and uncertainty. A troubled heart lacks peace
and often an absence of calm assurance. One answer to a troubled heart is a friend who will provide wise counsel.

The one who dubbed our era *The Aspirin Age* didn't miss it
far. It's true that we live in a time when huge numbers of the
world's population use aspirin or some other medication to relieve pain, much of which is stress related. But medicine cannot
relieve the deep pain of a troubled heart for the multitudes who
are seeking inner peace. That takes a friend who tunes in to our
troubles, and precious few of us are even aware of others'
struggles.

The importance of sensitivity to others' needs can scarcely be
exaggerated. Even though you may not be deep in Bible knowledge, you should realize that you can be used effectively by
God as a counselor, friend, and interested listener in the lives
of others—just because you know the Lord Jesus Christ! Naturally, the deeper your knowledge of His Word, the sharper will
be your discernment and the wiser will be your counsel. Job's

counselors, for example, dealt him misery and spoke unwisely (you might take the time to read Job 13:3–4; 16:2; 21:34).

One of Solomon's sayings (Prov. 20:5) points out the value of a wise counselor.

> A plan in the heart of a man is like a deep water,
> But a man of understanding draws it out.

Look also at Proverbs 18:4:

> The words of a man's mouth are deep waters;
> The fountain of wisdom is a bubbling brook.

Those sayings tell us that there is within our inner beings a pool of water—often *troubled* water! Also notice that the mouth brings forth the substance of that pool thanks to the *man of understanding* who draws it out.

For example, you may feel deeply about the circumstances in which you find yourself. You cannot fully think through the depths of your feelings without the aid of one who "draws out" those feelings. And how important it is to have such people nearby!

Does that describe *you*? If so, you will be willing to take the time that is necessary to minister in this way. Personally, I believe this is exactly what Paul has in mind when he writes: "Bear one another's burdens, and thus fulfill the law of Christ" (Gal. 6:2).

Because the daily grind of a troubled heart is so common, we tend to overlook it in others. We often think we're the only ones who struggle with it. Not so! It's all around us. And as I mentioned earlier, it wears many faces. For example, I find these six specified in Solomon's sayings:

1. A "deceitful" heart.

> Deceit is in the heart of those who devise evil,
> But counselors of peace have joy. [12:20]

2. A "heavy" heart.

> Anxiety in the heart of a man weighs it down,
> But a good word makes it glad. [12:25]

The Hebrew verb from which *anxiety* is translated, literally means "to be anxious, fearful, worried." You can detect a worried heart rather easily. It shows up on one's face.

3. A "sorrowful" heart.

> Even in laughter the heart may be in pain,
> And the end of joy may be grief. [14:13]

4. A "backsliding" heart (carnality).

The backslider in heart will have his fill of his own ways,
But a good man will be satisfied with his. [14:14]

5. A "proud" heart.

Everyone who is proud in heart is an abomination to the Lord;
Assuredly, he will not be unpunished. [16:5]

Before destruction the heart of man is haughty,
But humility goes before honor. [18:12]

6. An "angry" heart.

> The foolishness of man subverts his way,
> And his heart rages against the Lord. [19:3]

Perhaps you wonder *how* you can detect these troubles. Look at Proverbs 20:11–12:

> It is by his deeds that a lad distinguishes himself
> If his conduct is pure and right.
> The hearing ear and the seeing eye,
> The Lord has made both of them.

As you notice, the Lord says He has given you hearing ears and seeing eyes. I urge you to *use them!* Listen carefully. Watch the person with whom you speak. Be sensitive. This, of course, implies that *you* talk very little, especially during the initial contact. Now read Proverbs 16:23–24:

> The heart of the wise teaches his mouth,
> And adds persuasiveness to his lips.
> Pleasant words are a honeycomb,
> Sweet to the soul and healing to the bones.

God will be pleased to use your words as His instruments, if you allow Him to control what you say. It would be wise of you to claim the promise God gave to Moses in Exodus 4:12: "Now then go, and I, even I, will be with your mouth, and teach you what you are to say." Claim that all week long.

Who knows? You may be the one God wants to use this week in the life of another who can't seem to get beyond the grind of a troubled heart.

R EFLECTIONS ON A TROUBLED HEART

1. This week is a good time to stop, look, and listen.

   a. *Stop* long enough to pray. Ask God for His wisdom to see beyond the grind . . . to realize you are not alone in your troubles . . . to have a renewed sense of inner relief.
   b. *Look* around. Become aware of the circle of acquaintances that is larger than your own personal world. Be sensitive. Discern turmoil in others . . . even in your friends.
   c. *Listen.* Instead of launching a barrage of verbal missiles, just ask a few questions, then (without offering advice) listen. Patiently and graciously hear them out. When our words are few, they become more valuable.

2. Go back to those six examples of a troubled heart from Proverbs. Which one is *your* most frequent battle? Does anybody know it? Can you say you are truly accountable? Have you given anyone permission to step into your private world? Just as others need a "counselor-friend," so do you. How about reaching out and asking someone you respect and trust to enter your secret world? Yes, you'll need to choose the person(s) carefully . . . but begin the search this week.

3. Check out a reliable book on counseling from a local library or preferably your church library. Begin reading it soon. Think of ways to implement some of the techniques presented in the book. One word of caution, however: Be sure that the author is committed to biblical principles and truly loves Christ as Lord. It is so important that we know a counselor's underlying faith before we embrace the concepts and techniques he (or she) espouses.

There are six things which the
 Lord hates,
 Yes, seven which are an
  abomination to Him:
Haughty eyes, a lying tongue,
And hands that shed innocent blood,
A heart that devises wicked plans,
Feet that run rapidly to evil,
A false witness who utters lies,
And one who spreads strife among
 brothers. [6:16–19]

The tongue of the wise makes knowledge
 acceptable,
But the mouth of fools spouts
 folly. [15:2]

The lips of the wise spread knowledge,
But the hearts of fools are not so. [15:7]

THE GRIND OF AN UNCONTROLLED TONGUE

(PART ONE)

Solomon's sayings have a lot to say about what we say. In fact, "tongue," "mouth," "lips," and "words" are mentioned in Proverbs almost 150 times. That means on an average of just under five times in each of the thirty-one chapters, those words occur. Seems to me any subject mentioned that often calls for at least two weeks of our attention. Let's do that.

A key statement on the subject of the tongue is located in Proverbs 15:2, which says:

> The tongue of the wise makes knowledge acceptable,
> But the mouth of fools spouts folly.

That's one of those "contrastive couplets," isn't it? It mentions "the wise" in contrast to "fools." Interestingly, the way they use their tongues is a dead giveaway of their identity. You and I realize, of course, that the root problem is not in the mouth but in the heart—the person deep within us. Jesus taught that:

> "The good man out of the good treasure of his heart brings forth what is good; and the evil man out of the evil treasure brings forth what is evil; for his mouth speaks from that which fills his heart." [Luke 6:45]

Like a bucket draws water from a well, so the tongue dips down and pours out whatever is in the heart. If the source is clean, that is what the tongue communicates. If it is contaminated, again, the tongue will expose it.

Using the key statement of Proverbs 15:2 as our outline, let's focus this week on the wrong uses of our tongue . . . and next week on the right uses.

I have never known anyone who has not at some time struggled with using his (or her) tongue in a wrong manner *or* who has not suffered the brunt of another's tongue. Few grinds are more painful!

As I read through Solomon's sayings, I find at least five unhealthy ways an uncontrolled tongue reveals itself. If this issue of an uncontrolled tongue is one of your "daily grinds," let me urge you to pay close attention.

1. Deceitful flattery.

> Bread obtained by falsehood is sweet to a man,
> But afterward his mouth will be filled with gravel. [20:17]

> He who rebukes a man will afterward find more favor
> Than he who flatters with the tongue. [28:23]

What is flattery? Nothing more than insincere compliments expressed with deceitful motives. It is excessive praise verbalized in hopes of gaining favor in the eyes of another. A good rule to follow: Don't do it. Stay clear of it. In fact, it is better to rebuke another in love than to flatter deceitfully.

2. Gossip and slander.

> A worthless person, a wicked man,
> Is the one who walks with a false mouth,
> Who winks with his eyes, who signals with his feet,
> Who points with his fingers;
> Who with perversity in his heart devises evil continually,
> Who spreads strife. [6:12–14]

> He who conceals hatred has lying lips,
> And he who spreads slander is a fool. [10:18]

> A fool's mouth is his ruin,
> And his lips are the snare of his soul.
> The words of a whisperer are like dainty morsels,
> And they go down into the innermost parts of the body. [18:7–8]

He who goes about as a slanderer reveals secrets,
Therefore do not associate with a gossip. [20:19]

Who hasn't been hurt by the uncontrolled tongue of a gossip? But wait. What, exactly, is meant by gossip? It is a false or exaggerated report maliciously discussed and/or circulated about a person. Throughout Scripture, God reserves some of His severest words for gossips as He condemns this habit.

I would also include here the importance of confidentiality. Those who can be trusted with sensitive information are rare!

3. <u>Arguments, striving, angry words</u>. Take the time to read Proverbs 14:16–17; 15:4; 17:14; 18:6; 25:15; 29:11. You'd also profit from a careful examination of the following sayings:

Do not associate with a man given to anger;
Or go with a hot-tempered man,
Lest you learn his ways,
And find a snare for yourself. [22:24–25]

An angry man stirs up strife,
And a hot-tempered man abounds in transgression. [29:22]

By "arguments" and "striving" I do *not* mean the expression of differing opinions or even disagreement. Intelligent thinking and unguarded, open conversation include the freedom of expression, which involves periodic differences of opinion. Arguments and striving, however, have to do with attitudes such as stubbornness and rigidity. This inevitably arouses anger—the kind of anger that is displeasing to the Lord. It is not so much a question of *do* you disagree, but *how* you disagree.

How easy to form the habit of striving! Haven't you seen husbands and wives who argue, simply out of habit? Entire homes are set on edge when this attitude pervades.

Read over each proverb listed above. If they describe you, your homework is overdue!

4. <u>Boasting and foolish jesting</u>.
First, let's consider *boasting*. The next two verses will help clarify what I mean:

> In the mouth of the foolish is a rod for his back,
> But the lips of the wise will preserve them. [14:3]
>
> Like clouds and wind without rain
> Is a man who boasts of his gifts falsely. [25:14]

It is subtle how we shine our own halos. How desperately we want to be noticed! We hint about it, we "feed" on compliments, we even brag with spiritual phrases, yet we know that our hidden motive is to exalt ourselves.

Link all this with Proverbs 6:16–17:

> There are six things which the Lord hates,
> Yes, seven which are an abomination to Him:
> Haughty eyes, a lying tongue. . . .

Listed first on God's "hate list" are haughty eyes. And haughty eyes are the indication of a prideful spirit so often seen in those who boast.

Now, let's address *foolish jesting*. Read Proverbs 10:21; 15:7; 18:7. Ponder especially 18:7:

> A fool's mouth is his ruin,
> And his lips are the snare of his soul.

By "foolish talk" I have in mind talk that is not edifying—silly, useless, foul and/or profane verbiage. (I'm certainly not including tasteful and wholesome humor.) God warns us that the lips of the fool are the "snare" of his soul. How often we have been snared!

A verse from the Letter to the Ephesians vividly warns us:

Let no unwholesome word proceed from your mouth, but only such a word as is good for edification according to the need of the moment, that it may give grace to those who hear. [4:29]

5. Verbosity.

> When there are many words, transgression is unavoidable,
> But he who restrains his lips is wise. [10:19]

Verbosity means excess verbiage—talking too much and saying too little. One who is verbose usually feels compelled to give his comment. He is also "hard of listening." He feels constrained to fill silent segments of conversation with talk, words without significance. He interrupts without hesitation. A number of years ago I discovered that I never learned anything while I was talking. Neither do you!

We have been thinking about the wrong uses of our tongue. The scene has not been pleasant; has it? I hope that rehearsing these five unpleasant examples will encourage you to put the clamps on the muscle in your mouth. Next week, let's focus on some correct, healthy uses of the tongue. Frankly, I'm ready for the positive. Aren't you?

REFLECTIONS ON AN UNCONTROLLED TONGUE

(PART ONE)

This has been enormously convicting! Since that is true, let's consider three *brief* reflections for the week.

1. Think before you say anything. If it won't contribute, say nothing.

2. Each morning this week, as you look at yourself in the bathroom mirror, don't forget to look at your *tongue.* Hold your mouth open long enough to realize that slab of skin, membranes, and muscles has the power to injure . . . to stab . . . to kill. Pray for control.

3. Cultivate the lost art of listening all week long. Deliberately talk less. By the end of the week you'll be amazed at how much you have learned!

The mouth of the righteous flows
    with wisdom,
    But the perverted tongue will be
      cut out.
The lips of the righteous bring forth what
    is acceptable,
But the mouth of the wicked, what is
    perverted. [10:31–32]

The eyes of the Lord are in every place,
Watching the evil and the good. [15:3]

A man has joy in an apt answer,
And how delightful is a timely
    word! [15:23]

Bright eyes gladden the heart;
Good news puts fat on the bones.
He whose ear listens to the life-giving
    reproof
Will dwell among the wise. [15:30–31]

Pleasant words are a honeycomb,
Sweet to the soul and healing to the
    bones.   [16:24]

A joyful heart is good medicine,
But a broken spirit dries up the bones.
    [17:22]

Like apples of gold in settings of silver
Is a word spoken in right circumstances.
Like an earring of gold and an ornament
    of fine gold
Is a wise reprover to a listening
    ear.   [25:11–12]

Better is open rebuke
Than love that is concealed.
Faithful are the wounds of a friend,
But deceitful are the kisses of an
    enemy.   [27:5–6]

THE GRIND OF AN UNCONTROLLED TONGUE

(PART TWO)

Since Solomon says so much about the tongue, it was impossible to digest all that wisdom during one week's time. And since this slippery little fellow we call the tongue gives us so much trouble so often, it seemed appropriate to return to the subject for a second look. After all, James 3:2 states:

> For we all stumble in many ways. If anyone does not stumble in what he says, he is a perfect man, able to bridle the whole body as well.

In other words, a controlled tongue is the hallmark of maturity. And how few there are, it seems, who qualify!

All last week we gave thought to some of the unwholesome and detrimental uses of the tongue. We uncovered no fewer than five wrong ways the tongue can be used:

1. Deceitful flattery
2. Gossip and slander
3. Arguments, strife, and angry words
4. Boasting and foolish jesting
5. Verbosity

What a convicting list! As a matter of fact, I know of very few subjects *more* convicting than this one.

But there certainly are right ways the tongue can be used. This week, let's focus on those as we let Solomon's sayings add soothing oil to the daily grind of an uncontrolled tongue. You may recall Solomon's saying from Proverbs 15:2, 7, which we looked at last week:

> The tongue of the wise makes knowledge acceptable,
> But the mouth of fools spouts folly.
>
> The lips of the wise spread knowledge.

Just as we found five wrong uses, there are also five ways "the lips of the wise" can bring benefit to others.

1. Wise counsel and sound advice.

> The lips of the righteous bring forth what is acceptable. [10:32]
>
> The lips of the wise spread knowledge. . . . [15:7]
>
> Without consultation, plans are frustrated,
> But with many counselors they succeed. [15:22]
>
> Prepare plans by consultation,
> And make war by wise guidance. [20:18]

It would also be worth your time to read and meditate on Proverbs 25:19, 26, and 28. These three additional sayings look at the results of listening to unwise, unsound advice. We have all experienced both sides of counsel—wise and unwise. How can anyone adequately measure the great benefits of wise, timely counsel?

Obviously, one without God cannot give you God's viewpoint, even though he may have beneficial words of human wisdom. We must use great discernment when seeking others' counsel. You may be surprised to read that not even the aged are always reliable:

> The abundant in years may not be wise,
> Nor may elders understand justice. [Job 32:9]

2. Reproof, rebuke, spiritual exhortation.

> A fool rejects his father's discipline,
> But he who regards reproof is prudent. [Prov. 15:5]

Stern discipline is for him who forsakes the way;
He who hates reproof will die. [15:10]

He whose ear listens to the life-giving reproof
Will dwell among the wise.
He who neglects discipline despises himself,
But he who listens to reproof acquires understanding. [15:31–32]

Faithful are the wounds of a friend,
But deceitful are the kisses of an enemy. [27:6]

He who rebukes a man will afterward find more favor
Than he who flatters with the tongue. [28:23]

How rare yet how essential reproof is! Can't you think of
occasions when someone wisely yet firmly rebuked you . . .
and you became a better person because of it? Look again at
Proverbs 27:6. I will amplify it, using the Hebrew text as a basis
for my words:

Trustworthy are the bruises caused by the wounding of one
who loves you; deceitful is the flattery of one who hates you.

This tells us several things:

- The one who does the rebuking should be one who *loves*
  the one he rebukes.

- The "bruise" that is left lingers on. It is not soon forgotten.

- Friendship should include the freedom to mention a criticism.

- Not all compliments come from the right motive.

So much of this matter has to do with discernment and discretion. There is the right *way* and the right *time* (not to mention
the right *motive*) for such an act. God certainly is not pleased
with criticism and/or rebuke from anyone and everyone at any
time he pleases.

No finer passage of Scripture on the subject of timing our
words can be found than Proverbs 25:11–12:

> Like apples of gold in settings of silver
> Is a word spoken in right circumstances.
> Like an earring of gold and an ornament of fine gold
> Is a wise reprover to a listening ear.

3. Words of encouragement.

> A man has joy in an apt answer,
> And how delightful is a timely word! [15:23]
>
> Bright eyes gladden the heart;
> Good news puts fat on the bones. [15:30]
>
> Pleasant words are a honeycomb,
> Sweet to the soul and healing to the bones. [16:24]

By "encouragement" I mean sincere expressions of gratitude given honestly to another individual (usually in private). We so seldom do this, yet it is one of the signs of a mature, godly individual.

Do you express encouragement to those closest to you? Your wife or husband? How about your children? Your teacher? Your secretary? Someone who does a quality job for you? However, we should guard against doing it *too much*. That cheapens the encouragement and makes it appear insincere. Like too large a gem on a ring, encouragement, when overdone, lacks elegance and charm.

4. Witnessing, teaching, comforting.

The mouth of the righteous is a fountain of life. . . . [10:11]

The tongue of the righteous is as choice silver,
The heart of the wicked is worth little.
The lips of the righteous feed many,
But fools die for lack of understanding. [10:20–21]

The fruit of the righteous is a tree of life,
And he who is wise wins souls. [11:30]

The words of a man's mouth are deep waters;
The fountain of wisdom is a bubbling brook. [18:4]

Death and life are in the power of the tongue [18:21a]

Deliver those who are being taken away to death,
And those who are staggering to slaughter, O hold them back.
If you say, "See, we did not know this,"
Does He not consider it who weighs the hearts?
And does He not know it who keeps your soul?
And will He not render to man according to his work? [24:11–12]

Who can accurately measure the benefits gleaned from the tongue of a godly teacher, well-versed in the Scriptures? Or, how could we gauge the depth of comfort received from the lips of a close friend during a period of grief or affliction? And what about the one(s) who told you about Christ? Remember the help you received from the gloriously good news of the Lord Jesus Christ? My, what a tremendous help!

Stop and consider this: The gospel is believed *only* when words have communicated it. The words may be written or spoken, but words are an integral part of the plan. To one who shares Christ, the tongue is essential.

Your tongue can serve no better function in life than that of faithfully, consistently communicating Christ.

5. A good sense of humor.

A joyful heart makes a cheerful face,
But when the heart is sad, the spirit is broken. [15:13]

All the days of the afflicted are bad,
But a cheerful heart has a continual feast. [15:15]

By a sense of humor, please understand that I am *not* referring to silly, foolish talk or to distasteful, and ill-timed jesting. By humor, I mean well-chosen, properly timed expressions of wit and amusing, funny statements. I am so convinced of the value of wholesome humor, I believe one who lacks it will not be as capable a leader or as good a communicator as he (or she) could be.

There are special times when a sense of humor is needed, such as in lengthy, tense, and heated meetings, or when a serious atmosphere has settled in the home over a long period of time, or following extremely difficult experiences in our lives.

How quickly and how easily we forget to laugh! And yet, how healthy laughter is. Look at that last phrase of the final saying I quoted above. The Hebrew text literally says that the cheerful heart *"causes good healing."*

How do you measure up, my friend? Honestly now, have you become so serious you can no longer enjoy yourself (and others)? Let's face it, if there is one, general criticism we Christians must accept without argument, it is that we have become altogether too serious about everything in life. We exclude or ignore most every opportunity for a good, healthy laugh! We're "uptight," far too intense, and much too critical of ourselves and others. As a result, our tolerance and understanding are extremely limited. May God loosen us up! And may He ultimately enable us to live beyond the grind of an uncontrolled tongue.

R EFLECTIONS ON AN UNCONTROLLED TONGUE
(PART TWO)

1. Turn to the New Testament in your Bible and read James 3:1–12 slowly and aloud. Do that *at least three times* this week. After each reading, sit quietly and talk with the Lord about how much you want Him to gain full control over your tongue.

2. Make a list of two ways you could use your tongue in a more helpful manner.

   (a) _____

   _____

   (b) _____

   _____

   How about implementing both before the week is over?

3. A final suggestion *must* deal with improving your sense of humor. In all honesty, have you become rather testy? Maybe a bit too tedious, even negative? Perhaps it is due to too many hours at work. Burnout always robs us of our humor. It may stem from your serious temperament or your circumstances. Enough of that! Take a few extra hours off this weekend. Deliberately focus on the brighter side of life. Select a humorous book to read or a comedy on television or at the movies . . . and let your hair down! People who cultivate a healthy sense of humor give themselves permission to enjoy life. Start there.

Better is a dish of vegetables where
    love is,
Than a fattened ox and hatred
    with it. [15:17]

Better is a little with righteousness
Than great income with injustice. [16:8]

Better is a dry morsel and quietness with
    it
Than a house full of feasting with
    strife. [17:1]

THE GRIND OF DISCONTENTMENT

Many folks eat their hearts out, suffering from the contagious "If Only" disease. Its germs infect every slice of life.

> If only I had more money
> If only I could make better grades
> If only we owned a nicer home
> If only we hadn't made that bad investment
> If only I hadn't come from such a bad background
> If only she would have stayed married to me
> If only our pastor were a stronger preacher
> If only my child were able to walk
> If only we could have children
> If only we *didn't* have children
> If only the business could have succeeded
> If only my husband hadn't died so young
> If only I would've said "No" to drugs
> If only they had given me a break
> If only I hadn't had that accident
> If only we could get back on our feet
> If only he would ask me out
> If only people would accept me as I am
> If only my folks hadn't divorced
> If only I had more friends

The list is endless. Woven through the fabric of all those words is a sigh that comes from the daily grind of discontentment. Taken far enough, it leads to the dead-end street of self-pity—

one of the most distasteful and inexcusable of all attitudes. Discontentment is one of those daily grinds that forces others to listen to our list of woes. But they don't for long! Discontented souls soon become lonely souls.

I am so pleased that Solomon did not overlook discontentment. On three separate occasions he wrote sayings for all of us to read, especially when we are tempted to feel sorry for ourselves. You may have already noticed that all three are "comparative couplets" where the former things named are "better than" the latter. For example:

> Better is a dish of vegetables where love is,
> Than a fattened ox and hatred with it. [15:17]

Who needs a T-bone steak? So what's the big deal about chateaubriand for two if it must be eaten in an absence of love? Several years ago I smiled as I read about a gal at a cocktail party trying to look happy. A friend noticed the huge sparkling rock on her finger and gushed, "My! What a gorgeous diamond!"

"Yes," she admitted, "it's a Callahan diamond. It comes with the Callahan curse."

"The Callahan curse?" asked her friend. "What's that?"

"Mr. Callahan," she said with a frown.

Solomon asks, "What good is it to have more and more of anything if hatred is part of the package?"

Here's another eloquent rebuke:

> Better is a dry morsel and quietness with it
> Than a house full of feasting with strife. [17:1]

We've seen that, too. Lots of people and partying, constant coming and going, endless activity and loads of food . . . but strife. No thanks. How easy to be fooled by all the noise and smoke! A simple bowl of oatmeal served in a tranquil setting is far better.

> Better is a little with righteousness
> Than great income with injustice. [16:8]

Can't miss the point of that one either. Anything—*anything*—that requires injustice to get won't bring satisfaction. Just "a little" with righteousness outstrips the Taj Mahal with injustice. Who cares if his bank account is stuffed and his investment portfolio is impressive if he has to live with a guilty conscience? It's like sleeping on a coat hanger. Every move you make is another reminder that something is wrong.

The rich *and* the poor must hear this. Those who want (and have) much and those who feel they need more are equally in need of this counsel. Discontentment rarely has anything to do with one's financial status. Greed is cancer of the attitude, not caused by insufficient funds but by inappropriate objectives. Some will *never* be satisfied, no matter how much they have. Discontentment is a sneaky thief who continues to disrupt our peace and to steal our happiness. Ever so subtly it whispers "more . . . more . . . more . . . more . . ."

Look at the words of 1 Timothy 6:6–10, 17–19 very carefully, as if you are reading them for the first time:

> But godliness actually is a means of great gain, when accompanied by contentment. For we have brought nothing into the world, so we cannot take anything out of it either. And if we have food and covering, with these we shall be content. But those who want to get rich fall into temptation and a snare and many foolish and harmful desires which plunge men into ruin and destruction. For the love of money is a root of all sorts of evil, and some by longing for it have wandered away from the faith, and pierced themselves with many a pang. . . .

> Instruct those who are rich in this present world not to be conceited or to fix their hope on the uncertainty of riches, but on God, who richly supplies us with all things to enjoy. Instruct them to do good, to be rich in good works, to be generous and ready to share, storing up for themselves the treasure of a good foundation for the future, so that they may take hold of that which is life indeed.

As the Chinese philosopher Lao-Tzu once said:

> There is no calamity greater than lavish desires.
> There is no greater guilt than discontentment.
> And there is no greater disaster than greed.

R EFLECTIONS ON DISCONTENTMENT

1. As you read through that "if only" list, perhaps *your* particular discontentment was missing. If so, acknowledge it here. Openly admit the one longing you have nursed for most of your life.

2. Now go back and read those words from the Chinese philosopher. How do they apply? In what way can you say you are willing to address your secret longing? And while we're at it, is there ever a proper place for being discontented? Explain your answer, especially in light of the words "if we have food and covering . . . be content."

3. Jesus, on more than a few occasions, spoke directly to the issue of always wanting more. In His immortal Sermon on the Mount, He stated "You cannot serve God and mammon" (Matt. 6:24). What is the difference between "earning" and "serving" money? One more thought: If Jesus were to live on earth today, where do you think He would be employed? What kind of car would He drive? How much money would He earn? Do you think He would periodically fly first class? Would He ever feel a slight sting of discontentment? Why? Or why not?

For the commandment is a lamp,
and the teaching is light;
And reproofs for discipline are the
way of life,
To keep you from the evil woman,
From the smooth tongue of the
adulteress.
Do not desire her beauty in your heart,
Nor let her catch you with her eyelids.
For on account of a harlot one is reduced
to a loaf of bread,
And an adulteress hunts for the precious
life.
Can a man take fire in his bosom,
And his clothes not be burned?
Or can a man walk on hot coals,
And his feet not be scorched?
So is the one who goes in to his
neighbor's wife;
Whoever touches her will not go
unpunished. [6:23–29]

The one who commits adultery with a
woman is lacking sense;
He who would destroy himself does it.
Wounds and disgrace he will find,
And his reproach will not be blotted
out. [6:32–33]

THE GRIND OF
LUSTFUL
TEMPTATIONS

Solomon shoots straight.

I find that rather refreshing in our day of gray definitions and bold rationalizations. The sayings you just read are timeless and no less relevant today than they were when the ink was still wet. Our battle with lustful temptations is intense. There is always the opportunity to fall . . . the snares to trip us up. Whether it's in the area of fortune, fame, power, or pleasure— lust wages a mighty war in our souls. And many there are who surrender to it.

Let me remind you that these words and warnings appear in another of the "My son" accounts. As a father, Solomon wanted to leave trustworthy counsel for his son to read and heed. Perhaps he wrote these words with an extra amount of passion since his own father David had suffered the consequence of yielding to lustful temptations many years earlier. Though David's adultery happened before Solomon's birth, no one can doubt that he was ever aware of the consequences that came in the wake of the king's compromise. Solomon was reared in a context that never let him forget his father's moral failure.

Solomon begins with the standard of Holy Scripture:

> For the commandment is a lamp, and the teaching is light;
> And reproofs for discipline are the way of life. [6:23]

That is always the place to find one's standard . . . God's perfect and Holy Word. Not the media. Not others' opinions.

Not the books written by fellow strugglers. Not even our own conscience, which can be seared, calloused, or prejudiced. The "lamp" of God's precepts, the "light" of His teaching—*these* provide us with unfailing direction. Furthermore, as we learned earlier, His reproofs goad us into line and intensify our discipline.

So then, what do we learn from Solomon's sayings when we're faced with the lure of a lustful lifestyle? How do we live beyond the grind of this kind of temptation?

1. Stay away from "the evil woman" (or man).

2. Guard against the "smooth tongue" that invites you in.

3. Refuse to entertain secret desires of the opposite sex's beauty.

4. Don't let those alluring eyes captivate you.

Now, wait just a minute! *Why* would Solomon take such a hard stand on resisting lust's appeal? Without the slightest hesitation, the wise man sets forth the truth, which so few stop to think through today. As we read these sayings, we find several specific reasons:

First, the adulteress goes for "the precious life," which, when snared, is reduced to zero. The backwash is undeniable. To name only a few of the consequences:

Loss of character	Injury to his career
Loss of self-respect	Smearing of his name
Loss of others' respect	Embarrassment to his church
Loss of his family	Draining of his finances
Loss of his testimony	Possibility of disease
Loss of his joy and peace	Beginning of secrecy

Second, the hot fire of punishment will begin and never be fully extinguished. Burn scars are among the most obvious and painful. The one who yields to lustful temptations "will not go unpunished."

Third, it reveals the "lack of sense"; a self-destructive process is begun.

Fourth, "wounds and disgrace" will never be fully erased. Solomon isn't through!

He goes even further, describing in lurid detail how lust appears so appealing, so accepting, so safe . . . yet in the end, it is like "an arrow" and "a snare."

> At the window of my house I looked out through the lattice. I saw among the simple, I noticed among the young men, a youth who lacked judgment. He was going down the street near her corner, walking along in the direction of her house at twilight, as the day was fading, as the dark of night set in.
> Then out came a woman to meet him, dressed like a prostitute and with crafty intent. (She is loud and defiant, her feet never stay at home; now in the street, now in the squares, at every corner she lurks.) She took hold of him and kissed him and with a brazen face she said: "I have peace offerings at home; today I fulfilled my vows. So I came out to meet you; I looked for you and have found you! I have covered my bed with colored linens from Egypt. I have perfumed my bed with myrrh, aloes and cinnamon. Come, let's drink deep of love till morning; let's enjoy ourselves with love! My husband is not at home; he has gone on a long journey. He took his purse filled with money and will not be home till full moon."
> With persuasive words she led him astray; she seduced him with her smooth talk. All at once he followed her like an ox going to the slaughter, like a deer stepping into a noose till an arrow pierces his liver, like a bird darting into a snare, little knowing it will cost him his life. [Prov. 7:6–23, NIV]

Wake up! Let the truth be heard, my friend. When the escapade ends, gross consequences follow . . . and *they* never end.

This is a day when many are becoming soft on those who fall morally. At the risk of overkill, let me ask you: Do you find Solomon soft? Stop and meditate on the final six words in the scripture you just read: ". . . it will cost him his life." I call that about as severe a consequence as one can imagine.

Now is the time to come to terms with temptation. The daily grind may not fully go away, but it need not be considered an overwhelming battle.

R EFLECTIONS ON LUSTFUL TEMPTATIONS

1. Because Solomon shoots straight, I see no reason to back off and trade diplomacy for truth. A good place to start is with a few pointed questions:

   - Are you flirting with lust or resisting it? Do you encourage sexual come-ons?

   - Have you worked out a plan for lust to keep a foot in the door? Be painfully honest.

   - Is there some secret sin you are harboring? Someone you're meeting with? Magazines? Video cassettes? How about those hotel late-night TV movies? Or cable television channels?

   I plead with you; run for your life from those flames of temptation. If you don't, they are sure to grow hotter as the months pass.

2. You may be dangerously close to sexual fire. It could be so close that you find yourself unable to back off. It may call for professional help. *Get it.* Contact a pastor for reference if you don't know whom to see . . . or call someone you respect and start back toward purity. Let me urge you, also, to burn whatever you have hidden away—make a *clean* sweep of it! Tell your illicit partner it is over. Do that even if you don't feel like doing it. Act now.

3. I have already mentioned the importance of being accountable. Once again, I must affirm how valuable it would be
for you to allow another trusted individual (or two) into
the secret chambers of your life. In order for this to happen, you need to be the one who makes the first move.
Even if you don't have a major battle in this area, you *still*
need a point of accountability. An accountability group
forms a safety net. A few trusted friends who love you too
much to let you exist in a self-made world of secret struggles and personal blind spots can become your best in-
surance investment. Living beyond the daily grind of
lustful temptations will require team effort. Start building
your team!

Go to the ant, O sluggard,
Observe her ways and be wise,
Which, having no chief,
Officer or ruler,
Prepares her food in the summer,
And gathers her provision in the harvest.
How long will you lie down, O sluggard?
When will you arise from your sleep?
"A little sleep, a little slumber,
A little folding of the hands to rest"—
And your poverty will come in like a
  vagabond,
And your need like an armed
  man. [6:6–11]

The soul of the sluggard craves and gets
  nothing,
But the soul of the diligent is made
  fat. [13:4]

Commit your works to the Lord,
And your plans will be
  established. [16:3]

The mind of man plans his way,
But the Lord directs his steps. [16:9]

Do not love sleep, lest you become poor;
Open your eyes, and you will be satisfied
  with food. [20:13]

The plans of the diligent lead surely to
  advantage,
But everyone who is hasty comes surely
  to poverty. [21:5]

THE GRIND OF PROCRASTINATION

Pro·cras·ti·nate: To put off intentionally and habitually, post-
pone . . . to put off . . . reprehensibly the doing of something
that should be done.

—Webster's Seventh New Collegiate Dictionary

Thanks, Webster.

Not that we needed a definition, but sometimes it helps to
nail things down. When we procrastinate, we deliberately say
"later" but usually think "never." It's the mañana syndrome:
"Someday, we gotta get organized." Which, being interpreted, is
really saying, "Who cares if it *ever* gets done?" People who procrastinate have no definite plans to accomplish the objective.
They simply push it into the slimy ooze of indefiniteness, that
murky swamp where the thought of good intentions slips in
over its head.

Is your daily grind procrastination? Then Solomon's sayings
to the rescue!

First off, Solomon assures us that we have all the mental
equipment we need to do the deed.

> The plans of the heart belong to man,
> But the answer of the tongue is from the Lord. [16:1]

That ability to plan is unique to mankind. "Orderly thinking"
(16:1, MLB) is ours and ours alone. We have a built-in capacity

to think things through . . . to plan things out. Horses don't. Rabbits can't. Chickens won't. But you and I can *and should.*

Second, Solomon affirms we can also have the *desire* to get the thing done.

> Commit your works to the Lord,
> And your plans will be established. [16:3]

We even have divine assistance available. But please don't kid yourself; this is not automatic. A desire doesn't guarantee accomplishment. I recall another saying of Solomon:

> The soul of the sluggard craves and gets nothing,
> But the soul of the diligent is made fat. [13:4]

Deep within our beings rest rival foes: Sluggard vs. Diligence. The fight is on. Both have desires, you understand. Even Sluggard "craves," but he accomplishes zilch. He doesn't follow through. He postpones: "Maybe someday."
But Diligence?

> The plans of the diligent lead surely to advantage,
> But everyone who is hasty comes surely to poverty. [21:5]

Then why don't we always overrule Sluggard and give the nod to Diligence? Why do we opt for procrastination more often than not? I have thought about that a lot (even while sitting here, realizing I needed to get at it). Here are my conclusions:

- Either we set goals that were unwise or unrealistic
- Or we attempted to do something that was not God's will
- Or we allowed Sluggard to win when he arm-wrestled Diligence!

So? Surprisingly, Solomon says we need to take a trip out to an anthill. In fact, God *commands* us to do so!

> Go to the ant, O sluggard,
> Observe her ways and be wise,

Which, having no chief, officer or ruler,
Prepares her food in the summer,
And gathers her provision in the harvest.
How long will you lie down, O sluggard?
When will you arise from your sleep? [6:6–10]

Ouch! I find it more than a little humiliating to think of standing six feet above a tiny insect and being told to bend down and learn from its ways. But what lessons the ant teaches us! Those tiny pedagogues model several valuable messages:

- They don't need some superintendent over them.
- They get the essentials done first.
- They work ahead of time so they can relax later.
- They do it all without fanfare or applause.

What happens if we fail to follow the ant's example?

- We continue to procrastinate.
- We begin to resemble "a vagabond."
- We ultimately become dependent on others.

Furthermore, we miss one of life's most delightful rewards, which Solomon describes in these words:

Hope deferred makes the heart sick,
But desire fulfilled is a tree of life. . . .
Desire realized is sweet to the soul. [Prov. 13:12, 19]

Our hearts get "sick" when we keep putting our hope on hold. What is it that is so "sweet to the soul"? Accomplishment. For example:

- A garage cleaned spic and span.
- The storm windows attached before winter's first blast.
- Those twenty pounds gone from our bodies.
- The whole yard mowed . . . and trimmed.
- The room addition finished (yes, that includes *paint!*).
- A car waxed.
- A new dress made.
- Pictures labeled and placed in the photo album.
- The chapter written!

R EFLECTIONS ON PROCRASTINATION

1. Take the Scriptures literally. Go out to the closest anthill and watch. Watch very carefully. If you look closely you will see those tiny creatures handling a load much larger and heavier than their own bodies. Furthermore, you'll see none of them kicking back, arguing with each other, or procrastinating. Diligent creatures, those ants.

2. Perhaps what keeps most of us from getting a big job done is one of two things:
   a. Getting started
   b. Spelling out a plan

   Think about both for a few moments. Why not plunge in right away? Better still, how about writing down a procedure. Organize the workload—you know the age-old motto: Plan your work, then work your plan. That's not very clever or creative, but it is still effective.

3. Fill in the blanks:
   - I need to finish _____.
   - What keeps me from it is _____

     and _____.
   - By _____ (time) on _____ (date), I will complete that project.

   When you do, reward yourself! Your "realized desire" deserves loud applause.

By wisdom a house is built,
And by understanding it is
established;
And by knowledge the rooms are
filled
With all precious and pleasant
riches.   [24:3–4]

THE GRIND OF
DOMESTIC
DISHARMONY

Of all the "grinds" that eat away at our peace, none is more nagging, more draining, more painful than disharmony at home. The sarcastic infighting. The negative putdowns. The stinging stares. The volatile explosions of anger . . . occasionally, even brutality and abuse. A TV blaring in the living room, a stack of dishes in the sink. Doors slammed shut. Desperate feelings of loneliness.

Those descriptions may portray the dwelling where you live. It is possible that you have gotten to the place where you look for excuses not to be there, or to be home only as little as possible. You sometimes wonder what can be done to restore harmony . . . to make things different. You probably think that change is impossible. I have good news: It is not.

Solomon, in two simple-sounding verses (24:3–4), tells us we need three essential ingredients in order to turn a house into a home—but what powerful ingredients they are!

1. "By *wisdom* a house is built. . . ."

Wisdom is seeing with discernment. The original Hebrew word emphasizes accuracy, the ability to sense what is beneath the surface. Wisdom refuses to skate across the surface and ignore what is deep within. It penetrates.

2. "By *understanding* it is established. . . ."

Understanding is responding with insight. Instead of fighting back and taking comments personally, understanding insightfully weighs things with perspective.

3. "By *knowledge* the rooms are filled with all precious and pleasant riches."

Knowledge is learning with perception. It includes things like a teachable spirit, a willingness to listen, a desire to discover . . . to find out what is really there. Knowledge forever pursues the truth.

So much for the basic building materials every home must have. What about the results? What happens when wisdom, understanding, and knowledge team up and go to work? Again . . . three results are spelled out by Solomon, each corresponding to a separate "ingredient." You will notice that these words have nothing to do with physical materials or tangible creature comforts. A home doesn't have to have a two-car garage or a matching sofa and chair in the living room or wall-to-wall carpet. What is essential? Wisdom, understanding, and knowledge.

1. By wisdom a house is *built* (v. 3).

The Hebrew term for built suggests "to restore." It is the idea of *re*building something so that it flourishes once again.

2. By understanding it is *established* (v. 3).

The word translated "established" means "set in order." It's the idea of putting something back into an upright position . . . something that was once leaning, falling, or twisted.

3. By knowledge the rooms are *filled* with all precious and pleasant riches (v. 4).

When Solomon wrote "by knowledge the home is *filled,*" he used a term that meant fulfillment, ever-abundant satisfaction. The constant pursuit of the truth makes that happen. And those "precious and pleasant riches"? Those would be the things that last. To name a few: happy memories, positive and wholesome attitudes, feelings of affirmation, acceptance, and esteem, mutual respect, good relationships, and depth of character.

Sounds so wonderful, doesn't it? Almost too ideal to be possible? No, God never dangles theoretical carrots in front of us, mocking us with unattainable possibilities.

Is your home beginning to deteriorate? Are those living in the home lacking a team spirit, a mutual commitment to relationships? Since you cannot force others to change, start with yourself. Begin to demonstrate those three ingredients that have the ability to transform a house virtually in shambles into a home of purpose and harmony.

Yes . . . start with yourself.

REFLECTIONS ON DOMESTIC DISHARMONY

1. Write out Proverbs 24:3–4 on some paper in your own handwriting. Tape the piece of paper onto your bathroom mirror. Since the words flow rather easily, commit them to memory this week. Each morning and each evening, as you review those thoughts, tell the Lord you want them to become a reality in your home. Ask Him to show you ways you can demonstrate wisdom, understanding, and knowledge. Don't make a public announcement of your plan, just begin quietly. Stay at it.

2. As you drive (or walk) home each evening this week, mentally prepare yourself for whatever you may have to face. Remind yourself to remain calm and considerate, nondefensive, cooperative, and thoughtful. Each day this week do something (or *say* something) that will encourage each member of your family. Watch the Lord honor your unselfishness. It may be remarkable how He begins to lift you beyond your daily grind of domestic disharmony.

3. Perhaps you now live alone . . . but you learned many of these principles from both your parents or one of them. Before the week has ended, write or call. Express your gratitude for the things you learned. Be specific as you state your appreciation. You may even add a few lines you read from this section of the book as you describe why you are so thankful.

TRANSITION

Congratulations! You have not only finished the first twenty-six weeks of our readings and reflections in the songs and sayings of Scripture, you have reached the halfway mark in our year together. It has been quite a journey, hasn't it? You have faced some tough issues head on, and you have come to terms with several areas of your life that have needed attention. Good for you!

Our studies these past weeks have not been simple projects, but rather searching ones. That's the way God planned it. The songs of David and the sayings of Solomon were never meant to be shallow little jingles or cute and clever axioms. With inspired persuasion, they push their way into our life, they probe the secret recesses of our heart . . . they refuse to be ignored. As Scripture states, "There is no creature hidden from His sight, but all things are open and laid bare to the eyes of Him with whom we have to do" (Heb. 4:13).

As helpful as these weeks together may have been, our journey is incomplete. We have *another* twenty-six weeks to go! We need to return to those songs and, again, listen to the sweet singers of Israel. Their compositions await more of our time and attention; and, finally, we want to hear more counsel from the wise king whose proverbs provide the oil we need to handle life's demanding grinds.

Let me encourage you to start at the beginning of Book II with renewed determination and strong reliance on our heavenly Father. Living beyond the daily grind calls for both. I commend you for staying with me to the midway point. I think you will find the latter half of the journey just as rewarding and adventuresome as the former—maybe more!

And now . . . let's press on with fresh confidence and hope.

NOTES

Introduction

1. "Without a Song" words and music by Edward Eliscu, William Rose and Vincent Youmans. Copyright © 1929 (renewed 1957) Miller Music Corporation and Vincent Youmans Co., Inc. Published by Miller Music Corporation by arrangement with Vincent Youmans Co., Inc. All Rights of Miller Music Corporation assigned to SBK Catalogue Partnership. All rights administered by SBK Miller Catalog and Vincent Youmans Co., Inc. International copyright secured. Made in USA. All rights reserved. Used by Permission.

Section One

1. Joseph M. Scriven [1855], "What a Friend We Have in Jesus."
2. Immanuel Kant, *Critique of Practical Reason* [1781].
3. F. B. Meyer, *The Shepherd Psalm* (Grand Rapids, MI: Fleming H. Revell Company, 1895), 26.
4. Haddon W. Robinson, *The Good Shepherd*, formerly *Psalm Twenty-Three* (Chicago: Moody Press, 1968), 23.
5. Charles W. Slemming, *He Leadeth Me, The Shepherd's Life in Palestine* (Fort Washington, PA: Christian Literature Crusade, 1964), 64 pages.
6. Haddon W. Robinson, *The Good Shepherd*, 52.
7. F. B. Meyer, *The Shepherd Psalm*, 162.
8. Haddon W. Robinson, *The Good Shepherd*, 59.
9. J. Oswald Sanders, *Spiritual Leadership* (Chicago: Moody Press, 1967), 141.
10. Dr. and Mrs. Howard Taylor, *Hudson Taylor's Spiritual Secret* (Chicago, IL: Moody Press, 1958), 107.
11. George Keith [1787], "How Firm a Foundation."
12. Arthur Porritt, *John Henry Jowett* (London: Hodder and Stoughton, 1924), 290.
13. George Matheson [1882], "O Love That Will Not Let Me Go."
14. George W. Robinson [1838–1877], "Loved with Everlasting Love."
15. Martin Luther [1529], "A Mighty Fortress Is Our God"; translated by Frederick H. Hedge [1852].
16. Charles Schulz, "Peanuts" (New York: United Media). Copyright by Charles Schulz.
17. From *If* by Amy Carmichael. Copyright 1938 Dohnavur Fellowship (London: S.P.C.K.; Fort Washington, PA: Christian Literature Crusade). Used by permission.

LIVING BEYOND THE DAILY GRIND

BOOK II

CONTENTS

INTRODUCTION

Here is more good news for those who are struggling to live beyond the grinding hassles of everyday living. In this second volume of *Living Beyond the Daily Grind*, we pick up our year-long journey through selected Psalms and Proverbs at week twenty-seven, applying the soothing oil of these songs and sayings of Scripture to such daily difficulties as ingratitude, sorrow, excuse-making, praise-less times, envy, financial problems, motherhood, and many others.

When I began this project many months ago, I had no idea how extensive it would become. Now that I realize its broad dimensions, I find myself grateful for fresh strength to see it through to completion.

My approach in this second volume will be the same as in the first—practical and relevant rather than analytical and scholarly. From my experience of more than two and a half decades in ministry, I have learned that the quickest way to put the truth of Scripture into people's lives is both through their heart and through their head. This is especially true of the Psalms and the Proverbs. God has preserved these songs and sayings not simply for the purpose of intellectual stimulation but for their practical application as well. If we are ever going to put biblical principles into action, we must deliberately resist the temptation to substitute analysis for appropriation.

This is not to say that we should drift and dream our way through Scripture, spiritualizing this phrase or that, hoping that a few ideas will inadvertently lodge in our minds like floating sticks snagged on a river bank. On the contrary, God's Book deserves our serious concentration as we seek to apply its wisdom to the nagging and inescapable pressures with which we live. At the same time, however, we must not miss the beauty of its poetry as we pursue the practicality of its message. Keeping this balance can be tricky.

In one of his lesser known works, *Reflections on the Psalms,* C. S. Lewis addresses the need for this balance that I am attempting to describe. I could not agree more with his observations.

> In this book, then, I write as one amateur to another, talking about difficulties I have met, or lights I have gained, when reading the Psalms, with the hope that this might at any rate interest, and sometimes even help, other inexpert readers. I am "comparing notes," not presuming to instruct. . . .
>
> What must be said, however, is that the Psalms are poems, and poems intended to be sung: not doctrinal treatises, nor even sermons. Those who talk of reading the Bible "as literature" sometimes mean, I think, reading it without attending to the main thing it is about; like reading Burke with no interest in politics, or reading the *Aeneid* with no interest in Rome. That seems to me to be nonsense. But there is a saner sense in which the Bible, since it is after all literature, cannot properly be read except as literature; and the different parts of it as the different sorts of literature they are. Most emphatically the Psalms must be read as poems . . . if they are to be understood; no less than French must be read as French or English as English. Otherwise we shall miss what is in them and think we see what is not.

The approach we took in Book I will continue in this book as well—one reading a week, with an emphasis on carrying out the suggestions that appear in the Reflection section at the end of each reading. The first thirteen weeks will focus on selections from the Psalms, and the last thirteen weeks, on the Proverbs.

I commend you for your faithful diligence. There are many who graze through the Bible in a random manner, nibbling here and yon with only a passing interest in words on a page. Few are those who drink deeply and consistently from the streams of living water. May our Lord richly reward you for your commitment. Ultimately, may He use the pages that follow to help you to continue living beyond the daily grind.

Chuck Swindoll
Fullerton, California

The Songs In Scripture

Psalm

A Psalm of David, when he was in the wilderness of Judah.

O God, thou art my God; I shall
seek Thee earnestly;
My soul thirsts for Thee, my
flesh yearns for Thee,
In a dry and weary land where there is
no water.
Thus I have beheld Thee in the
sanctuary,
To see Thy power and Thy glory.
Because Thy lovingkindness is better
than life,
My lips will praise Thee.
So I will bless Thee as long as I live;
I will lift up my hands in Thy name.
My soul is satisfied as with marrow and
fatness,
And my mouth offers praises with joyful
lips.

When I remember Thee on my bed,
I meditate on Thee in the night watches,
For Thou hast been my help,
And in the shadow of Thy wings I sing
for joy.
My soul clings to Thee;
Thy right hand upholds me.

But those who seek my life, to destroy it,
Will go into the depths of the earth.
They will be delivered over to the power
of the sword;
They will be a prey for foxes.
But the king will rejoice in God;
Everyone who swears by Him will glory,
For the mouths of those who speak lies
will be stopped.   [63:1–11]

THE GRIND OF
RITUAL
RELIGION

How easy it is to fall into the trap of "ritual religion"! So many Christians know little of a vital, fresh, day-by-day relationship with the Lord. I did not say an *inactive* relationship. Christians have never been more active! The tyranny of the urgent is no theoretical problem. Many a believer leaves the treadmill of three or more activities every Sunday only to enter a full week of meetings, appointments, functions, rehearsals, clubs, engagements, banquets, studies, committees, and retreats. I heartily agree with the one who said:

> Much of our religious activity today is nothing more than a cheap anesthetic to deaden the pain of an empty life![1]

I write not out of bitterness but out of a deep desire that we cultivate a consistent and meaningful walk with the Lord Jesus Christ—one that exists without needing to be pumped up and recharged with unending activities. I would wish that we all might know our Lord in such a significant way that this divine companionship, this healthy vertical relationship, knows fewer and fewer ups and downs. We *must* find ways to live beyond the grind of ritual religion that is devoid of a personal, daily relationship with the Lord.

In *The Pursuit of God*, perhaps his finest book (my second copy is almost worn out), A. W. Tozer points out:

I want to deliberately encourage this mighty longing after God. The lack of it has brought us to our present low estate. The stiff and wooden quality about our religious lives is a result of our lack of holy desire. Complacency is a deadly foe of all spiritual growth. Acute desire must be present or there will be no manifestation of Christ to His people. He waits to be wanted. Too bad that with many of us He waits so long, so very long, in vain.

Every age has its own characteristics. Right now we are in an age of religious complexity. The simplicity which is in Christ is rarely found among us. In its stead are programs, methods, organizations and a world of nervous activities which occupy time and attention but can never satisfy the longing of the heart. The shallowness of our inner experience, the hollowness of our worship, and that servile imitation of the world which marks our promotional methods all testify that we, in this day, know God only imperfectly, and the peace of God scarcely at all.[2]

David's ancient song, Psalm 63, has to do with what it means to hunger, to thirst and long for God—to be fully satisfied with Him alone. It is not a song of activity but of quietness . . . not a song designed to give the drum beat to busy feet but to thirsty souls—genuinely hungry saints!

By the way, are you one? Have you finally come to the end of rat-race religion? Have you decided to leave the hurry-worry *sin*drome and find complete satisfaction in the Savior, in the worship of Him alone? If you have, you are rare. In fact, you are almost extinct! But, if you have, this ancient song is for you. If you have not, it will sound mystical, perhaps even dull. David's quiet song, you see, is written for the few who are still hungry—for those who prefer depth to speed.

SUPERSCRIPTION

Very simply, the superscription reads: "A Psalm of David, when he was in the wilderness of Judah."

David composed this ancient hymn. But he was not in a temple or a worshipful tabernacle; he was in the wilderness

. . . alone, removed, obscure, separated from every comfort and friend. He was acutely acquainted with thirst, hunger, pain, loneliness, and exhaustion—but these were not his basic needs, as we shall see.

EXPOSITION

As in many of the psalms, the first verse sets the tone and gives the composition its theme.

> O God, Thou art my God; I shall seek Thee earnestly;
> My soul thirsts for Thee, my flesh yearns for Thee,
> In a dry and weary land where there is no water.

Right away we see that he was not seeking literal food, water, comfort, or rest—he was seeking a deep communion with his Lord. The "dry and weary land" is a vivid picture of our world today. So few, so very few believers are living victoriously. So many, so very many in this world are captivated with "stuff" and the pursuit of more and more. As a result, the inner barrenness of soul is beyond belief. The land is indeed "dry and weary," but that only makes the yearning stronger! Since "there is no water" in that kind of land, David longs for his thirst to be quenched from above.

The next verse begins with "Thus." This is a very significant connective. The idea here is "So then . . ." or "Therefore. . . ." David longs for God. Nothing around him can satisfy that longing. He says, in effect, "So then, since nothing around me cultivates a sense of closeness and companionship, I will cultivate it myself." Actually, the *Thus* of verse 2 introduces several things David does to satisfy his inner longing for a deep walk with his Lord. I find *five specific things* the songwriter does to find such satisfaction. They appear in the balance of his song:

1. He mentally pictures the Lord (v. 2).

> Thus I have beheld Thee in the sanctuary,
> To see Thy power and Thy glory.

When he says, "I have beheld Thee," we understand he means just that; he perceives his glorious Lord in his thoughts. The verse mentions the Lord's "power" and "glory." He imagines these things clearly in the thought processes of his mind. He spends time in the wilderness framing a mental picture of the Lord in power and glory on His heavenly throne. He takes the scriptures he knows regarding the Lord God and allows them to "sketch" in his mind a mental image of Him. In other words, he sets his mind upon and *occupies himself with the Lord.* That is a great way to remove the wearisome ritual from religion.

We all have vivid imaginations. In fact, these imaginations can get us into trouble if they are not kept under control. Ugly pride or lust, hatred or jealousy can feed our minds vivid pictures which can lead to terrible sins. This is precisely the case of "committing adultery in the heart" which our Savior mentions in Matthew 5:28. Lustful imaginings can ultimately result in illicit acts of passion.

David gives us a remedy: Spend those leisure moments picturing the Lord Himself. Or, in the words of the apostle Paul: "Set your mind on the things above, not on the things that are on earth" (Col. 3:2).

The next time you're tempted to allow your mind to paint the wrong mental picture, remember Psalm 63:2.

2. He expresses praise to the Lord (vv. 3–5).

> Because Thy lovingkindness is better than life,
> My lips will praise Thee.
> So I will bless Thee as long as I live;
> I will lift up my hands in Thy name.
> My soul is satisfied as with marrow and fatness.
> And my mouth offers praises with joyful lips.

I don't want to be spooky or come across the least bit vague about this matter of praise. Obviously, praise is important since the psalms are full of it. Look back over these verses. Verse 3 says it is something "my lips" do. In verse 5 they are "joyful lips." Verse 4 says it is to be done "as long as I live," so it isn't a once-a-week matter. An additional hint is given in verse 3, where God's "lovingkindness" prompts David to praise his Lord. Praise "satisfies his soul," according to verse 5.

Yes, praise is a deeply significant aspect of our personal worship, and we are remiss if we ignore it. Unfortunately, many are afraid of praise because they associate it with some sort of wild, uncontrolled, highly emotional "praise service," in which individuals faint, scream, jump around, and dance uncontrollably in the aisle. Listen, praise is important! It is not limited to public meetings or televised religious services. Praise is to flow from within us. Praise gushes forth and refreshes us. Actually, praise is an aspect of *prayer*. Let me explain:

Prayer could be divided into five parts:

a. *Confession* (read Prov. 28:13; 1 John 1:9). Dealing completely with sins in our lives—agreeing with God that such-and-such was wrong, then claiming forgiveness.
b. *Intercession* (read 1 Tim. 2:1–2). Remembering others and their needs in prayer.
c. *Petition* (read Phil. 4:6; Heb. 4:15–16). Bringing ourselves and our needs to God. Remembering them and requesting things of the Lord for ourselves.
d. *Thanksgiving* (read 1 Thess. 5:18). Prayer that expresses gratitude to God for His specific blessings and gifts to us.
e. *Praise* (read 1 Chron. 29:11–13). Expressions of adoration directed to God without the mention of ourselves or others—only God. We *praise* God by expressing words of honor to Him for His character, His name, His will, His Word, His glory, etc.

Husband, when you were dating your wife-to-be, can you remember doing this? You looked at her hair . . . and you expressed praise over her hair. You praised her for her beauty, her choice of perfume and clothing, and her excellent taste. You probably ate some of her cooking—and praised her for it. You observed the way she talked and expressed herself, and again you praised her. Praise came naturally because that was a genuine, stimulating part of romance. By the way, I hope you haven't *stopped* praising her! Praise is greatly appreciated by your wife, and likewise by our Lord. He frequently tells us in His Word of its importance to Him.

3. He meditates on the Lord (v. 6).

> When I remember Thee on my bed,
> I meditate on Thee in the night watches.

To meditate means "to muse, to ponder." According to Psalm 49:3, the mouth speaks wisdom but when the heart meditates upon God's Word, *then* comes understanding.

I find it noteworthy that in this sixth verse David refers to the night watches and being on his bed when he meditates. This points up a very helpful fact. One of the best times to ponder God's Word and allow the mind to dwell upon it is when we retire at night. That's the time David said he remembered the Lord. Restless, fretful nights are calmed by moments of meditation.

4. He sings for joy (vv. 7–8).

> For Thou hast been my help,
> And in the shadow of Thy wings I sing for joy.
> My soul clings to Thee;
> Thy right hand upholds me.

David was in the wilderness. He had no audience, nor did he seek one. God was the single object of his worship and it was to Him his soul would cling. To strengthen the relationship between himself and his Lord, David *sang* for joy. Rare but blessed are those disciples of David who are relaxed enough in God's presence to break forth in song. Singing brings joy to our hearts.

One of my most unforgettable experiences having to do with a song sung in solitude occurred when I was in the Marine Corps, stationed on Okinawa. A missionary, whom I had come to appreciate because of his spiritual investment in my life, was undergoing a severe, crucial trial. I knew of it because he had shared it with me. I watched him to see how he would respond. He didn't seem discouraged nor did he lose his zeal. One evening I went to his home and was told by his wife that he was down at his little office in Naha, the capital city. I took the bus that rainy night and arrived a couple of blocks from his office. Stepping off the bus, I began splashing my way toward his office. Before long I began to hear singing. I realized it was his voice. The hymn was familiar. I remember the words so clearly:

> O to grace how great a debtor,
> Daily I'm constrained to be!
> Let Thy goodness, like a fetter,
> Bind my wandering heart to Thee. . . .[3]

It was my missionary friend, singing before his Lord all alone at his study-office. It was at times like that he found strength and joy in the midst of his trials. He had learned the truth of this verse in Psalm 63. In "the shadow of [God's] wings" my friend sang for joy. As I listened I felt as if I were standing on holy ground.

5. He rejoices in his God (vv. 9–11).

> But those who seek my life, to destroy it,
> Will go into the depths of the earth.
> They will be delivered over to the power of the sword;
> They will be a prey for foxes.
> But the king will rejoice in God;
> Everyone who swears by Him will glory,
> For the mouths of those who speak lies will be stopped.

David closes this psalm of worship with a pen portrait of his situation. To our surprise, he wasn't absolutely alone, because verse 9 testifies of those who sought his life to destroy it. Nor was he free from criticism and slander, according to the last verse. But the most surprising of all is that small portion that reads: "But the king will rejoice in God. . . ."

Who will soon be king? David! He is saying that the threatening circumstances would not steal his joyful spirit. As the king-elect, he would not doubt his Lord's protection. What an enviable determination!

Are you as determined as young David to live beyond the grind of religious ritual? I encourage you to cultivate such a spontaneous relationship with your God that you never again fall into the predictable mold of empty religion. Once you have tasted the real thing, you'll never be satisfied with plateaus of phony piety. You will want only to be in "God's presence," regardless of your location. It is the most refreshing place to be on Planet Earth, even though, at the time, you may find yourself "in the wilderness."

REFLECTIONS ON RITUAL RELIGION

1. Can you define "ritual religion"? How does it differ from true spirituality that includes authentic worship and meaningful praise? Describe the contrast in these two columns:

Ritual Religion	True Spirituality

2. Evaluate your religious activities for the next few minutes. Make a mental list of your weekly schedule. After naming each one, ask some hard questions:

   - Is this vital to my relationship with Christ?
   - Does this encourage me to grow deeper in my walk?
   - Am I doing this for the right motive?
   - What would happen if I stopped this activity?
   - Should I? Am I really willing to do so?

3. Deliberately change some longstanding habits for the purpose of adding freshness to your relationship with Christ.

   - Drive to church a different route.
   - Change your time of meeting with the Lord each day this week.
   - Pray after a meal instead of before it.
   - Sit in a different place at church on Sunday.
   - Add a hymn or praise song to your devotions.
   - Use another version of the Scripture for a month.

   See what a creature of habit you have become without realizing it?

Psalm

He who dwells in the shelter of
    the Most High
    Will abide in the shadow of the
    Almighty.
I will say to the Lord, "My refuge and my
    fortress,
My God, in whom I trust!"
For it is He who delivers you from the
    snare of the trapper,
And from the deadly pestilence.
He will cover you with His pinions,
And under His wings you may seek
    refuge;
His faithfulness is a shield and bulwark.

You will not be afraid of the terror by
    night,
Or of the arrow that flies by day;
Of the pestilence that stalks in darkness,
Or of the destruction that lays waste at
    noon.
A thousand may fall at your side,
And ten thousand at your right hand;
But it shall not approach you.
You will only look on with your eyes,
And see the recompense of the wicked.
For you have made the Lord, my refuge,

Even the Most High, your dwelling place.
No evil will befall you,
Nor will any plague come near your tent.

For He will give His angels charge
   concerning you,
To guard you in all your ways.
They will bear you up in their hands,
Lest you strike your foot against a stone.
You will tread upon the lion and cobra,
The young lion and the serpent you will
   trample down.

"Because he has loved Me, therefore I
   will deliver him;
I will set him securely on high, because
   he has known My name.
He will call upon Me, and I will answer
   him;
I will be with him in trouble;
I will rescue him, and honor him.
With a long life I will satisfy him,
And let him behold My
   salvation." [91:1–16]

THE GRIND OF
ENEMY ATTACK

Enemy attack? I can imagine a few of you who just read these words are saying to yourself, "sounds pretty treacherous to me. . . . But I'm not sure I know much about such things." I understand. There was a time in my life when I would have entertained similar thoughts. No longer, however. You may be surprised to know that there are many in God's family who have encountered demonic assaults, especially those who have served Christ in regions where the powers of darkness are commonplace. But in no way are enemy attacks limited to those dark corners of the world.

My wife and I have often talked about how we can sense the invisible presence of the adversary. There are subtle yet distinct hints that evil forces are at work. There is a heaviness in one's spirit, a lingering realization that what we are dealing with is more than another human being could be causing. Usually there are unexplainable coincidences and at the same time superhuman feelings of oppression that bear down on the mind. We have noticed that during such attacks our attempts to pray for relief are strangely thwarted. It's eerie! There aren't necessarily noises in the night or furniture moving across the floor, but sleep is often disturbed. A breaking free from the insidious attack is beyond one's own ability to make happen. Wicked, vile thoughts (even suicidal promptings) can accompany these assaults. There is no mistaking the source—the enemy of our souls is behind such ungodly grinds in life. How grateful I am for this song in Scripture. It, like few other scriptural passages, comes to grips with enemy attacks and gives us hope to get beyond them.

Every ancient song, like every great hymn, has its own special "tone." The magnificent hymn "And Can It Be?" has a tone of *assurance*. The lovely "Guide Me, O Thou Great Jehovah" has a tone of *dependence and trust*. The moving strains of "O Sacred Head, Now Wounded" carry a tone of *passion and pain*, while "I Am His, and He Is Mine" conveys *love and acceptance*. Psalm 91 has a unique tone in its message as well. We discover this by reading it through and looking for words or phrases that communicate similar thoughts. Let me list some:

Verse 1:   *shelter*
Verse 2:   *refuge . . . fortress*
Verse 4:   *refuge . . . shield*
Verse 5:   *terror by night . . . arrow . . . by day*
Verse 6:   *pestilence . . . destruction*
Verse 7:   *a thousand may fall*
Verse 9:   *refuge*
Verse 11: *guard*
Verse 15: *rescue*

There can be little doubt about the "tone" of Psalm 91; it is warfare, battle, conflict, fighting. It is a song for battle in that it conveys an atmosphere of daily, oppressive enemy attack.

Who is the enemy? Israel's national foes? No. A human being who is opposing the writer? I don't believe so. An actual, visible war on a bloody battlefield? No, I doubt it. Look at several more verses as we identify the enemy:

Verse 3:   *the trapper*
Verse 8:   *the wicked*
Verse 10: *evil*

Then consider the promise of angelic assistance (vv. 11–12) as well as divine deliverance (vv. 14–15).

I firmly believe that this song deals with our spiritual

enemies, *the Devil and his demons.* It talks about a battle in the unseen spiritual realm. This explains our need for angelic and divine intervention. Because our enemy, in this case, is supernatural in strength, we need supernatural help. This also helps us understand the promise of *absolute* deliverance from "the pestilence" that stalks day and night . . . and the *full* protection that is provided us (vv. 5–7). I find no other explanation, realistic or accurate, for these verses defy defeat. In no other realm could we claim such absolute protection and deliverance.

I hesitate to spell out the full spectrum of enemy attacks. Neither space nor time to explain all the details are sufficient. But perhaps an example or two would help. There are certain people whose presence throbs with evil. Being near them unleashes depressing powers which are both frightening and unavoidable. I have encountered these individuals throughout my ministry and have never forgotten the attacks. Frequently the people have trafficked in mind-bending occult practices and/or have been heavily involved in the drug culture. I have seen weird, even bizarre things occur in my family during such times. Fitful nightmares, passionate outbursts of rebellion and arguments, a heavy cloud of depression, strange accidents, and uncharacteristic marital disharmony can follow in the wake of these attacks. I shudder as I recall those awful times.

Keep this in mind as we dig into Psalm 91. The tone is *warfare* and the enemy is our evil adversary who comes at us with persistent regularity.

OUTLINE

Let me suggest four distinct parts to Psalm 91:

I. Protection amid Evil (vv. 1–4)
II. Attitude toward Evil (vv. 5–10)
III. Assistance against Evil (vv. 11–13)
IV. Security from Evil (vv. 14–16)

PROTECTION AMID EVIL

Because the first four verses are crucial to the rest of the psalm, let's take our time as we develop them.

A very important fact to remember is that we as believers in the Lord Jesus Christ are not removed from the *presence* of wickedness. In fact, our Savior prayed specifically: "I do not ask Thee to take them out of the world, but to keep them from the evil one" (John 17:15).

This verse alerts us to a significant truth—God has planned that we continue to live in a hostile, wicked, non-Christian world system (*kosmos*) but be protected all the while. He deliberately did not remove us from an atmosphere of hostility.

As I mentioned earlier, He has made possible a plan of *insulation* not *isolation*. God isn't interested in our isolating ourselves, hidden away like pious hermits in a cave, but rather that we live courageously on the front lines, claiming His insulation amid an evil environment.

Now then, in order for us to enjoy the benefits of insulation, we must live in the light of Psalm 91:1–4. The secret, of course, is in our *dwelling* in the shelter of the Most High—our abiding in His shadow habitually.

The word *dwells* (v. 1) is translated from the Hebrew *yah-shaav*, meaning "to remain, sit, abide." There is a permanence conveyed in the original term. We would say, "live in conscious fellowship with, draw daily strength from—let Him habitually have first place." That is the applied truth of the Hebrew text. The idea is developed further with the mention of "the shelter" in verse 1. This original word is *sah-thaar*, meaning "cove, covert, secret hideaway." It is therefore a place of vertical nearness and divine intimacy.

Before going any further, let me emphasize that Psalm 91 is written to *dwellers*. It promises deliverance and protection not to everyone, but to *dwellers*, those who draw daily, habitual strength from their Lord as they sustain an intimacy of fellowship and nearness with Him. Don't forget that!

We are told in the last part of verse 1 that as this close

fellowship is maintained, we shall ". . . abide in the shadow of the Almighty." Now we come upon a different Hebrew term translated *abide*. It is *loon*, meaning "to lodge, pass the night." It conveys a periodic rest or stopover for lodging.

What is verse 1 actually saying? Simply this: If we who know the Lord Jesus Christ will dwell in conscious fellowship with Him (keeping our sins confessed and forsaken, and walking in moment-by-moment dependence upon Him), we shall enjoy the benefits of living under His protective care on those occasions when rest and lodging are needed. If we maintain our walk with Him, we can count on Him and His deliverance at periodic times when the going gets rough.

This explains why verse 2 says:

> I will say to the Lord, "My refuge and my fortress,
> My God, in whom I trust!"

A "refuge" is a place of rest. A "fortress" is a place of defense. Notice that this does not say the Lord will *provide* these things. Rather, it says that the Lord *is* these things. This is why our dwelling in Him is essential . . . because it is *in Him* alone that we will find rest and defense. Take time to consider the last word in verse 2—*trust*. It is a translation of the same Hebrew term as the one in Proverbs 3:5 which we studied in the previous volume.

> Trust in the Lord with all your heart,
> And do not lean on your own understanding.

It means a total trust, as if resting all one's weight on something else. When one is crippled, he must trust his crutches. That is the kind of trust our Lord wants from us.

Verses 1 and 2 deal with who God is, but verses 3 and 4 deal with what God does. Basically, there are three things named:

a. He delivers: from the snare of the trapper and from the deadly pestilence
b. He covers: with His pinions/under His wings
c. He shields: by His faithfulness

The Hebrew sentence structure enables us to point out particular emphases in our study from time to time. In this case, the emphatic part of verses 3–4 is "He." The New American Standard Version renders it, ". . . it is He. . . ." The idea is emphatic: "He, alone" or "He it is, not anyone else!" Practically speaking, you will find no absolute assistance or deliverance from anyone else—only your Lord in whom you trust.

Now, one at a time, let's look at the specific things He provides for us in times of enemy attack.

1. He delivers from the snare of the trapper.

I want to remind you once again that this promise is directed to the "dweller." Not everyone—not even every Christian—is promised deliverance. If you wish to be delivered, you must dwell! If you are now under satanic/demonic assault, the way to deliverance is dwelling—drawing power and triumph through His name and His victory at Calvary. I shall deal with the specifics of this later.

Look at the word *deliver*. It is translated from *nah-tzaal*, meaning "to snatch away." This original term appears in Psalm 34:19: "Many are the afflictions of the righteous; / But the Lord *delivers* him out of them all" (emphasis mine).

How great is His deliverance!

This third verse goes on to say that we will be "snatched away" from a "snare." Literally, it means a "bird trap." My Webster's dictionary says that a trap is ". . . something by which one gets entangled, something deceptively attractive. . . ."

But remember, we need not be victims! It is He alone—our glorious, all-conquering Lord—who "snatches us out" as we dwell in Him.

He delivers also from "the deadly pestilence." Literally, "from a death of destruction." One translation renders this "from a violent death." This, of course, is the ultimate result of our being ensnared. Never doubt it; the devil plays for keeps. If possible, he will take us to a violent death, as Saul, who took his own life (1 Sam. 31:4; 1 Chron. 10:13–14) and Judas, who did the same (Luke 22:3; Matt. 27:5). Satan's ultimate desire is our destruction. He is happy when a self-inflicted, violent death smears the testimony of a Christian. Our Lord promises deliverance from such a death.

2. He covers with His pinions/under His wings.

The Lord is here pictured as an immense bird keeping close watch over its brood. Both Psalm 36:7 and Psalm 57:1 mention the protection we have under our Lord's "wings." The prophet Isaiah includes God's promise that we are dearer to Him than a nursing child is to his mother (49:15–16). What comfort!

Back in the nineteenth century, William O. Cushing put this vivid word picture into a poem:

> Under His wings I am safely abiding;
> Though the night deepens and tempests are wild,
> Still I can trust Him:
> I know He will keep me;
> He has redeemed me, and I am His child.
>
> Under His wings, under His wings,
> Who from His love can sever? . . .[4]

3. He shields by His faithfulness.

The psalmist has pictured our Lord's protection in three distinct ways in verses 3 and 4. First, in the scene of a trapper. Second, in the scene of a bird and her brood. Now, in the scene of a battle. Here he assures us that we are guarded by His faithful presence.

Now let's consider the balance of this psalm.

ATTITUDE TOWARD EVIL

I find two invincible attitudes we are to exhibit toward evil:
1. No fear (vv. 5–6).

> You will not be afraid of the terror by night,
> Or of the arrow that flies by day;
> Of the pestilence that stalks in darkness,
> Or of the destruction that lays waste at noon.

Look over the descriptive terms that portray our enemy's tactics: *terror . . . arrow . . . pestilence . . . destruction.* All these describe satanic and demonic assaults against us. Notice also that these assaults take place at any time of the day or night. Our enemy will stop at nothing to make us afraid! Intimidation is one of his sharpest darts.

Child of God, we need not fear! Martin Luther was right when he wrote:

> And tho' this world, with devils filled,
> Should threaten to undo us;
> We will not fear, for God hath willed
> His truth to triumph through us:
> The prince of darkness grim,
> We tremble not for him;
> His rage we can endure,
> For lo! his doom is sure,
> One little word shall fell him![5]

The late, great Charles Haddon Spurgeon's comment is equally reassuring:

> When Satan's quiver shall be empty thou shalt remain uninjured by his craft and cruelty, yea, his broken darts shall be to thee as trophies of the truth and power of the Lord thy God![6]

2. Faith (vv. 7–10).

> A thousand may fall at your side,
> And ten thousand at your right hand;
> But it shall not approach you.
> You will only look on with your eyes,
> And see the recompense of the wicked.
> For you have made the Lord, my refuge,
> Even the Most High, your dwelling place.
> No evil will befall you.
> Nor will any plague come near your tent.

I see *faith* written between each line, don't you? Our Lord expects us to stand firmly on His Word—His promises—His strength. Read Ephesians 6:10–11, 16 at this juncture, my friend. You'll see that the "shield of faith" is able "to extinguish *all* the flaming missiles of the evil one" (emphasis mine). Remember, faith demands an *object.* Like love and mercy, faith cannot exist alone. In this case, faith's object is God's written Word. Our Lord and Savior has recorded His truth for us to claim when the going gets rough. Nothing else can hold us together and keep us from panic in the way that specific verses and passages of written Scripture do. If you fail to set your heart upon God's Word, you'll soon weaken in your resistance and ultimately succumb to the traps of the enemy. You will have to fight ignorance and superstition and even a few of your uneasy feelings if you're going to walk by faith, child of God.

There are at least four specific biblical truths for the Christian to claim when undergoing or seeking release from satanic/demonic attacks.

1. The Cross. Go to verses that declare Satan's defeat at Calvary. Read them orally: Colossians 2:13–15, Hebrews 2:14–15, and 1 John 3:8.

2. The Blood. As you consider and claim Satan's defeat at the Cross, call to mind specific passages dealing with the *blood* of the Lord Jesus Christ: Romans 5:8–9 and Revelation 12:10–11.

3. The Name. As you seek deliverance and strength amid your battle, verbally state the *full name* of the *Lord Jesus Christ* as your refuge and sovereign God: Proverbs 18:10 and Philippians 2:9–10.

4. The Word. Stand firmly upon God's written Word, as our Lord did when the Devil tempted Him to yield to his traps: Matthew 4:4, 7, 10 and Ephesians 6:11, 17.

If you will use this as a practical guide and claim each one *by faith,* you will be among the righteous ones who are *bold as a lion* (Prov. 28:1), and you will find that you can live beyond the grind of enemy attacks.

ASSISTANCE AGAINST EVIL

For He will give His angels charge concerning you,
To guard you in all your ways.
They will bear you up in their hands,

Lest you strike your foot against a stone.
You will tread upon the lion and cobra,
The young lion and the serpent you will trample down (Ps.
   91:11–13).

These verses assure us of angelic assistance when we face attacks from supernatural realms. It makes sense. Satan and the demons are supernatural beings—so are angels. We need supernatural help when dealing with supernatural enemies. By the way, for further information on angels, read Psalm 103:19–21 along with Hebrews 1:14.

Now let's look closely at verses 11–13. The psalmist states three distinct activities of the angels on our behalf.

1. Angels are given "charge" of us (v. 11). The term *charge* is from the Hebrew *tzah-wah,* which means "to appoint, install, give command of." Angels are actually *appointed* to us, given command of certain earthly individuals. Consider Matthew 18:10. It reads:

See that you do not despise one of these little ones, for I say to you, that their angels in heaven continually behold the face of My Father who is in heaven.

Give some thought to the possessive "their." In other words, children have *their own* angels—unseen guardians—who are actually *appointed* by God. The same is true of adults (Acts 12:15). We have been appointed angelic assistance. In numerous yet invisible ways, they come to our aid.

2. Angels "guard" us in all our ways (v. 11). The Hebrew *shah-maar* means "to keep, watch over, observe, preserve, take care of." Angels are overseers of God's people. Like silent sentries, they stand guard over us, preserving our steps.

My wife and I frequently smile as we call to mind those days when our four active children were young. How very, very busy the angels must have been who were assigned to them! I am personally convinced they heaved a sigh of relief when our children finally grew from the age of endless, reckless activity to a more mature lifestyle. Believe me, we frequently thank the Lord that we had at least four unseen baby sitters who assisted us twenty-four hours a day, seven days a week back then!

3. Angels "bear you up" in their hands (v. 12). The verb *nahsah* actually means "to lift, to carry, take up." Here in Psalm 91 it means "to support, sustain." This rounds out the picture, doesn't it? Angels are appointed to us, and they watch over us, preserving us and guarding us from demonic assault. At times, it is necessary for them to support and sustain us, even as Elisha and his servant were assisted in 2 Kings 6:15–17 (please stop and read).

SECURITY FROM EVIL

We have almost finished this rather extensive journey through Psalm 91. For thirteen verses the songwriter has been speaking. Now, *God* speaks . . . the Lord declares six "I wills":

> I will deliver him (v. 14).
> I will set him securely on high (v. 14).
> I will answer him (v. 15).
> I will be with him in trouble (v. 15).
> I will rescue him and honor him (v. 15).
> I will satisfy him (v. 16).

What a list of promises! Child of God, these are addressed to *you*. Look at that initial phrase and concluding phrase in verse 14: "Because he has loved Me . . . because he has known My name." The Lord says that those who love Him and those who know Him have this secure hope in Him. The Hebrew term used for "love" is unusual and rare. Most often it is used with reference to "attaching something to something." The Hebrew term includes the idea of attaching a saddle to a horse. It would be acceptable to render Psalm 91:14: "Because he clings affectionately to Me. . . ."

The Lord's "I wills" are not for everybody. But then, they weren't meant to be. God gives these promises to dwellers, "clingers," believers who, by faith, wrap themselves around their Savior. What a way to live! As a matter of fact, it's the *only way to live!*

CONCLUSION

May I ask: Do *you* know the Lord Jesus Christ personally? Has there ever been a time in your life when you took Christ at His Word and asked Him to take over the controls of your life, to enthrone Himself within you? He wants to be your Lord and Savior, but He waits for your decision. He really doesn't want you to perish. He wants to satisfy you with a meaningful, full, abundant life. Won't you invite Him in right now? Act now. The Lord Jesus Christ is ready to enter your life. Just utter a prayer of invitation as soon as you conclude this study. Don't delay. Please receive Christ now. When you have Him living within, no enemy attack will ever again have the power to overcome you.

REFLECTIONS ON ENEMY ATTACK

1. Even though our examination of this great song was lengthy and a bit detailed, I don't want you to miss its practical relevance. Like few other scriptures, it addresses the believer's assurance of victory over our adversary's attacks. You may be going through the grind of demonic oppression. There may be a person whose presence is clearly an evil force in your life. You may be fighting off thoughts of injuring yourself or taking your own life. Perhaps you got involved in the world of occult practices years ago and you still fight those forces from the past. What an exhausting battle that can be! Remind yourself of two wonderful facts:

   • You have no reason to fear.
   • Your faith will overcome all enemy attacks.

   Repeat those two statements again and again.

2. You may need even more reassurance. Turn back to this magnificent song and circle the three promises God gives you.

   Verse 10a: No evil will befall you.
   Verse 10b: No plague will invade your home.
   Verse 11: Angelic assistance will guard you.

Remind yourself of those three promises as you retire for a night's rest this very evening. The enemy of our souls prefers "night attacks," so don't be surprised if he uses the darkness to frighten you.

3. Read this psalm aloud and in its *entirety* each day this week. Along with the psalm, read Romans 8:31–39 and 1 John 4:4; 5:18–21. Literally, *claim those truths* today. This is a heavy subject, but one we need to deal with without any uneasiness.

Psalm

A Psalm for Thanksgiving.

Shout joyfully to the Lord, all the
earth.
Serve the Lord with gladness;
Come before Him with joyful
singing.
Know that the Lord Himself is God;
It is He who has made us, and not we
ourselves;
We are His people and the sheep of His
pasture.

Enter His gates with thanksgiving,
And His courts with praise.
Give thanks to Him; bless His name.
For the Lord is good;
His lovingkindness is everlasting,
And His faithfulness to all
generations.   [100:1–5]

THE GRIND OF
INGRATITUDE

In these days of abundance and wealth, it is our tendency
to become ungrateful and presumptuous. Affluence abounds
in our American culture. Many a family has a driveway full
of cars, a house full of gadgets, appliances, personal television
sets and telephones, and a refrigerator full of food. Life isn't
simply easy-going, it's downright luxurious!

Please don't misunderstand. Having an abundance is not
a sin, in and of itself. Throughout the pages of Scripture we
find examples of people who were both wealthy and godly:
Abraham, Job, Joseph, David, Solomon, Josiah, Barnabas,
Lydia, to name a few. But we also find some who became en-
amored of their wealth and lost sight of the Lord and His right
to rule their lives. As I have said on numerous occasions, there
is nothing wrong with having nice things . . . but there is
everything wrong when nice things have us. Ingratitude and
presumption can quickly rob our lives of generosity and humility. Here is a song that will bring back a spirit of thankfulness
and joyful gratitude.

Every time I read through the One Hundredth Psalm, I think
of Vacation Bible School! Do you have the same reaction? For
some reason I was memorizing all or part of Psalm 100 every
summer of my childhood in VBS. As I think of that, I also remember the three Bible school teachers who resigned when
they learned they would have *me* in their department! Needless
to say, I was not a "model child" in church. Take heart, Sunday
school teachers! You could be teaching a potential pastor as

you labor with a group of busy, noisy children. I thank God for those who were longsuffering with me!

Psalm 100, however, is not just a "Bible school psalm." Nor is it directed to children only. As we take a closer look at this favorite old hymn, three questions come to mind.

Question One: *To whom is it addressed?* Read verses 1 and 5 once again. You'll find that it is addressed to *all the earth* (v. 1), to *all generations* (v. 5). Psalm 100 is for the whole world—all ages and stages. It is broad in its scope. Its message is universal. We are to understand that God wants *all* people in every era to hear and apply its message.

Question Two: *Of whom does it speak?* Verses 1–3, along with verse 5, give us the answer. Psalm 100 speaks of *the Lord.* His name appears no less than four times. One of those times He is declared to be God Himself. This psalm directs our attention to *Jehovah,* the Old Testament personal name for God. You cannot appreciate Psalm 100 (nor can you apply its message) if you are not intimately acquainted with the One of whom it speaks. Being thankful—really thankful—begins with being rightly related to the Giver of everything.

Question Three: *How is it arranged?* Let your eyes graze back over the lovely meadow of this psalm. Do you notice its arrangement? Since the Psalms were originally written as hymns, they are poetic in form. That doesn't mean they rhyme, but it does mean that they follow a certain style, a "meter" or "beat." Each psalm is independent of all the others. Like our present-day hymns, each one has a distinct message and arrangement.

Psalm 100 is composed of seven commands or imperatives. Following these commands a final verse appears that sums up God's character, giving us the reason for the commands. Let's work our way through the psalm by keeping this arrangement in our minds.

THE COMMANDS

1. Shout joyfully to the Lord.

This is quite a beginning! In fact, the Hebrew is very explicit, leaving out the term "joyfully," for literally it says: *Shout to the*

Lord! The word *shout* comes from a Hebrew word meaning "to raise a shout, to give a blast" (as on a trumpet). In our modern day we use certain terms to express approval:

Right on!	Fantastic!
Far out!	Wonderful!
All right!	Praise God!
Great!	Amen!

These are "shouts" or verbal expressions of thanksgiving. God says to all the earth-dwellers, "Shout words of joyful approval to me!"

Haven't you come to realize this? At certain times God does things about which we cannot keep quiet. He takes care of little details or some problem, and we suddenly sense that He has come to our assistance. Don't accept this silently. Shout to Him. Lift up your voice in praise! By doing so we counteract that grind of ingratitude that so easily can climb aboard.

2. Serve the Lord with gladness.

A healthy sign of the grateful life is *serving*. Few things do a better job of interrupting the daily grind of ingratitude than serving others. Ponder this portion of God's Word. In doing God's work, we serve Him, not the local church, not the superintendent of some department, not the pastor or some board. We serve the Lord. It is *He* we worship and for *Him* we labor— not man! And please observe that this kind of service is not irksome, nor does it come from guilt. The verse says it is *with gladness*. The Hebrew term for this phrase was used when talking about pleasant things that gave happiness.

How very, very rare it is to find service with gladness in churches today. Many people serve in order to relieve their guilt or to quiet their conscience. Some serve because they feel obligated or forced. The vast majority of Christians think only in terms of service in a local church and miss the concept of serving Christ's Body—the universal church. Yet the Body has needs, aching needs, numerous needs, many of them outside particular local church functions.

There is the service of encouragement, fellowship, giving (time as well as cash), being involved with others in helping those who are in need, discipleship, sharing the Lord, bearing others' burdens, and on and on. Oh, that gladness might characterize our service!

3. Come before Him with joyful singing.

We have already considered this idea of singing on several occasions, so there is no need to add much to my previous remarks. Let me simply emphasize the word *joyful*. I get the picture that God prefers to have us happy people, rejoicing in His presence, for He has mentioned it in each line of this psalm thus far.

Are you joyful? Really now, is your face pleasant—is a smile frequently there? Do your eyes reveal a joyful spirit within? When you sing, in church for example, is it *with joy?* The next chance you get, glance at the fellow in the next car on the freeway. He is *never* smiling! Look at the lady ahead of you or behind you at the grocery store. No smile . . . no joy.

I was humming and smiling the other day as I was shopping and several people stared at me! One even asked why I was happy. I had a choice opportunity to talk about why I was happy and to share with him the One who gave me joy.

Lighten up, Christian! Dress up your testimony with a genuine spirit of joy! Happiness is truly contagious.

4. Know that the Lord Himself is God. . . .

> Know that the Lord Himself is God;
> It is He who has made us, and not we ourselves;
> We are His people and the sheep of His pasture. [v. 3]

Our worship of the Lord God is to be intelligent. We are to *know* certain things in order for this to be true. This third verse lists three things we need to keep in mind:

• *We are to know that God is our Lord.* We quickly acknowledge Christ as our Savior—but so slowly do we submit ourselves to Him as our *Lord.* Immediately, He accepts us into His family as we believe He died and arose for us . . . but only after years of stubborn struggling it seems, do we finally allow Him *first place* as our sovereign Lord. We are to know that the One we worship is the Lord, our God.

• *We are to know that He has made us.* I see two things of practical importance here. First, God made, designed, and formed us just as we are. We are to keep that in mind. We look precisely like He planned for us to look. He made us, inside and out, literally. No person can joyfully live his life and shout praises to God until he accepts himself as God has made him. Second, God is still "making" us—He is not through. We are not self-made people. No one is! A wonderful thought is tucked away in the first part of Philippians 2:13. I want to quote from *Kenneth Wuest's Expanded Translation:* "For God is the One who is constantly putting forth His energy in you. . . ."[7]

You see, God is still working. He is not finished by any means, child of God. Please cooperate. Please be patient.

• *We are to know that we are His sheep, that we belong to Him.* It is awfully easy to want to be the shepherd. So, we must be reminded that we are His sheep; we belong to Him. He is in charge. As sheep, we are to submit.

5. <u>Enter His gates with thanksgiving, and His courts with praise.</u>

What was in the psalmist's mind? To what do the "gates" and "courts" refer? I believe he had the *temple* in mind. That was the place where he approached God's presence, for God's glory literally filled the temple, according to 2 Chronicles 5:14 and 1 Kings 8:10–11. The temple had its gates and its courts, both of which gave access to the presence of God.

Today we have no such earthly phenomena. In light of that, how do we enter His gates and His courts? What is our access to His presence today? The answer is *prayer.* Hebrews 4:16 invites us to "draw near" to God's throne. Through prayer we come into the very presence of God. And this psalm tells us to do it with two things accompanying our coming—thanksgiving and praise.

6. <u>Give thanks to Him.</u>

Because this sixth command is so closely linked with the fifth, I mention it before applying the point. Giving thanks is repeated so that we will not miss its importance.

If you're looking for "signs of the last days," you will probably not think of looking for *ingratitude*, but you should. It is listed in 2 Timothy 3:1–5 right along with the more popular and obvious "signs." We have become an ungrateful, thankless generation! Small wonder God repeats the importance of giving thanks in Psalm 100.

7. Bless His name.
The word *bless* is from *bah-rack*, meaning "to kneel." The idea is to show honor and homage to God—His name is higher than any other name on earth.

REASONS FOR THE COMMANDS

> For the Lord is good;
> His lovingkindness is everlasting,
> And His faithfulness to all generations. [v. 5]

Why obey these seven commands? The answer is connected to His character:

Because He is good.
Verse 3 told us "He is God" and this final verse tells us "He is good." The original Hebrew term, *tobe* means "pleasant, agreeable, delightful." How different from the present-day concept many people have of God. He is not an irritated Sovereign of heaven who takes delight in smashing our lives and frowning on our happiness—like some celestial Bully with a club in His hand. No! He is good. His commands are best for us. His ways are perfect.

Because His lovingkindness is everlasting.
God loves and accepts us as we are. Knowing what will best encourage us and give us real happiness, He leads us into His way by giving us His commands in this song. His unqualified love and acceptance are behind His every command.

Because He is faithful forever.
He is not partial. The God who commands is fair and faithful to *all* generations. He doesn't play favorites. His commands will result in benefits (if obeyed) because He is faithful.

Turn, finally, to Ephesians 5:1. Read the verse slowly. *The Amplified Bible* renders it: "Therefore be imitators of God—copy Him and follow His example—as well-beloved children [imitate their father]."

It is not enough to read that God is pleasant, agreeable, loving, accepting, faithful, and impartial. *We are to mimic our Father!* In fact, we are *commanded* to do so in Ephesians 5:1. Why not start today? Give up your self-centered way of life and stretch your spiritual wings! God, by His indwelling Holy Spirit, longs to live out His character through you . . . and He longs to start right now. As He does so, the grind of ingratitude will slowly fade into oblivion.

REFLECTIONS ON INGRATITUDE

1. In your own words, define gratitude.

   _____

   _____

   _____

2. Do a little reviewing of the things God has provided for you. In the words of the old gospel song, "Count your many blessings, name them one by one." List some of them below. You'll be surprised how it will help you live beyond the grind of ingratitude.

   Blessings at home:

   Blessings at church:

   Personal blessings:

Take the time throughout the week to express your gratitude to God. Your cup is full and running over, isn't it?

3. Don't limit your gratitude to God. Think about five or six people who have meant much to you. Before the week has run its course, write each one a note of appreciation. Express your thanks briefly but sincerely. For all you know, one (or more) of them could be going through an intensely difficult trial at this very moment.

Psalm

A Psalm of David

I will sing of lovingkindness and
    justice,
To Thee, O Lord, I will sing praises.
I will give heed to the blameless way.
When wilt Thou come to me?
I will walk within my house in the
    integrity of my heart.
I will set no worthless thing before my
    eyes;
I hate the work of those who fall away;
It shall not fasten its grip on me.
A perverse heart shall depart from me;
I will know no evil.
Whoever secretly slanders his neighbor,
    him I will destroy;
No one who has a haughty look and an
    arrogant heart will I endure.

My eyes shall be upon the faithful of the
    land, that they may dwell with me;
He who walks in a blameless way is the
    one who will minister to me.
He who practices deceit shall not dwell
    within my house;
He who speaks falsehood shall not
    maintain his position before me.
Every morning I will destroy all the
    wicked of the land,
So as to cut off from the city of the Lord
    all those who do iniquity.   [101:1–8]

THE GRIND OF
AIMLESSNESS

Some people seem to drift aimlessly through life, headed in no specific direction. Without clearly defined objectives, it is not surprising that many adopt a lifestyle that lacks definition and purpose.

I know a few folks who sort of take life as it comes . . . no big deal. Reminds me of the time I had been invited to a college campus to speak. On my way to the meeting hall, I met a fellow who was obviously apathetic. Hoping to put a little spark into his plans beyond graduation, I asked him a few probing questions. I'll never forget his answer to my first one: "Where are you going . . . what are your plans?" With hardly a hesitation, he answered back, "Plans? Well, uh, I'm going to lunch." How typical of those caught in the grind of aimlessness! They live from one meal to the next. Without much concern beyond that evening's television programs, they drift through life like a skiff in a swamp.

The psalmist chose not to live a life without purpose. Aside from David's slump into disobedience, he served the Lord as His man for many, many years. He was indeed "a man after God's own heart." For the most part, he lived a godly life. This brings us to Psalm 101. Perhaps more than any other passage of Scripture, these eight verses explain David's *spiritual philosophy of life*. In fact, an appropriate title for Psalm 101 might be: *David's Statement of Faith*. This song represents his credo. It declares his spiritual aims.

He committed himself to these things without reservation. Not that he never fell short, but he always had the standard before him. In this psalm there is not the slightest trace of diplomatic compromise or vacillation . . . only simple, straightforward, devout words. He subscribed to this "profession of faith," and in doing so he became God's man of the hour. All who hope to live beyond the grind of aimlessness would do well to observe how David declared himself. As before, we want to survey the psalm before working our way through it.

Psalm 101 could be called "the psalm of wills and shalls." I count at least ten "I wills" or "I shalls." This tells us that the psalm is very *personal*. In fact, it begins with a series of *resolutions* and ends with several *declarations*. Let's use Joshua 24:15 as the basis for our outline. It is the famous statement: ". . . choose for yourselves today whom you will serve: . . . but as for me and my house, we will serve the Lord."

For four verses David implies "as for me . . ." and lists his *resolutions* in five "I wills." Following that, in verses 5–8, he turns to his kingdom, implying "as for my house . . . ," and lists seven different types of people as he makes *declarations* about each one. An outline could look like this:

I. As for Me: Resolutions (vv. 1–4)
    A. I will sing (v. 1)
    B. I will give heed (v. 2a)
    C. I will walk (v. 2b)
    D. I will set (v. 3)
    E. I will know (v. 4)
II. As for My House: Declarations (vv. 5–8)
    A. Slanderer (v. 5a)
    B. Proud (v. 5b)
    C. Faithful (v. 6a)
    D. Blameless (v. 6b)
    E. Deceiver (v. 7a)
    F. Liar (v. 7b)
    G. Wicked (v. 8)

AS FOR ME: RESOLUTIONS

I once heard the president of a seminary express his concern over the school by saying, "I fear we may be turning out graduates with a great number of *beliefs* but not enough *conviction*." Conviction gives beliefs a backbone. David wasn't satisfied with a nice set of theological beliefs floating around in his head; he pinned them down to concrete convictions. It's as though he is saying in verses 1–4, "I'm committed to this purpose. . . ." In these four verses he lists four great qualities the believer *must* possess in order to maintain clear direction. Each one *assaults* an aimless mindset.

Consistency

> I will sing of lovingkindness, and justice,
> To Thee, O Lord, I will sing praises. [v. 1]

Observe what he sings about: lovingkindness and justice. For both of these things he expressed praise. I suggest that "lovingkindness" has reference to times of blessings, prosperity . . . the "good life." It would include times when all is going well. The "justice," on the other hand, suggests times of adversity, difficulty, and problems . . . the "real life." For both of these experiences, David praised his God. He resolved that he would be *consistent* in his praise no matter what his circumstances might be.

How important it is to be consistent in our praise to God! We are quick to sing praises to Him when we enjoy good health, financial success, happiness, freedom from pressure, and accomplishing some enviable achievement . . . but rarely do we praise Him for "justice," for the hard times when our tunnel of troubles seems so long.

On the heels of losing virtually everything, Job remained consistent. He remarked: "Shall we indeed accept good from God and not accept adversity?" (Job 2:10).

He refused to be fickle and inconsistent. To Job the Lord was to be praised as much for "taking away" as for "giving" (Job

1:21). Like Job, David resolved to be consistent in his praise to God, whether times were good or bad.

Integrity

> I will give heed to the blameless way.
> When wilt Thou come to me?
> I will walk within my house in the integrity of my heart
>   [Ps. 101:2]

The first part of this verse has to do with *public* integrity as David says, literally, "I will give heed unto the way of integrity." You may recall that the original Hebrew term translated *integrity* means "to be finished, whole, complete." It carries with it the idea of being totally honest, thoroughly sound. The king of Israel knew that his life before the people *had* to be solid and honest for the kingdom to remain strong.

The second part of this verse has to do with *private* integrity—he mentions being sound in "my house" and "my heart." Integrity is like an iceberg in that what shows is only a very small part of the hidden whole.

Humility

> I will set no worthless thing before my eyes;
> I hate the work of those who fall away;
> It shall not fasten its grip on me. [v. 3]

David resolves to remove everything that might catch the affection of his heart and turn his gaze off the Lord and onto himself. He claims that he will not allow a single thing to capture his attention and tempt him to exalt himself. He resolves to avoid every unworthy aim and ambition. To do less would inevitably lead to his "falling away" from fellowship with his Lord.

Pride is such a senseless sin! It defies logic for any Christian to be arrogant and gripped in the jaws of conceit. Paul implies this in 1 Corinthians 4:6–7, which says:

Now these things, brethren, I have figuratively applied to myself and Apollos for your sakes, that in us you might learn not to exceed what is written, in order that no one of you might become arrogant in behalf of one against the other.

For who regards you as superior? And what do you have that you did not receive? But if you did receive it, why do you boast as if you had not received it?

Read that again! Whatever you and I have we were *given*. Since we were given that particular thing, why boast as though we deserve the credit? Of the seven things God says He hates (Prov. 6:16–19), can you remember the *first* on His "hit list"? It is "haughty eyes" . . . that arrogant, proud appearance which God says He will abase (Ps. 18:27).

Years ago I learned a little poem (source unknown). It puts us in our place, especially when we begin to think of ourselves as indispensable:

Sometime when you're feeling important,
Sometime when your ego's way up,
Sometime when you take it for granted that you are the
    prize-winning 'pup';
Sometime when you feel that your absence would leave an
    unfillable hole,
Just follow these simple instructions,
And see how it humbles your soul.
Take a bucket and fill it with water,
Put your hand in it up to your wrist.
Now pull it out fast and the hole that remains is the measure of
    how you'll be missed.
You may splash all you please as you enter,
And stir up the water galore,
But STOP and you'll find in a minute,
It's back where it was before.

Purity

A perverse heart shall depart from me;
I will know no evil. [v. 4]

David has resolved thus far that he will be a man of consistency, integrity, and humility. Now he resolves to be a man of purity—knowing no evil. This has to be one of the reasons God called David "a man after My own heart." Rare indeed are those people in this world who could say what David says in this fourth verse.

David's son Solomon also wrote of the value of personal purity in Proverbs 11:19–21:

> He who is steadfast in righteousness will attain to life,
> And he who pursues evil will bring about his own death.
> The perverse in heart are an abomination to the Lord,
> But the blameless in their walk are His delight.
> Assuredly, the evil man will not go unpunished,
> But the descendants of the righteous will be delivered.

Don't miss the last part of that passage. A pure life is actually a spiritual investment, the dividends being enjoyed by your children. God has a *purity layaway plan* . . . which you establish now and your descendants later cash in on.

I cannot overemphasize the value of a pure life. We have an inordinate curiosity about perversion and evil. We are not only aware of wickedness, but we are drawn to it with interest. The news media capitalize on this interest by highlighting the evil in our world. They have found that public interest is high when it comes to impure, wicked activities. David realized, however, that "a perverse heart" would only lead to a weakening of his spiritual life.

My wife, Cynthia, and I know a young man who was in training for the ministry. He met and married a girl who had been gloriously saved out of an impure past. She had been a call girl, a harlot of the street, connected with an organized ring of prostitutes in a large city. During those years she went to the depths of wickedness and shame. Through a series of events, she heard the gospel and came, by faith, to Christ. After her conversion and subsequent marriage to our minister friend, she found herself in an entirely new environment. Instead of evil there was purity and wholesome living. On one occasion, she shared with

Cynthia the tremendous adjustment she faced and the difficulty of fully forgetting her past. She wanted to, but evil had a way of lingering in her mind. Perhaps that is the reason David resolved to "know no evil." This world's system puts a brand upon us that is the next thing to impossible to erase. How much better it is to be pure and inexperienced than to be scarred by impure memories that are quick to play back their reruns at a moment's notice.

AS FOR ME AND MY HOUSE: DECLARATIONS

Now the composer changes direction. David no longer looks *within*, he looks *around*. He considers the people of his kingdom and declares his position regarding several different types . . . seven in all.

Slanderer

Whoever secretly slanders his neighbor, him I will destroy.
[v. 5a]

The term *destroy* comes from a Hebrew word meaning "to put an end to." The idea is that David would put an end to and silence the slanderer. He would not tolerate slander!

Proud

No one who has a haughty look and an arrogant heart will I endure. [v. 5b]

David also declares that he cannot abide an arrogant person. You will notice that pride reveals itself in the *face*, "a haughty look . . . " but its source is in the *heart*, "an arrogant heart." Proverbs 21:4 (please read) also links the proud heart with a haughty appearance.

One of the practical problems connected with pride is dealing with its byproduct: *argumentation*. Show me a proud person—

really haughty—and I'll show you one who brings contention and arguments into almost every situation. Pride must have its say and its way! Listen again to Solomon, the wise: "Through presumption comes nothing but strife" (Prov. 13:10).

Faithful

> My eyes shall be upon the faithful of the land. [Ps. 101:6a]

While David couldn't endure the proud, he longed to dwell with the faithful of the land. He had discovered that the faithful person is usually easy to get along with . . . cooperative . . . teachable . . . and best of all, trustworthy.

I came across an interesting thought in my study of the Scriptures. On two occasions in the Book of Proverbs the same question is asked—once with regard to men and the other with regard to women.

The question: Who can find? The thought behind the question: This is so rare, you can hardly find one! Now look at Proverbs 20:6 for the *man*, then Proverbs 31:10 for the *woman*. Among men it is hard to find *faithfulness* ("who can find a trustworthy man?"). Among women it is hard to find *strength of character* (the literal meaning of the original word translated "excellent" in Proverbs 31:10—"an excellent wife who can find?").

Blameless

> He who walks in a blameless way is the one who will minister to me. [Ps. 101:6b]

David admits that there is a certain category of people who minister to him, who serve him. He says that they are the "blameless" people—not perfect but people of integrity.

In my opinion, this is the single most important trait to be found among ministers—among all those who minister, counsel, teach, and serve others. Integrity is absolutely indispensable in the lives of God's servants. When integrity breaks down, one forfeits the right to lead in a high-profile capacity.

Deceiver

> He who practices deceit shall not dwell within my house. [v. 7a]

David's original term for *dwell* in this verse is different from the previous verse. Here it means "to come near." He is saying that the hypocrite/deceiver will not even *come near* his house. Deception has to do with keeping back the full story or hiding the real motive behind an action. It is the act of deliberately causing someone to be misled. If you have ever dealt with a deceiver, you know why David felt so strongly about this.

Liar

> He who speaks falsehood shall not maintain his position before me. [v. 7b]

The king had a policy: No liar will be established in a position of authority! He would not tolerate lying.

By the way, this is a good business policy. You are unwise if you tolerate an employee in your business who is a liar. Perhaps you have tried to work with a liar. If so, you know the impossibility of sustaining a harmonious, secure relationship in that situation.

Wicked

> Every morning I will destroy all the wicked of the land,
> So as to cut off from the city of the Lord all those who do
> iniquity. [v. 8]

This is quite a conclusion! He has mentioned several types of people and forcefully declared himself regarding each one, but this is the strongest of all. It seems certain that David believed in capital punishment. He knew that it was a God-ordained principle established once and for all as a definite tool to be used by government to maintain law and order (Gen. 9:5–6).

We live in a day when society is often blamed for the crimes of lawbreakers—felonies and misdemeanors alike. And even parents have been seen as guilty for their children's crime. Our whole basis of judgment has shifted from the objective, clear-cut assertions of Scripture to the subjective, shifting sands of human viewpoint and feeling. Oh, that we might return as a nation to God's truth, God's methods, God's pattern of dealing with those who do iniquity!

Well, there you have it—David's credo. There was no question as to where he stood on things that matter. With simplicity and objectivity, he stated his convictions. Aimlessness was not a word in his vocabulary, nor should it be in ours.

REFLECTIONS ON AIMLESSNESS

1. Is aimlessness one of the "daily grinds" you can't seem to shake? See if you can figure out why. Uncertain about your career? Disturbed over a few unwise decisions? Preoccupied with the fear of taking a risk? Talk this over with someone you respect. Do that this week for sure. Ask the individual to pray for you . . . to trust God with you that He would clarify your objectives and give you a sense of renewed assurance.

2. Select a person in history you admire because of his or her accomplishments. Go to the library and check out a copy of that person's biography. Read it during the next several weeks, taking special note of how the individual became focused in his energy and direction. Make a few notes of your own. We are often stimulated by the example of those we admire. Strong leaders are usually readers of biographies.

3. What a powerful "statement of faith" is Psalm 101! David wrote his in the form of a song. Let me challenge you to write out your own credo. First, think through where you stand . . . those areas that have no "wobble room" in your list of convictions. Then, write them down.

   Here is my statement of faith:

   I resolve:

   I declare:

Psalm

I love the Lord, because He hears
My voice and my supplications.
Because He has inclined His ear to
 me,
Therefore I shall call upon Him as long
 as I live.
The cords of death encompassed me,
And the terrors of Sheol came upon me;
I found distress and sorrow.
Then I called upon the name of the Lord:
"O Lord, I beseech Thee, save my life!"

Gracious is the Lord, and righteous;
Yes, our God is compassionate.
The Lord preserves the simple;
I was brought low, and He saved me.
Return to your rest, O my soul,
For the Lord has dealt bountifully with
 you.
For Thou hast rescued my soul from
 death,
My eyes from tears,
My feet from stumbling.
I shall walk before the Lord
In the land of the living.
I believed when I said,
"I am greatly afflicted."

I said in my alarm,
"All men are liars."

What shall I render to the Lord
For all His benefits toward me?
I shall lift up the cup of salvation,
And call upon the name of the Lord.
I shall pay my vows to the Lord,
Oh may it be in the presence of all His
    people.
Precious in the sight of the Lord
Is the death of His godly ones.
O Lord, surely I am Thy servant,
I am Thy servant, the son of Thy
    handmaid,
Thou hast loosed my bonds.
To Thee I shall offer a sacrifice of
    thanksgiving,
And call upon the name of the Lord.
I shall pay my vows to the Lord,
O may it be in the presence of all His
    people,
In the courts of the Lord's house,
In the midst of you, O Jerusalem.
Praise the Lord.   [116:1–19]

THE GRIND OF SORROW AND GRIEF

It is easy for those who are strong and healthy to forget how many tears of sorrow and grief are shed every day. All around this aching world—perhaps in your own home or in your heart this very week—sadness abounds. Tears fall. Grief has you in its grip. And it can happen so fast.

Just last week I spoke with a young man on our support staff at the church I serve as senior pastor. He was all smiles about his future, such a contagious fellow. But before nightfall that same day he was killed in an automobile-motorcycle collision. Today his family grieves his absence. Such is the groan of humanity. To omit the subject of sorrow and grief in a two-volume book on life's daily grinds would be inexcusable.

We don't know the details, but the composer of the ancient song you just read found himself in a grievous circumstance. Did you catch the clues as you read through his lyrics? He states that "the cords of death encompassed" him as well as "the terrors of Sheol" (the grave). He admits that he "found distress and sorrow" in whatever he was enduring. A few lines later he declares that he was "brought low" and the Lord rescued his "eyes from tears." Somehow his God put him back on his feet so firmly and brought back his perspective so clearly, he was able to write: "Precious in the sight of the Lord / Is the death of His godly ones" (Ps. 116:15).

Amazing! From the pit to the pinnacle . . . from agony to

ecstasy. The same one who begins the song in the dark valley of sorrow and grief (vv. 1–2) ends it in the most magnificent statement of praise a Jew could utter: "Hallelujah!" (v. 19, MLB).

The psalmist, after passing through the deep valley of grief, sits down and recounts his experience. The song is his personal testimony; first, of his love for the Lord who saw him through the turbulent waters of distress, sorrow, and grief (vv. 1–11); and second, of his desire to return his thanks to the Lord for seeing him through it all (vv. 12–19).

In outline form, the song could appear:

I. I love the Lord! (vv. 1–11)
   A. Because He hears me (vv. 1–2)
   B. Because He rescues me (vv. 3–6, 8–11)
   C. Because He cares for me (v. 7)
II. What shall I render to the Lord? (vv. 12–19)
   A. I shall proclaim His benefits (vv. 12–13)
   B. I shall pay my vows (vv. 14, 18–19)
   C. I shall praise His name (vv. 15–17)

I LOVE THE LORD!

Let's take a few moments this week to probe a little deeper into a song of sadness. To begin with, go back to that opening line, "I love the Lord, because . . ." (v. 1). In the nineteenth century a young English girl, Elizabeth Barrett, suffered a spinal injury at age fifteen, which left her a semi-invalid for many years afterward. Although she regained strength prior to her marriage to Robert Browning in 1846, she was hesitant to burden him with a frail, crippled wife. Her love for him was beautifully expressed in her work *Sonnets from the Portuguese* as she wrote the immortal words: "How do I love thee? Let me count the ways. . . ." She then held nothing back as she described the depth of her love. In the same way the psalmist says that to his Lord in his expressions of affection.

Why did he love the Lord? He counts the ways.

Because He Hears Me

> I love the Lord, because He hears
> My voice and my supplications.
> Because He has inclined His ear to me,
> Therefore I shall call upon Him as long as I live. [vv. 1–2]

1. He hears my voice.
2. He inclines His ear to me.

These are two distinct responses, not one and the same. The first, "He hears," simply means that when the psalmist speaks, God listens; God pays attention to what he has to say. The second, *He inclines,* is from the Hebrew *nahtah,* meaning "to bend, turn aside." It is more of an intimate term than *hear.*

For example, Solomon uses it in Proverbs 7:21 to describe the response of a man who is seduced by a harlot and "turns aside" to her. It appears in 1 Kings 11:4 to describe how Solomon's wives "turned away" his heart after other gods. The psalmist says that he loves the Lord because God "bends down," as it were, and "turns aside" from His infinite work . . . as He pays close attention to him in his sorrow and grief. God *never* turns His back on those who cry out to Him through tears. On the contrary, He "bends an ear."

Because He Delivers/Rescues Me

> The cords of death encompassed me,
> And the terrors of Sheol came upon me;
> I found distress and sorrow.
> Then I called upon the name of the Lord:
> "O Lord, I beseech Thee, save my life!"
> Gracious is the Lord, and righteous;
> Yes, our God is compassionate.
> The Lord preserves the simple;
> I was brought low, and He saved me. [vv. 3–6]

For Thou hast rescued my soul from death,
My eyes from tears,
My feet from stumbling. I shall walk before the Lord
In the land of the living. I believed when I said,
"I am greatly afflicted."
I said in my alarm,
"All men are liars." [vv. 8–11]

Some tragic circumstance had surrounded the writer. Some terrible, painful experience caused him to say that he was near death. Grief, sorrow, and difficulty were his companions, which explains why he confesses to a great deal of distress and even crying.

I believe Spurgeon best captures the pathos of the psalmist's situation as he writes:

> As hunters surround a stag with dogs and men, so that no way of escape is left, so was David enclosed in a ring of deadly griefs. The bands of sorrow, weakness, and terror with which death is accustomed to bind men ere he drags them away to their long captivity were all around him. . . . Horrors such as those which torment the lost seized me, grasped me, found me out, searched me through and through, and held me a prisoner. . . . these were so closely upon him that they fixed their teeth in him as hounds seize their prey.[8]

The marvelous part of it, however, is that the Lord delivered him; He rescued him. Though reduced in strength, slandered in character, depressed in spirit, sick in body, and grief-stricken, the psalmist testifies that the Lord stuck by his side! He always will. God doesn't ditch us; He doesn't leave the sinking ship; He doesn't retreat when the enemy increases strength. Our Lord is a specialist when it comes to deliverance, and you can claim that fact this moment!

We are not surprised to see that the psalmist says he will therefore "walk before the Lord" (v. 9) because of His deliverance. It is a natural reaction or desire to spend time with someone who stayed with us during some painful experience we endured.

Because He Cares for Me

> Return to your rest, O my soul,
> For the Lord has dealt bountifully with you. [v. 7]

Look at that! The words *dealt bountifully* are a translation of the Hebrew *gah-maal*, which means "to deal fully/completely" with something or someone. Frequently, it suggests the idea of "rewarding." Today we would say, "Because the Lord takes such good care of me, I will love Him in return." In other words, God leaves nothing out when He provides for us, when He takes care of us, when He surrounds us with His watchful care.

Having been lifted up and sustained in his grief, the songwriter then asks: "What shall I render to the Lord?"

WHAT SHALL I RENDER TO THE LORD?

In other words: How can I return my thanks? What will possibly suffice as proof of my gratitude? God has done so very, very much, how can I adequately render my appreciation to Him? How can I possibly repay? In response to that question, he offers three answers: (1) proclaim His benefits, (2) pay my vows, and (3) praise His name. Let's consider each one.

I Shall Proclaim His Benefits

> I shall lift up the cup of salvation,
> And call upon the name of the Lord. [v. 13]

What does "I shall lift up the cup of salvation . . ." mean? In the Old Testament the word *cup* is frequently used to denote plenty and abundance. You may remember that in Psalm 23:5 David claims that his "cup overflows." The term *salvation* actually appears in the Hebrew Bible in the plural—*salvations*. We would grasp the meaning better if we'd render it "deliverances." The psalmist is expressing praise to God for His abundant and numerous deliverances. So, literally, he says, "In the name of

Jehovah I shall proclaim." It is the idea of openly declaring that God is his Deliverer.

Moses does this in Deuteronomy 32:1–4:

> "Give ear, oh heavens, and let me speak;
> And let the earth hear the words of my mouth.
> Let my teaching drop as the rain,
> My speech distill as the dew,
> As the droplets on the fresh grass
> And as the showers on the herb.
> For I proclaim the name of the Lord;
> Ascribe greatness to our God!
> The Rock! His work is perfect,
> For all His ways are just;
> A God of faithfulness and without injustice,
> Righteous and upright is He."

This matter of making a public proclamation in honor of the Lord is important. It is good. It is healthy. It is biblical. God floods our lives with abundance . . . yet so few Christians share their experiences publicly, so few Christians "proclaim His benefits." (Unfortunately, we live in a day of spiritual secret-service agents. I sometimes think of them as Lady Clairol Christians: nobody knows but God!) Let's stop holding our praise to ourselves. Share your Savior . . . don't be ashamed or shy. If you want to render something of value to the Lord, proclaim His benefits! It may surprise you how much it helps you to live beyond the grind of sorrow and grief.

I Shall Pay My Vows

> I shall pay my vows to the Lord,
> O may it be in the presence of all His people, . . . [v. 14]

> I shall pay my vows to the Lord,
> O may it be in the presence of all His people,
> In the courts of the Lord's house,
> In the midst of you, O Jerusalem.
> Praise the Lord! [vv. 18–19]

A vow is a solemn promise to which you commit yourself before God. The vows found in the Bible are quite serious and binding. I also notice that biblical vows were always voluntary . . . but once made, they became compulsory. We may want to forget our vows today, but God never does.

The psalmist is saying that he can render his gratitude to the Lord by keeping his promises, preferably before the public. I recently discovered an excellent passage of Scripture regarding vows.

> Do not be hasty in word or impulsive in thought to bring up a matter in the presence of God. For God is in heaven and you are on the earth; therefore let your words be few. . . . When you make a vow to God, do not be late in paying it, for He takes no delight in fools. Pay what you vow! It is better that you should not vow than that you should vow and not pay. Do not let your speech cause you to sin and do not say in the presence of the messenger of God that it was a mistake. Why should God be angry on account of your voice and destroy the work of your hands? [Eccles. 5:2, 4–6]

Serious, isn't it? The Bible says that it is better not to vow at all than to vow and not keep your word.

I Shall Praise His Name

> Precious in the sight of the Lord
> Is the death of His godly ones.
> O Lord, surely I am Thy servant,
> I am Thy servant, the son of Thy handmaid,
> Thou hast loosed my bonds.
> To Thee I shall offer a sacrifice of thanksgiving,
> And call upon the name of the Lord. [Ps. 116:15–17]

Finally, the psalmist declares his thanks and praises God's name in appreciation for all His goodnesses. I have a question: Why does he mention "the death of His godly ones" here? I think the answer is connected to his tragic experience mentioned earlier in verses 3–4, 6, and 8. In fact, I believe the psalmist had been delivered from death, perhaps as a lone survivor. In verse 16, he mentions himself as "the son of Thy handmaid" from whom he had been "loosed." In other words, he had been loosed from the bonds of death, if I interpret this correctly. I suggest that the calamity and grief mentioned earlier quite probably snuffed out the life of several of his loved ones, quite likely including his mother—which resulted in his tears and grief (v. 8), sorrow and disillusionment (vv. 10–11). Even in these circumstances, he rendered his praise to God.

That is the way it ought to be. Our praise and thanksgiving should be expressed *regardless*. Not until we learn to give thanks *in everything* will we discover God's most basic lessons for our lives—even in times of distress—even in times of sorrow and grief.

REFLECTIONS ON SORROW AND GRIEF

1. Have you or a close friend of yours recently traveled through the deep dark vale of sorrow and grief? If so, there is a fragility and tenderness in your life that such experiences bring about. Answer several questions:

   a. Have you fully expressed your grief?
      (Don't hurry . . . try not to deny its depths.)
   b. Are you being honest about your feelings?
      (It is easy to put up a false front of strength.)
   c. Do you still entertain some anger . . . maybe even feelings of cynicism?
      (Take another look at the psalmist's words in verse 11.)
   d. Can you bring yourself to admit your need for others?
      (They are there . . . awaiting your invitation.)

2. How long has it been since you literally made a list of the Lord's benefits? Start with a clean sheet of paper, address it to the Lord your God, and as Elizabeth Barrett Browning once did, begin with these words at the top: "How do I love thee? Let me count the ways. . . ." Then list fifteen to twenty of His benefits. Psalm 103 will help get your list started.

3. A vow, as we were reminded in the song, is a serious thing. Think back over the vows of your life . . . those times when you made promises to the Lord, either publicly or privately. Have you kept them? Do you need to return and come to terms with one or two? Do that this week.

Psalm

Aleph.

How blessed are those whose
    way is blameless,
    Who walk in the law of the
        Lord.
How blessed are those who observe His
    testimonies,
Who seek Him with all their heart.
They also do no unrighteousness;
They walk in His ways.
Thou hast ordained Thy precepts,
That we should keep them diligently.
Oh that my ways may be established
To keep Thy statutes!
Then I shall not be ashamed
When I look upon all Thy
    commandments.
I shall give thanks to Thee with
    uprightness of heart,
When I learn Thy righteous judgments.
I shall keep Thy statutes;
Do not forsake me utterly!   [119:1–8]

Mem.

O how I love Thy law!
It is my meditation all the day.
Thy commandments make me wiser than
    my enemies,
For they are ever mine.
I have more insight than all my teachers,
For Thy testimonies are my meditation.
I understand more than the aged,
Because I have observed Thy
    precepts.   [119:97–100]

THE GRIND OF
LOW ENTHUSIASM

Interesting word, enthusiasm. It is from two Greek terms, *en* (meaning "in") and *theos* (meaning "God")—in other words, enthusiasm represents the presence of God in one's life. That makes sense. The truth of God applied to our circumstances brings a burst of enthusiasm nothing else can provide.

New homes, boats, cars, and clothes give us a temporary "high"—until the payments grind on. A new job is exciting, but that dries up in a few months. A new marriage partner makes us feel "up" until reality begins to erase the fun memories of a fantasy honeymoon. All those things may eventually leave us feeling responsible or disappointed or disillusioned . . . sometimes even a little bored. But not when we put "God in"?

Psalm 119—the longest song in the ancient hymnal—is a song that is full of "God in" kind of statements. Over and over it affirms the value of having God's Word in our lives. It keeps pounding away on that theme with a heavy, powerful beat to the music. There is one statement after another announcing the joys, the fresh motivation, the unique benefits of God's Book in our lives. Let's get a grasp of the whole song before we concentrate our attention on a few select stanzas.

OVERVIEW

Length

As I have mentioned, this is the longest song. Not only that, it is the longest chapter in the whole Bible—176 verses. No other chapter even comes close in length.

Structure

Find a Bible and locate Psalm 119. You will notice that the verses of this lengthy song are divided into twenty-two sections, eight verses each. Each section has a title, such as "Aleph," "Beth," "Gimel," etc. These words are really not words at all, but the letters that comprise the Hebrew alphabet. There are twenty-two letters in all, which explains the song's composition in twenty-two sections. Every section of this ancient hymn was originally written with each verse in that section beginning with the same Hebrew letter. In other words, all eight verses in the "Aleph" section of the Hebrew Bible, originally began with that same letter—"Aleph." This poetical structure (called "acrostic" or "acronym") greatly eased the discipline of committing the entire psalm to memory.

Theme

As I have implied, the psalm carries as its theme the *Word of God*. I have found only a very few verses that fail to mention the Scriptures. There are several synonyms employed by the composer that refer to the written Scriptures. Some are:

Word	Testimonies
Law	Judgments
Ways	Statutes
Paths	Commandments
Precepts	Ordinances

An old German version of the Bible places the following description at the head of Psalm 119: "This is the Christian's Golden ABCs of the praise, love, power, and use of the Word of God."

Purpose

The psalmist desires to give praise to God for His Word, and then he states how we are to behave in relation to it.

APPLICATION

Many well-meaning folks are seeking what I would call a "spiritual high" . . . sort of an emotional narcotic that will quiet the pain of their aching, monotonous lives. As a result, you will find people driving miles and miles to attend nightly meetings or standing in long lines to experience some high-level delight that will send them back home on the crest of ecstasy. But all this inevitably leads to emotional hangovers. God's Word—His written Truth—provides the Christian with all the nutrients and true enthusiasm he (or she) can absorb. Coupled with the indwelling Holy Spirit's motivating power, God's Word can virtually transform a life *without a single hangover*—guaranteed!

Believers need to get back to the basics! If Psalm 119 says anything, it says we must be willing to sink our shafts down into His Book and stand *alone* on the principles it contains. Pour over it. Pray over it. Read it. Study it. Memorize sections of it. Meditate upon it. Let it saturate your thinking. Use it when problems arise. Filter your decisions through it. Don't let a day pass without spending time alone with God, listening to the silent voice of His eloquent Word.

Please . . . please heed my counsel! All other attempts to gain spiritual growth lead to frustration. I know; I've tried many of them. And with each one my enthusiasm waned; with God's Word it never has! Nothing enables us to live beyond the grind of low enthusiasm like a daily application of His Word to our situation—absolutely nothing!

Look at an example. Turn to Psalm 119:97–100. I want to reinforce my point by considering the songwriter's words regarding the benefits of consistent scriptural input.

> O how I love Thy law!
> It is my meditation all the day.
> Thy commandments make me wiser than my enemies,
> For they are ever mine.
> I have more insight than all my teachers,
> For Thy testimonies are my meditation.
> I understand more than the aged,
> Because I have observed Thy precepts.

He exclaims, "I love your Word!" He declares his affection for what God has said and has allowed to be written and preserved. Nothing on earth compares to the power of God's Word.

I once came across a powerful quote by Daniel Webster that illustrates what the composer is saying here in verse 97. In the presence of Professor Sanborn of Dartmouth College, Mr. Webster laid his hand on a copy of the Scriptures as he said,

> This is THE Book. I have read through the entire Bible many times. I make it a practice to go through it once a year. It is the Book of all others for lawyers as well as divines; and I pity the man who cannot find in it a rich supply of thought and rules for his conduct. It fits man for life; it prepares him for death.[9]

In verses 98–100, the psalmist speaks of the superiority of the Word over three sources of truth held in high esteem by the world.

1. The Word makes us wiser than our enemies.

> Thy commandments make me wiser than my enemies,
> For they are ever mine. [v. 98]

The world places great importance on knowledge gained from *experience*. In this case, the songwriter mentions experience in dealing with our enemies. But he says that the one who has a grasp of the Word is wiser than his enemies. I feel my enthusiasm beginning to grow with that thought.

2. The Word gives us more insight than all our teachers.

> I have more insight than all my teachers,
> For Thy testimonies are my meditation. [v. 99]

The world also emphasizes the importance of getting knowledge from *education*. But the Lord says that the one who knows the Word possesses more insight than his educators. My enthusiasm is increasing.

3. The Word causes us to have more understanding than the aged.

> I understand more than the aged,
> Because I have observed Thy precepts. [v. 100]

The world embraces enormous respect for *old age* . . . claiming that age equals understanding. But verse 100 declares that one who obeys God's Word can actually have more understanding than an aged individual. In Job 32:8–9, we find a similar observation: "But it is a spirit in man, / And the breath of the Almighty gives them understanding. / The abundant in years may not be wise, / Nor may elders understand justice."

What have we found? We have found that a knowledge and application of the written truths of the Word will better equip us for life than our experiences, our teachers, and even the aged! High-level enthusiasm grips me!

I notice something else. Glance over verses 98–100 again. Three things become a reality in the lives and thinking of those who absorb the Word: wisdom, insight, and understanding.

To illustrate the meaning and distinction of each, I will use a simple diagram:

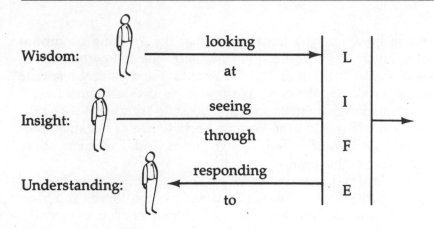

Wisdom: looking at → L

Insight: seeing   I
                     through   F

Understanding: ← responding   E
                     to

Wisdom, as we learned previously, means the ability to *look at* life and its difficulties from God's point of view. As I learn more of the Word of God and begin to get a grasp of its practical principles, I also glean the ability to look at life from God's viewpoint. I begin to see my circumstances as opportunities He has designed to develop me and train me as His vessel. This removes bitterness and irritation from my life and replaces them with gratitude and enthusiasm!

Insight means the ability to *see through* life and its difficulties from God's viewpoint. In other words, as I grow in the Word, I gain the ability to penetrate beyond the *surface level* of irritations and problems. I am given insight to see the real causes for certain situations, much like God can see beneath the outer mask (1 Sam. 16:7). Make no mistake about it, teachers can communicate knowledge, but the Word alone can give you insight.

Understanding means the ability to *respond to* life's situations/difficulties from God's viewpoint. As I get a hold on the Word, I discover how to react when things don't turn out my way. I find that my attitude is as important to God as my activity . . . often more so!

Before we end this study and take up a new one, let's set these three realities in concrete by looking at a problem from life.

Let's imagine that you recently got a job that has proven to be less than you expected. You prayed for employment, then, lo and behold, this job opened up. You were grateful. After a few weeks, however, you have found that the working conditions leave much to be desired. Furthermore, the fellow employees are all non-Christian and petty. Your first and *natural* response would be disappointment, perhaps even disillusionment. This would lead to daily irritations and possible arguments with others. Your life would soon become a whole pile of negative, pessimistic assaults on others—maybe even God. Exit: motivation. Enter: low enthusiasm.

How much better to apply some basic, biblical principles! Let's say that you were now getting into the Word. You soon come across the fact that God is working on you personally. You are His personal "project." His plan is to develop you into a mature, stable person. He has your good at heart. Nothing is "coincidental" in the Christian life . . . all things (even your job!) work together for good.

Suddenly, it dawns upon you that your job, with all its limitations and irritations, is a perfect place for God to mature you and make you patient. You begin to anticipate each day as another opportunity to grow in grace toward others and submission to Him. Wisdom helps you look at your situation from His viewpoint.

Then, those who work around you don't bother you so much because God's Word has begun to teach you how to see through their surface problems. You now see that their verbal assaults are indicative of a deeper problem of inner unrest. You also learn that you need not take their abuse personally, for it really isn't directed at you personally. Almost overnight, your *insight* has saved you from an ugly, irritating, retaliatory spirit. Instead of arguing with them, you find that you are interested in *helping* them.

You have now begun to respond to your once-irritating occupation with a positive attitude. Time spent in the Letter of James, for example, has resulted in your being very careful about what you say and how you behave before the lost . . . and in your doing a diligent job regardless of the circumstances. What has happened? You have gleaned *understanding*. Furthermore, you have begun to enjoy and accept the challenge of your situation because you know it is exactly where the Lord wants you. It is an ideal place for making Christ known.

God's Word is for *you*, my friend, not just the theologian or the pastor; it's for you! There is no situation that you cannot face if you are really serious about spending time on a regular basis in the Book of books! And a great place to start is Psalm 119, especially if the grind of low enthusiasm has begun to take its toll.

REFLECTIONS ON LOW ENTHUSIASM

1. On a scale of one to ten, ten being best, how high would you rate your daily level of enthusiasm? A nine? Perhaps five? Would you have to say two? Do you find that your day begins better than it ends? Do you see yourself a victim of circumstances? Are you to the point of wondering if *anyone* could be enthusiastic living with all the stuff you have to put up with? All this week, focus every spare moment you have on Psalm 119. Leave your Bible open to it so you can return to it quickly and easily. As you read, pray. Ask God to bring back a fresh, authentic supply of "God-in" enthusiasm.

2. Remember the imaginary illustration I ended with in the applicational part of this week's reading? It was based on the wisdom, insight, and understanding mentioned in Psalm 119:98–100. Go back and re-read those verses and that closing example. Then, this week, write an *actual* example from your own life. In what way are you finding wisdom, insight, and understanding at work in your life?

3. Tell one other person this weekend about something you learned from reading this song. Explain your project of reading through Psalm 119, then state at least one thing that has brought back some much-needed enthusiasm.

A Song of Ascents, of Solomon

Unless the Lord builds the house,
They labor in vain who build it;
Unless the Lord guards the city,
The watchman keeps awake in
   vain.
It is vain for you to rise up early,
To retire late,
To eat the bread of painful labors;
For He gives to His beloved even in his
   sleep.

Behold, children are a gift of the Lord;
The fruit of the womb is a reward.
Like arrows in the hand of a warrior.
So are the children of one's youth.
How blessed is the man whose quiver is
   full of them;
They shall not be ashamed,
When they speak with their enemies in
   the gate.   [127:1–5]

A Song of Ascents

How blessed is everyone who fears the
    Lord,
Who walks in His ways.
When you shall eat of the fruit of your
    hands,
You will be happy and it will be well
    with you.
Your wife shall be like a fruitful vine,
Within your house,
Your children like olive plants
Around your table.
Behold, for thus shall the man be blessed
Who fears the Lord.

The Lord bless you from Zion,
And may you see the prosperity of
    Jerusalem all the days of your life.
Indeed, may you see your children's
    children.
Peace be upon Israel!   [128:1–6]

THE GRIND OF
FAMILY LIFE

Maybe it doesn't sound very spiritual, but some phases of family living can be a grind! Rearing a household of busy children, maintaining good communication, living unselfishly with others day in and day out under the same roof, remaining positive and affirming, dealing with strong wills, and handling some of the other domestic challenges can be a first-class chore! Hats off to all who do their very best. To set the record straight, it is worth all the effort. Someday, parents, those children will "rise up and call you blessed." Don't count on it too soon . . . I said *someday*! I am pleased to discover that the ancient songs in God's eternal hymnal do not omit words of encouragement for families.

Periodically, we come across psalms that fit together, forming a unit or a progression of thought. This is true of Psalms 22, 23, and 24. It is also true of Psalms 90 and 91 as well as Psalms 111 and 112. One psalm sets the stage, we might say, while the next completes the picture.

This is precisely what we find in the two songs we are highlighting this week. Both have to do with life in the *home*. They are domestic psalms. How do we know that? Look at 127:1— it refers to the building of the house. Then 127:3–5 mentions children. The third verse of Psalm 128 pictures the wife, the home, and children again, and Psalm 128:6 even traces the progression of time to one's grandchildren. If you think upon this theme, you also observe the psalmist's idea of

national strength being connected to the strong family unit
in Psalm 128:5. A nation remains only as strong as her
families. A crumbling family life is one of the signs of a crumbling culture.

Evangelist Billy Graham in his book *World Aflame,* writes discerning yet serious words concerning America:

> The immutable law of sowing and reaping has held sway. We
> are now the hapless possessors of moral depravity, and we seek
> in vain for a cure. The tares of indulgence have overgrown the
> wheat of moral restraint. Our homes have suffered. Divorce has
> grown to epidemic proportions. When the morals of society are
> upset, the family is the first to suffer. The home is the basic unit
> of our society, and a nation is only as strong as her homes. The
> breaking up of a home does not often make headlines, but it
> eats like termites at the structure of the nation.
>
> As a result of the mounting divorces, separations, and deser-
> tions, about twelve million of the forty-five million children in
> the United States [over one-fourth!] do not live with both parents.
> A vicious circle is set in motion. As the Bible says: "The Fathers
> have eaten sour grapes, and the children's teeth are set on edge"
> (Jer. 31:29).

As we turn to a brief examination of Psalms 127 and 128,
therefore, we turn to a most relevant portion of Scripture. In our
desperate national need, a return to our Judeo-Christian roots is
imperative. For it is these roots that will assist us toward mend-
ing the fracture of our domestic bones—the essential skeleton
of our great republic.

As I mentioned earlier, these two psalms form a progression.
They remind me of a historical mural that wraps its way around
a room, depicting a progressive story. The progression carries
us from the inception of a home all the way through to the
blessings of later years. Let me suggest a simple outline:

   I. Inception of the Home (127:1–2)
  II. Children Born within the Home (127:3–5)
 III. Training of the Children in the Home (128:1–3)
 IV. Blessings of Later Years beyond the Home (128:4–6)

I would urge you to pause right now and read both of the psalms again with this outline in mind.

Now then, let's see how it ties together.

INCEPTION OF THE HOME

> Unless the Lord builds the house,
> They labor in vain who build it;
> Unless the Lord guards the city,
> The watchman keeps awake in vain.
> It is vain for you to rise up early,
> To retire late,
> To eat the bread of painful labors;
> For He gives to His beloved even in his sleep. [127:1–2]

There are two major ideas conveyed in these two verses:

1. The Lord Himself is to be the center of our home (v. 1). There is an emphatic repetition of the phrase, "unless the Lord. . . ." As in the English, it is an *identical* repetition in the Hebrew Bible. What's more, it appears first in each sentence, adding even more emphasis to the thought. Of course, the idea is not that the Lord uses a hammer and nails so that He can literally "build the house," nor that He holds a weapon that He might literally "guard the city." The meaning is that He must be the very Foundation upon which a home is built before that home will stand firm. He must be the unseen Guardian of a city, trusted completely, before a city can be considered safe.

If such is not the case, all is "in vain" (also mentioned twice). In fact, in the Hebrew sentence structure, the words *in vain* appear first in each clause, emphasizing the emptiness of it all:

". . . *in vain* they labor who build it."

". . . *in vain* the watchman keeps awake."

Work, strive, fret, worry, plan, strain all you wish, but if the Lord is not the very *center* of your home, all your additional effort to make it strong is futile and worthless, Mom and Dad.

2. The Lord Himself must be the center of our life and work (v. 2). In keeping with the context of these two songs, verse 2

has reference to making a living—working long and hard hours. His point is that long, hard hours *by themselves* will never result in a godly, happy home—only "painful labors." And please note that if the Lord is *first* in our lives, He will reward us even in our sleep. A godly life includes times of rest and relaxation.

There is an ancient Greek motto that I learned many years ago. It says: "You will break the bow if you keep it always bent." That is worth some thought. Do I write to a parent who has become too busy, too hurried, too stressed out? God says He will reward you even in your sleep! Though you may feel too involved to back off and rest, you'd better! And on the other hand, if the Lord is not the very nucleus of your life, all the labor of a lifetime cannot serve as a substitute for Him. Long hours and painful labors, rising early and retiring late can never replace your allegiance to the Lord and His presence in your home. Money cannot replace Christ! Neither can things, or promises that circumstances will change "someday."

So let's get this straight, right at the foundation level of instruction on a happy home: *Christ must be first.* You must be a believer in the Lord Jesus Christ and you must marry one who is a believer if you wish to establish your home with full strength and stability . . . also if you hope to tap into the potential power for living victoriously.

CHILDREN BORN WITHIN THE HOME

> Behold, children are a gift of the Lord;
> The fruit of the womb is a reward.
> Like arrows in the hand of a warrior.
> So are the children of one's youth.
> How blessed is the man whose quiver is full of them;
> They shall not be ashamed,
> When they speak with their enemies in the gate. [127:3–5]

The songwriter grabs our attention with "Behold!" He says, in effect, "Pay attention . . . listen up!" These three verses take us a step further as they address the coming of children into the home, and the parents' proper attitude toward such.

Notice three titles the songwriter gives to children: (1) "gift," (2) "reward," and (3) "arrows." Each one calls for some analysis.

The term *gift* is a translation of the Hebrew word that means "property, possession . . . that which is shared/assigned." Children are the Lord's possessions and the property, which He graciously assigns to or shares with parents. Now this third verse doesn't say "some children" or even "most children," but simply "children," implying *all* children . . . *your* children! There is no such thing as an "accidental birth" or a "surprise pregnancy" from God's viewpoint. And wise are the parents who acknowledge the fact that their child is a personal gift from God. If you and I truly believe that each child is "assigned" by God, what a difference it can make with the child *we* may not have planned!

The word *reward* conveys the idea of pleasure—something given as a tangible proof of appreciation. Children are never to be viewed as punishment for God's displeasure—quite the contrary! The fruit of the womb is God's very personal trophy of His love, His choice reward.

The word *arrow* is equally meaningful. You'll notice that the word picture is that of a warrior with arrows in his hand. Imagine the scene. A warrior in battle doesn't stop to *make* his arrows, nor does he *ignore* them. He *uses* them. He *directs* them toward a target. A parent is responsible for the *direction* of his children. A child, like an arrow, is incapable of directing himself. It is the basic responsibility of parents to direct the early lives of their children. This makes a great deal of sense when you consider that a child is born in a state of depravity and inner sinfulness. You must stop here and read Psalm 51:5 along with Psalm 58:3. Both verses verify that children are born in a state of iniquity. Solomon's saying in Proverbs 22:15 underscores this fact: "Foolishness is bound up in the heart of a child; / The rod of discipline will remove it far from him." Children need parental authority.

What happens when a child isn't given direction? Let's allow Proverbs 29:15 to answer that question:

The rod and reproof give wisdom,
But a child who gets his own way brings shame to his mother.

A more literal translation of the verse would be, ". . . but a child left, brings shame to his mother." Left alone in his room to play? No. The thought is of a child left in the original condition in which he is born; a child who is not given direction will bring shame to his mother. Look at Proverbs 22:6 for a moment:

Train up a child in the way he should go,
Even when he is old he will not depart from it.

Without question, this is one of the most familiar verses in Proverbs, but how seldom it is correctly understood. The words *train up* come from the Hebrew term *kake*, meaning "palate, roof of the mouth, gums." The verbal form of this term was used to describe two different actions in two unrelated realms:

1. Newborn infants. The midwife in ancient times would take a newborn child into her arms, dip her finger in the juice of crushed dates, grapes, or olive oil and then reach inside the mouth of the infant and rub its palate or gums, causing the baby to suck as the flavor was tasted. In other words, she would *create a thirst* for the mother's milk. Then the infant would be placed on the mother's breast for nourishment.

2. Young horses. When a horse was wild, a rope was placed in its mouth as a bridle, and it was ridden until it became "broken" and submissive. In other words, the *self-will was broken* in the horse.

Both aptly describe what is involved in "training up" a child. It includes creating a thirst for the spiritual life. It also includes breaking the stubborn self-will and replacing it with a gentle, tender, submissive spirit.

Next, please observe that the parent is to do these things according to the child's way. The Amplified Bible helps capture the full meaning of the original Hebrew as it renders this portion of Proverbs 22:6 with the paraphrase: "in keeping with his individual gift or bent." In other words, the training administered by the parents is to be unique with each offspring. The parent, therefore, must know his child, must understand the "bent" of each one of his children and adapt his training for each according to that "bent." How does a parent come to know the bent of each child? According to Proverbs 20:11–12:

> It is by his deeds that a lad distinguishes himself
> If his conduct is pure and right.
> The hearing ear and the seeing eye,
> The Lord has made both of them.

Parents, we are responsible for listening to and looking at our children. Let's open our ears! Let's open our eyes! Think! Observe! We will never fulfill our part of Proverbs 22:6 correctly until we really come to *know each of our children.* God has given each child a unique makeup, a series of strengths and weaknesses. The wise parent learns the inward pattern of each child and fits his (or her) training to the need. How foolish to think that all kids are the same. They're not. Nor will they be directed correctly if the parent blindly and brutally disciplines without knowledge. We are to train each child according to "his way."

In case you think that all children in the same family have the same "bent," study Cain and Abel, Jacob and Esau, Absalom and Solomon, Isaac and Ishmael, and the children in *your own* family. According to Psalm 139:13–16, each child is uniquely planned and put together by God in the mother's womb. Wise are the parents who make a study of each one of the children born to them.

These are not new and novel thoughts on child-rearing. This process is explained in great detail in chapter 5 of my book *Growing Wise in Family Life.*[10]

Each child is to be viewed as a gift, a reward, and an arrow in our hands. Verse 5 of Psalm 127 says that we are to be happy when we have all the "arrows" God has designed for our quivers. And let me add a final thought: Not everyone has the same size quiver! The same Lord who gives fruit to the womb determines the size of each family quiver.

Perhaps you are fretting and chafing under the size of your quiver today. This is not what God desires. He wants you to be satisfied and happy, not frustrated and irritable. There is no joy like the joy that comes from God-given arrows in our divinely determined quivers.

TRAINING OF THE CHILDREN IN THE HOME

> How blessed is everyone who fears the Lord,
> Who walks in His ways.
> When you shall eat of the fruit of your hands,
> You will be happy and it will be well with you.
> Your wife shall be like a fruitful vine,
> Within your house,
> Your children like olive plants
> Around your table. [Ps. 128:1–3]

In Psalm 127 the arrows are in our hands, needing direction. As the songwriter continues his thoughts regarding the family in Psalm 128, he says that "everyone who fears the Lord" will be blessed or happy. The context is *the family*, remember—specifically, the children God gives. As the progression continues in Psalm 128:1–2, we see how each arrow is to be carefully directed: (1) in the fear of the Lord, and (2) walking in His ways. Again, you will notice, happiness will continue to be the surrounding atmosphere ("how blessed").

Parents who train their children according to biblical principles have the hope of ultimate happiness. As a matter of fact, verse 2 says your investment will allow you to "eat of the fruit of your hands" and "it will be well with you." The picture is, again, the hands (as it was in 127:4). Parents' hands enjoy the product of their labor as they "pick the fruit" of the domestic garden they have cultivated. As submission is caught, obedience taught, and understanding sought, the dividends come rolling in!

Verse 3 is such a pleasant picture. The father looks around the supper table. He sees his dear wife ("a fruitful vine") and children ("olive plants"). I notice that the children are not called "branches" but plants. This seems to emphasize that each offspring is independent, unique, one who will reproduce his own kind in later years. And the difference is also seen in that the mother is pictured as *a vine*, but the children as *olive plants*. This is a good and necessary distinction.

We, as parents, are unwise to assume that our children are put together exactly like we are. The father, for example, who is athletic, has a strong tendency to want that same tendency to emerge in his son, even to the point of forcing it. The same is true of a mother who is artistic. She persistently urges that talent in her daughter, but frequently that isn't the daughter's interest. Why? To answer with the songwriter's symbols: we are *vines*, but our children are *olive plants*. However, regardless of a child's talent (or lack of it), athletic ability (or lack of it), the training we give him or her must be that of *spiritual instruction* ("fear of the Lord"). A child *must be directed toward faith in the Lord Jesus Christ* and given an enormous amount of training in the principles of Scripture.

On occasion I have heard well-meaning young couples say that they are going to "let the children choose for themselves" when it comes to their spiritual lives. For fear of "warping their children" and "making fanatics out of them," some parents take a hands-off policy—an unfortunate mistake. As soon as the child's independent self-will emerges, he or she (dominated by a sinful nature) chooses to ignore the Lord, the local church, the instruction of the Scriptures, and the godly life. Remember, Solomon's warning? He declared that "Foolishness is bound up in the heart of a child" (Prov. 22:15). And also, as we saw earlier, David tells us that depravity—that inward undertow of evil—is part of the makeup of every child. My point is that a young child *cannot* "make up his own mind" correctly. His inner nature counteracts and overpowers godliness. Now I certainly do not believe in fanaticism. That is not our goal; but a balanced, victorious, growing spiritual life *is*. Without direction, a child will seldom (if ever) choose the path of obedience on his own.

If you think the grind of family life is a tough challenge, try to imagine the attitudes and atmosphere in your home if each child were told to just make up his (or her) own mind. The grind would become so severe, no one could endure the pressure!

LATER YEARS IN THE HOME

Behold, for thus shall the man be blessed
Who fears the Lord.

The Lord bless you from Zion,
And may you see the prosperity of Jerusalem all the days of your
  life.
Indeed, may you see your children's children.
Peace be upon Israel! [Ps. 128:4–6]

The domestic scene now reaches completion. The children are trained, raised, and launched from the nest. The psalmist paints a pleasant picture of serenity. In doing so, he mentions three realms of blessing:

1. Personal pleasure (v. 4). The psalmist says "for thus" happiness comes. For what? For all the hard work and consistent training invested by parents, happiness comes as God's reward. Believe me, if you determine to have Christ as the central figure of your home and His Word as the authority in rearing your children, you have your work cut out for you!

You will find that you'll be outnumbered, scoffed, considered strange by your neighbors (and a few teachers), criticized, misunderstood, and tempted to compromise. The very forces of hell will unleash their fury on you! You will be on your knees and in the Word regularly. But, if you maintain the standard (with love, gentleness, and consistency), God promises that you will look back in your twilight years and enjoy inward, personal pleasure. The converse is also true. If you relinquish your responsibilities as a parent, you can expect sad and serious consequences.

2. Civic benefits (v. 5). Even Zion will be blessed! Jerusalem will be prosperous and strong! The point is this: Your offspring will be used to make a dent in society—for good! All the days of your later life, you'll enjoy the fact that your earlier direction and private contribution to the home life of your children pay off in rich, public dividends.

3. National blessings (v. 6). Now, in this final verse, grandchildren arrive on the scene. You, the grandparent, see them,

and you witness a second-generation investment. Your own children pass on similar training so that the entire nation benefits and is blessed because the Lord, originally, was at the very center of your home.

CONCLUSION

Psalms 127 and 128 will not soon be forgotten, will they? They have encouraged us to establish the right foundation for our homes: the Lord Jesus Christ. They have instructed us to look upon the family as a God-given responsibility. We have been admonished to direct our offspring God's way, according to *His* prescribed plan. Finally, we have been promised personal, civic, and national blessings as a result of our efforts. If we apply these truths as God has spoken, the grind of family life will be greatly reduced. You can count on it!

I recently came across an anonymous piece that portrays the family as a garden. It suggests various things we can plant in our family relationships that will result in great benefits:

A family is like many things, perhaps most like a garden. It needs time, attention, and cultivation. The sunshine of laughter and affirmation. It also needs the rains of difficulties, tense moments, serious discussions about issues that matter. And there must be spade work, where hardness is broken loose and planting of fresh seeds is accomplished with lots of TLC. Here are some suggestions for fifteen rows worth planting:

Plant four rows of peas:

Preparedness
Perseverance
Promptness
Politeness

Then three rows of squash:

Squash gossip
Squash criticism
Squash indifference

Along with five rows of lettuce:	Let us be faithful
	Let us be unselfish
	Let us be loyal
	Let us love one another
	Let us be truthful
And three rows of turnips:	Turn up with a smile
	Turn up with a new idea
	Turn up with determination

And then? Well, from then on it's pretty simple. Water, weed, tend with care, and patiently watch the garden grow. Someday you'll look back and realize it was worth all the years of all the work and effort and prayer. Like a lovely garden, your family will be a thing of grateful pride, of seasonal beauty, of daily sustenance.

R EFLECTIONS ON FAMILY LIFE

1. Biblical instruction on the family is always insightful. That shouldn't surprise us, since God holds the patent on marriage and the establishment of a home. In light of that, return to Genesis in your Bible and read again the passages of primary reference on this subject. Take your time! Read Genesis 1:26–31 and 2:18–25. What stands out as *most* significant?

2. Think back to your original home—the place you were raised, the family unit from which you came. Ponder some positive scenes that are still vivid in your memory . . . a time when you (a) felt secure, (b) were affirmed, (c) learned a valuable—maybe painful—lesson, and (4) your whole family pulled together during a crisis. Do you still have a parent, a brother, or sister living? Give one a call (or write) and "relive" one of those scenes. Express your love. Explain what led you to contact him (or her).

3. Perhaps the most encouraging thought from our study of these two songs is that we are rearing our nation's future (128:5–6). Take some one-on-one time this week with each of your children and talk about the importance of this in tomorrow's world. Get specific. Include a few hugs of affirmation. Don't be afraid to include those great words . . . not just "Love ya!" but "I love you!" Finally, work hard to cultivate all those fifteen rows of very special plants. Someday, you'll be glad you did.

Psalm

A Song of Ascents

O Lord, my heart is not proud,
    nor my eyes haughty;
    Nor do I involve myself in
    great matters,
Or in things too difficult for me.
Surely I have composed and quieted my
   soul;
Like a weaned child rests against his
   mother,
My soul is like a weaned child within me.
O Israel, hope in the Lord
From this time forth and
   forever.   [131:1–3]

THE GRIND OF
IMPATIENT
ARROGANCE

Psalm 131 is one of the shortest chapters in the Bible—only three verses in length. If it is ever true, however, that good things come in small packages, this psalm is proof of that. Charles Haddon Spurgeon, that prince of preachers, said of Psalm 131:

> Comparing all the psalms to gems, we should liken this to a pearl; how beautifully it will adorn the neck of patience. . . . ![11]

He aptly describes this little psalm. It would be missed by the hurried reader and considered of almost insignificant value to one impressed with size and choice of terms, but it nevertheless contains a timely message.

David composes lyrics that address a hazardous and dangerous habit in this song: *impatient arrogance.* He is saying that he is not proud or haughty or interested in being seen, heard, or noticed. In fact, he is announcing his plan to move out of the limelight and away from that place of public attention.

Genuine humility isn't something we can announce very easily. To claim this virtue is, as a rule, to forfeit it. Humility is the fairest and rarest flower that blooms. Put it on display and instantly it wilts and loses its fragrance! Humility is one character trait that should be a "closet utterance," as W. Graham Scroggie puts it,[12] not something we announce from the housetop.

Perhaps you have already heard the humorous account of the

fellow who attempted to write about his own humility and had trouble choosing a title for his book. *Humility and How I Attained It* seemed inappropriate, as did *How I Became Very Humble.* He finally decided on *Me and My Humility*—and he inserted twelve full-page pictures of himself!

No, humility is not something to be announced. It simply belongs in one's life, in the private journal of one's walk with God, not in a book that looks like a testimony but comes across more like a "bragimony."

David, however, isn't bragging in Psalm 131. In fact, I don't think David had any idea that his meditations would ever be published and preserved down through the centuries for the world to read. He writes his song exclusively to the Lord (v. 1) and briefly states his convictions concerning his removal from the public eye.

We know nothing of what prompted the writing of this song. As we have already observed, the occasion leading to the writing of many of the ancient biblical songs remains a mystery. We can enter into the occasion in our imagination, however. Often we feel humbled and crushed after we have sinned and/or made a series of mistakes—after we have "blown it." At those times we are genuinely interested in finding the nearest cave and crawling in. At other times when we get a glimpse of our own pride and become sick of our deceptive attempts to cover it up, we fall before God and ask to be removed and made obscure. And then there are those occasions of heart-searching experiences: Times of sickness. Days of deep hurt. Painful waiting. Disappointing events. Loss of a loved one. Removal of a friend. Loneliness. Pressure. At those crossroads, the traffic of people seems overbearing, the flashing of lights seems so vain, and the noisy crowd, so repulsive. During such times one longs for obscurity and silence, humble communion with his Creator. Any of these occasions could have prodded the sweet singer of Israel to write this song of humility:

> O Lord, my heart is not proud, nor my eyes haughty;
> Nor do I involve myself in great matters,
> Or in things too difficult for me.

Surely I have composed and quieted my soul;
Like a weaned child rests against his mother,
My soul is like a weaned child within me.
O Israel, hope in the Lord
From this time forth and forever. [131:1–3]

In a matter-of-fact fashion, David addresses the Lord. Throughout the psalm he carries on a conversation with his God. Eight times in the first two verses he uses "I," "me," and "my." This, as we have said, is a page from his own journal.

Verse 1

O Lord, my heart is not proud, or my eyes haughty;
Nor do I involve myself in great matters,
Or in things too difficult for me.

You may remember that in the Hebrew Bible whatever appears *first* in a clause or sentence is frequently placed in that position for the purpose of *emphasis*. This is especially true when the phrase is rearranged and written in an awkward, strange manner. This is precisely what we find in verse 1.

There are three negatives set forth at the very beginning of three clauses: "Not proud" . . . "Not haughty" . . . "Nor do I involve myself." David is communicating the depth of his feelings. The structure of his words reveals strong passion. The terms do, too.

The term *proud* comes from *gah-bah*, meaning "to be high, exalted." He mentions his *heart* first—the root source of pride down deep within. He says that as deeply as God may wish to probe, He will not find a trace of a "high, exalted" attitude within him. God may "search" and "know my heart" (Ps. 139:23) all He wishes, declares David.

The term *haughty* comes from another word having a similar meaning—*room*. This Hebrew term means "to be lifted up, raised." The idea is that one who is proud within shows it in his *eyes*, which are "lifted up, raised." That is exactly what Proverbs 30:11–13 says:

> There is a kind of man who curses his father,
> And does not bless his mother.
> There is a kind who is pure in his own eyes,
> Yet is not washed from his filthiness.
> There is a kind—oh how lofty are his eyes!
> And his eyelids are raised in arrogance.

The "proud look" has to do with eyes that are "lifted up." We have all seen this among the pseudo-sophisticates and on the plastic masks worn by many of the Hollywood stars and television celebrities. David declares that both his heart and his eyes will stand the test of God's scrutiny.

There are two simple and quick ways God says the true condition of the heart is revealed. (Many of us may *think* we can hide it, but we cannot.) The first is through the eyes (as we have seen here) and the second is through the mouth (as Jesus says in Luke 6:45). Of course, one's life is another proof of one's heart condition, but that takes longer to observe. Keen counselors and wise people are careful to listen to words (what is said as well as what *isn't* said) and watch the eyes of others. You soon discover that the heart is like a well and the eyes and tongue are like buckets which draw water from the same well. If true humility is not in the heart, the eyes will show it.

David goes on to say that he does not involve himself in great matters nor difficult things. The idea here is that he doesn't pursue places of prominence or greatness. The simple fact is he doesn't *need* such a place in his life any longer. He is not only willing but pleased to be removed from the public platform of fickle applause.

This reminds me of another great man of God—Moses. According to Acts 7:22, he was educated in the finest schools Egypt had to offer. He was gifted with a powerful personality. He was a most impressive man. He was a mighty warrior—brave, brilliant, and even heroic. It was clear to many that he was destined to be the Pharaoh of the land. At age forty he killed an Egyptian and attempted to deliver his people (the Jews) by his own, powerful arm. Exodus 2:11–15 tells the whole story. This resulted in his fleeing Egypt and winding up in the Midian Desert . . . a hot, dry, forgotten place of obscurity, where he lived for another forty years—unknown and unapplauded. Think of it! Moses—a prominent member of the royal family—spending his days on the parched sands of a desert, suddenly and totally removed from people: shelved, sidelined, and silent. F. B. Meyer writes of this experience:

> But Moses was out of touch with God (in Egypt). So he fled, and crossed the desert that lay between him and the eastern frontier; threaded the mountain passes of the Sinaitic peninsula, through which in after years he was to lead his people; and at last sat wearily down by a well in the land of Midian. . . . and finally to the quiet life of a shepherd in the calm open spaces of that wonderful land, which, on more than one occasion, has served for a Divine school.
>
> Such experiences come to us all. We rush forward, thinking to carry all before us; we strike a few blows in vain; we are staggered with disappointment, and reel back; we are afraid at the first breath of human disapprobation; we flee from the scenes of our discomfiture to hide ourselves in chagrin. Then we are hidden in the secret of God's presence from the pride of man. And there our vision clears: the silt drops from the current of our life, as from the Rhone in its passage through the deep waters of Geneva's lake; our self-life dies down; our spirit drinks of the river of God, which is full of water; our faith begins to grasp his arm, and to be the channel for the manifestation of his power; and thus at last we emerge to be his hand to lead an Exodus.[13]

David, like Moses, chose to slip away and not involve himself in matters of greatness and public glamour. His, for a time at least, was to be a life of solitude and meditation.

Verse 2

How did David respond to this parenthesis of quietness, this back-row seat in the balcony? Was that capable and passionate man of war irritated and out of sorts because he had been reduced from captain of the team to spectator? Not in the least. Listen to verse 2 of Psalm 131:

> Surely I have composed and quieted my soul;
> Like a weaned child rests against his mother,
> My soul is like a weaned child within me.

There is not the slightest irritation in his words. The term *composed* means "to be smooth, even, level." The same Hebrew word used here also appears in Isaiah 28:25 with reference to a farmer's field that had once been rough and rugged but was now planted and "level." David is saying that his inner soul is not churning and stormy, but is calm and smooth. It is a beautiful description of tranquility and patience. The result is that he is "quieted" within; he is inwardly silent and still. He is like the words of the hymn by Jean Pigott that Hudson Taylor loved to sing while reaching the lost in inland China:

> Jesus, I am resting, resting
> In the joy of what Thou art;
> I am finding out the greatness
> Of Thy loving heart. . . .

Or perhaps more like the beloved Scandinavian hymn by Katharina von Schlegel:

> Be still, my soul! the Lord is on thy side;
> Bear patiently the cross of grief or pain;
> Leave to thy God to order and provide;
> In every change He faithful will remain.
> Be still, my soul! thy best, thy heavenly Friend
> Thro' thorny ways leads to a joyful end.

After the statement declaring his inner calm condition, David gives a tender illustration of a baby quietly resting on its mother—and twice he uses the word *weaned* to describe the child. The little tot is no longer striving and fretting with his mother for her milk . . . no longer demanding nor restless. All is calm. The roughness of self-will has been smoothed and is now calm and contented.

But wait! This isn't complete unless you see how the symbolic analogy fits into David's experience. Let's do that by answering three questions:

1. Who is the child? It is David's inward being.

2. Who is the mother? It is his public life . . . the familiar applause of people.

3. From what is it weaned? Clearly, it means he is weaned from the desire for prominence, the place of honor—the lime-light. "I no longer need that," says David. "I'm weaned!"

Verse 3

> O Israel, hope in the Lord
> From this time forth and forever.

As is true of all of us on special occasions, David had learned a truth that was so exciting he *had* to share it. He wanted his entire nation to enter into this joyous experience with him.

Please allow me a personal comment here. David's little song has been so comforting to me. I have loved its quiet peacefulness. I have needed its message. Perhaps you have, too. It is quite possible that God is "weaning" you away from every source of pride. You may have trusted in the fleeting silver and tinsel of this world, only to have it tarnish and melt in your hands. You may have believed in someone only to have him (or her) fail you and even turn against you. You, quite possibly, have fallen into the trap of self-exaltation and recently failed miserably. Maybe you've been accustomed to honor and public notice, but (like Moses) all that has passed, at least for a while. Perhaps your talent is no longer in de-mand . . . or your job is not now needed . . . or your coun-sel is no longer sought. "What's happening?" you may be asking. Arrogance refuses to accept such blows, but patience overrules and stills our souls at such times. But "Why?" you may wonder. God is answering your question in Psalm 131. You are being "weaned" from the mother of importance, pres-tige, public applause, honor . . . and (dare I say it?) *pride.*

Who does the weaning? The child? No, never. The act of weaning is done *to* the child, not *by* it. *God is responsible.* He is removing every crutch upon which you would lean . . . every crutch but Himself . . . so you will lean hard upon *Him* only, as Proverbs 3:5–6 says so beautifully. He is changing your diet to a new kind of food—from the milk of immaturity to the meat of genuine humility. And He wants you to learn this "from this time forth and forever."

R EFLECTIONS ON IMPATIENT ARROGANCE

1. Give your own definitions:

   Arrogance: _____

   _____

   Impatience: _____

   _____

   Quiet composure: _____

   _____

   Humility: _____

   _____

2. Take time to analyze how you are put together. Do you *have* to be in the center of attention in order to feel fulfilled? Why? Why not? Would others think of you as self-assured and confident . . . or arrogant? Why? Why not? One more: If you were suddenly sidelined by a serious accident or illness which removed you from the fast lane of activity, could you handle that without a great deal of adjustment? Why? Why not?

3. Can you think of someone you admire for his or her genuine humility? Isn't it remarkable how Christlike such a trait is? Go to the trouble of making a creative thank-you card that illustrates and expresses your gratitude . . . and see that the card gets into his (or her) hands *anonymously*. State in a few words (maybe your own poem?) your appreciation, but leave it unsigned.

By the rivers of Babylon,
There we sat down and wept,
When we remembered Zion.
Upon the willows in the midst
    of it
We hung our harps.
For there our captors demanded of us
    songs,
And our tormentors mirth, saying,
"Sing us one of the songs of Zion."

How can we sing the Lord's song
In a foreign land?
If I forget you, O Jerusalem,
May my right hand forget her skill.
May my tongue cleave to the roof of my
    mouth,
If I do not remember you,
If I do not exalt Jerusalem
Above my chief joy.

Remember, O Lord, against the sons of
    Edom
The day of Jerusalem,
Who said, "Raze it, raze it,
To its very foundation."
O daughter of Babylon, you devastated
    one,
How blessed will be the one who repays
    you
With the recompense with which you
    have repaid us.
How blessed will be the one who seizes
    and dashes your little ones
Against the rock. [137:1–9]

THE GRIND OF LINGERING CONSEQUENCES

No one can deny the relentless pain brought on by enduring the consequences of wrong actions. It may be as quick and simple as the sting following a swat from a parent's paddle or as lingering and severe as a prison sentence. Either one, however, is hard to bear. "The way of transgressors is hard" (Prov. 13:15, KJV).

The person who cheats on a mate and later leaves the marriage must ultimately endure the consequences. The child who runs away from home in a fit of rebellious rage must live with the painful ramifications. The politician who assures his voters of unrealistic and unachievable promises if elected must face his critics after election. The minister who compromises in the realm of ethics or morals must live with the private shame and loss of public respect. The list goes on and on.

Even though our day is characterized by an erosion of personal responsibility and attempts to soft-pedal or cover up the consequences of wrong, those very difficult days in the backwash of disobedience are nevertheless haunting realities. Sin still bears bitter fruit. Devastating consequences still await the transgressor. "Be not deceived . . . whatsoever a man soweth, that shall he also reap" (Gal. 6:7, KJV) is still in the Book. Few souls live more somber lives in the minor key than those who have disobeyed and must now endure the grind of lingering consequences.

And speaking of a somber, minor key, Psalm 137 comes to mind. Here is a mournful song! The composer is enduring the pain of past actions that led to his being among a group of captives. As a band of Jewish POWs, they have been taken by the Babylonians into a foreign land. Immediately, the scene is set:

> By the rivers of Babylon,
> There we sat down and wept,
> When we remembered Zion.

You can skim through the next eight verses and quickly detect other terms that reveal a prisonlike experience:

Verse 3: *our captors . . . our tormentors*
Verse 4: *a foreign land*
Verse 7: *Remember, O Lord, against the sons of Edom*
Verse 8: *O daughter of Babylon, you devastated one*

Why was a Hebrew writer in Babylon? What were the events that led to his and others' becoming captives of this foreign power? Believe me, it was no accident. It came to pass exactly as God had spoken through His prophet Jeremiah:

> Therefore thus says the Lord of hosts, "Because you have not obeyed My words, behold, I will send and take all the families of the north," declares the Lord, "and I will send to Nebuchadnezzar king of Babylon, My servant, and will bring them against this land, and against its inhabitants, and against all these nations round about; and I will utterly destroy them, and make them a horror, and a hissing, and an everlasting desolation. Moreover, I will take from them the voice of joy and the voice of gladness, the voice of the bridegroom and the voice of the bride, the sound of the millstones and the light of the lamp. And this whole land shall be a desolation and a horror, and these nations shall serve the king of Babylon seventy years." [Jer. 25:8–11]

Those prophetic warnings were spoken to the people of Judah. They had persisted in their disobedience for over three hundred years since the last days of Solomon's reign. The united kingdom of the Jewish nation had split after Solomon's death. A civil war followed. Ten of the twelve tribes of Israel settled in the north under King Jeroboam's leadership. Two settled in the south under King Rehoboam, Solomon's son. The civil war destroyed the Jewish unity and resulted in both groups ultimately falling captive to two foreign Gentile powers.

The northern kingdom is called "Israel" in Scripture and the southern kingdom is called "Judah." Israel had nineteen kings during her two-hundred-plus years before she fell to the Assyrians in 722 B.C. Judah had twenty kings (eight of them were righteous) until the Babylonians (also called Chaldeans) captured them and held them in bondage for seventy years, exactly as Jeremiah predicted. Psalm 137 was written during (or shortly after) Judah's captivity in Babylon.

Now that we have read the song and surveyed its historical background, let's draw an outline from it:

I. Memory of Captivity (vv. 1–3)
   —a personal section—
II. Devotion to the Lord (vv. 4–6)
   —a patriotic section—
III. Plea for Retribution (vv. 7–9)
   —a passionate section—

Few songs in Scripture begin with stronger emotions. The composer is absolutely dejected, feeling awful! He remembers the bitter humiliation, the stinging sarcasm he and his companions had to undergo. He even reminds us of a particular occasion when a representative of Babylon marched those Jews along a river and poked some cynical "fun" at them.

> By the rivers of Babylon,
> There we sat down and wept,
> When we remembered Zion.
> Upon the willows in the midst of it
> We hung our harps.
> For there our captors demanded of us songs,
> And our tormentors mirth, saying,
> "Sing us one of the songs of Zion." [vv. 1–3]

Can't you imagine that scene? With their heads hanging low, their shoulders slumped and tears streaming down their cheeks, those Jewish captives sat silent and gritted their teeth. Talk about a daily grind! This was the pit of pits. I can just hear the taunts of the Babylonian guard as he looked out over those downcast, depressed people of Judah.

"Hey, how about all you Jews joining in on one of those good ol' hymns of the faith! Let's hear it for dear ol' Jehovah! Sing it out, now . . . and as you sing, remember Zion!"

Oh, how that hurt! It hurt so deeply the writer remembered the precise words of his tormentor. This sad scene from Psalm 137 illustrates Galatians 6:7 better than any other Old Testament Scripture. I mentioned it earlier but it bears repeating:

Do not be deceived, God is not mocked; for whatever a man sows, this he will also reap.

The scoffers and critics of Christianity never stand any taller or shout any louder than when God's people publicly fall into sin and are forced to suffer the inevitable consequence. All Satan's hosts dance with glee when believers compromise, play with fire, then get burned. We've seen a lot of that sort of thing in recent years, haven't we? The secular media have a field day as God's people are forced to take it on the chin.

Those captives were getting just what they deserved, and they knew it. There was no more singing, no jokes, and no laughter in that embarrassed Jewish camp on foreign soil. One man describes the scene quite vividly:

This is the bitterest of all—to know that suffering need not have been; that it has resulted from indiscretion and inconsistency; that is the harvest of one's own sowing; that the vulture which feeds on the vitals is a nestling of one's own rearing. Ah me! this is pain! There is an inevitable nemesis in life. The laws of the heart and home, of the soul and human life, cannot be violated with impunity. Sin may be forgiven; the fire of penalty may be changed into the fire of trial; the love of God may seem nearer and dearer than ever and yet there is the awful pressure of pain; the trembling heart; the failing of eyes and pining of soul; the harp on the willows; the refusal to sing the Lord's song. [14]

Do you find yourself on "foreign soil" today? Are you reaping the bitter fruits of carnal sowing? Is your song gone? Are the consequences of your sins pressing upon you? Let me urge you to lay your heart bare before your Lord. Tell Him about it. Be certain that the cause of your dreadful experience is thoroughly confessed . . . and that you are not hiding or denying anything. Once you have claimed your Lord's forgiveness, let me urge you to claim His presence and quietly wait for relief. The consequences of sins—yes, even *forgiven* sins—are often difficult and sometimes lingering. The best way to ride out the storm is *on the rock* (Ps. 40:1–3). A humble and contrite heart is essential before you can expect any relief.

After relating the bitterness of that experience, the writer does a little self-analysis. His emphasis changes from without to within. He asks a very real question in verse 4 of Psalm 137: "How can we sing the Lord's song / In a foreign land?"

That is so true, so *very* true! Genuine singing is spontaneous; it cannot be forced. Nor will it joyfully burst forth from a broken heart or a guilty conscience. It comes as a direct result of the filling of the Holy Spirit, as Paul states in Ephesians 5:18–19:

> And do not get drunk with wine, for that is dissipation, but be filled with the Spirit, speaking to one another in psalms and hymns and spiritual songs, singing and making melody with your heart to the Lord.

In the same stroke of the pen that declares the importance of being Spirit-filled, the apostle Paul also mentions the singing heart.

Did it ever occur to you that just as certain animals cannot reproduce in captivity, neither can the believer? We are totally unable to have Christ's power, victory, and joy reproduced in us while we are still being held captive in the "foreign land" of carnality. Paul and Silas were chained in the Philippian jail, but the Christian melodies and songs rang out nonetheless. Physically and outwardly they were captives, but spiritually and inwardly they were free and full of joy (Acts 16:25–26).

And now in the next three verses of Song 137, with the zeal of a Jewish right-wing patriot, the psalmist states his devotion to his Lord and to the city of his homeland:

> How can we sing the Lord's song
> In a foreign land?
> If I forget you, O Jerusalem,
> May my right hand forget her skill.
> May my tongue cleave to the roof of my mouth,
> If I do not remember you,
> If I do not exalt Jerusalem
> Above my chief joy. [vv. 4–6]

Notice that the subject now changes from "we" and "our" to "I" and "my." He says that he will never, ever forget the blessings and benefits of being a citizen of Judah. He says that his song would be forever silenced—he would not skillfully play ("my right hand") nor spontaneously sing ("my tongue")—should he forget the marvelous benefits of home.

I believe the sixth verse could trouble some readers. He mentions exalting Jerusalem "above my chief joy." His "chief joy," of course, is that which gave him greatest joy. Why would he exalt a city above his greatest joy? We love our America, but certainly not necessarily more than any earthly joy. It would be strange to exalt America above our highest joy.

The answer is to be found in what the city of Jerusalem *represented* to the writer of this song. It was the place that contained the temple, the place of God's presence, and the center of worship. To be separated from Jerusalem was tantamount to being separated from God and the things of God. You see, in the Old Testament the things of God were spiritually connected to a *place*, Jerusalem. However, in the New Testament the things of God became spiritually connected to a *Person*, the Lord Jesus Christ. That is still true today. We worship a Person—not a building or a location.

The composer is saying that above and beyond his highest joy on earth is Jerusalem and all it represents.

Finally:

> Remember, O Lord, against the sons of Edom
> The day of Jerusalem,
> Who said, "Raze it, raze it,
> To its very foundation."
> O daughter of Babylon, you devastated one,
> How blessed will be the one who repays you
> With the recompense with which you have repaid us.
> How blessed will be the one who seizes and dashes your little ones
> Against the rock. [vv. 7–9]

It doesn't take a Bible scholar to discover that these are exceedingly emotional words. The writer feels passionate regarding the enemies of his beloved Zion. He mentions the ancient enemy of Edom in verse 7, then Babylon in verse 8. While brimming with zeal, he pronounces blessings upon those God may use to avenge the enemies for their brutal and unmerciful treatment of the Jews. The critic reads this (especially verse 9) and attacks the Old Testament for its outrageous God of wrath. If you and I were of that vintage, it is doubtful that the lyrics of Psalm 137 would seem barbaric.

You probably recall the Adolph Eichman trial of the past. One of our national periodicals covered the account in vivid detail. The journalist mentioned a Jewish man who had lost his parents and other close relatives in the horrible Nazi concentration camps. He stood abruptly to his feet in the audience of that courtroom and cursed Eichman. He was told to sit down and restrain himself, which he refused to do. As he was escorted by force from the room, he screamed words to this effect: "Let me get my hands on that Nazi pig . . . just for sixty seconds . . . let me have him that I may torture him with my own hands!" No one criticized that man who screamed those violent words. In fact, the magazine reporter expressed sympathy. Why? Because the man had suffered such a terrible loss, his memory was full and running over with rage. He longed for retribution.

Note that the psalmist doesn't ask that *he* himself might bring vengeance . . . only that God might see that in the end vengeance be poured out in the same way it had been brought upon Judah. If you will pause and read Isaiah 13:14–16, you will see that the Babylonians brutally murdered the little Jewish children before their parents' eyes. With passionate pleas, the writer of this song concludes with a request for similar retribution. He rests his case with God.

Did God respond? Did the Lord ever deal with Babylon and make it "an everlasting desolation" as He promised in Jeremiah 25:12? Yes, indeed! The Persians moved in upon the Babylonians and literally wiped Babylon off the face of the earth, so that it remains a desolation to this day.

Most any world atlas that bothers to mention Babylon will do so with an entry that reads something like: "Babylon, ruins of. . . ." Babylon is still a desolate, barren land of silence along the Bagdad railway, little more than a wind-whipped whistle stop for archaeologists en route to a dig in the rugged wasteland.

Psalm 137 is certainly relevant. It speaks to the believer who suffers the consequence of his sin . . . who tries in vain to "sing the Lord's song in a foreign land." It turns our hearts to Him alone, who can satisfy our deepest needs. It gives us a pattern to follow when we have been severely treated . . . and it reminds us that our God is fully able to bring vengeance upon those who revile and persecute and say all manner of evil against us falsely. As Romans 12:19–21 reminds us, God can and will handle our every desire for retribution, and He can do it in such a thorough way, we need only to step aside and let Him work.

If you are enduring the grind of lingering consequences following a time of disobedience in your life, you understand this song. As you read it, remember that you are not alone in your agonizing heartache. The pain may be severe and lingering, but the good news is this: It is *not* endless.

REFLECTIONS ON LINGERING CONSEQUENCES

1. Think of a few consequences from your past that you were forced to endure. Pause right now and thank the Lord for His grace. Instead of removing you from the earth, He sustained you. He, to this day, allows you to live. Call to mind the magnificence of His wondrous grace. Sing a few bars of "Amazing Grace" and listen again to the lyrics of that grand old hymn.

2. Let's make Psalm 137 a relevant, prophetic warning, not just a matter of historical record. The next time you are tempted to yield and let your carnal nature be satisfied, read the first five verses of this song. It would be a good idea to type those verses on a three-by-five card and clip it to the visor on your car or slide it beneath the glass on your desk. Underline the fourth verse in red.

3. Throughout the balance of this week, pray for any Christian you can think of who has fallen . . . a husband or wife, a politician, a minister, a career person, a physician, a nurse, an attorney, an author, a counselor, a musician, an artist, a camp director, a secretary—anyone! Ask God to bring each one back to Himself. Pray for wisdom and for discernment to know how to respond. Think of possible ways *you* might be able to help set the "captive" free.

Psalm

For the choir director.
A Psalm of David.

O Lord, Thou hast searched me
and known me.
Thou dost know when I sit
down and when I rise up;
Thou dost understand my thought from
afar.
Thou dost scrutinize my path and my
lying down,
And art intimately acquainted with all
my ways.
Even before there is a word on my
tongue,
Behold, O Lord, Thou dost know it all.
Thou hast enclosed me behind and
before,
And laid Thy hand upon me.
Such knowledge is too wonderful for me;
It is too high, I cannot attain to it.

Where can I go from Thy spirit?
Or where can I flee from Thy presence?
If I ascend to heaven, Thou art there;
If I make my bed in Sheol, behold, Thou
art there.
If I take the wings of the dawn,
If I dwell in the remotest part of the sea,
Even there Thy hand will lead me,
And Thy right hand will lay hold of me.
If I say, "Surely the darkness will
overwhelm me,
And the light around me will be night,"
Even the darkness is not dark to Thee,
And the night is as bright as the day.
Darkness and light are alike to
Thee.   [139:1–12]

THE GRIND OF
INSIGNIFICANCE

Most folks struggle with feelings of insignificance from time to time. Larger-than-life athletes, greatly gifted film and television stars, brilliant students, accomplished singers, skillful writers, even capable ministers can leave us feeling intimidated, over-looked, and underqualified. For some, feeling insignificant is not simply a periodic battle; it is a daily grind! We know deep down inside we're valuable; but when we compare ourselves, we often come out on the short end. A well-kept secret is that many of those athletes, celebrities, authors, and preachers who seem so confident struggle with the very same feelings that plague their admirers.

Because of our rapid population explosion, we are becoming numbers and statistical units rather than meaningful individu-als. Machines are slowly taking the place of workers. Computers can do much more, much faster, and with greater accuracy than even skilled specialists. Science doesn't help the problem. Our universe is viewed by scientists as being vast, so vast that this Earth is insignificant—a speck of matter surrounded by galaxies measured by light years rather than miles. The immensity of it all overwhelms an earthling at times and forces us to ask the age-old questions: Who am I? Why am I here? Where do I fit? What does it matter? This can result in an inner tailspin—one that increases rather than lessens, as we get older and the aware-ness of our surroundings expands. Perhaps you are among the many who are passing through what is called an "identity crisis."

If you are wrestling with this very real and puzzling perplexity, here is a song that is tailor-made for you. It is one of David's best! His lyrics describe the person who is standing alone and searching for answers regarding himself, his world, and his God. It provides the reader with a calm certainty that there is a definite link between himself and his Lord—that no one has been flung haphazardly or accidentally into time and space. This ancient song makes God seem real, personal, and involved because, in fact, *He is*. The crucial problems of international affairs and "global saturation" suddenly appear not half as crucial and the difficulties connected with one's identity crisis begin to fade as this wonderful song is understood.

Psalm 139 answers four questions. As we read through all twenty-four verses, we find that it falls neatly into four sections . . . six verses each. Each section deals with a different question. An outline might look something like this:

  I. How well does God know me? (vv. 1–6)
 II. How close is God to me? (vv. 7–12)
III. How carefully has God made me? (vv. 13–18)
IV. How much does God protect/help me? (vv. 19–24)

All twenty-four verses link us, God's creation, with our Creator. We are super-important to our Maker. We are not unimportant specks in space or insignificant nobodies on Earth, but rather the objects of His care and close, personal attention. If you take your time and think about each section, you'll find that the four questions deal with four of our most human and basic problems:

How well does God know me?
  (*The problem of identity*)

How close is God to me?
  (*The problem of loneliness*)

How carefully has God made me?
  (*The problem of self-image*)

How much will God protect/help me?
(*The problem of fear/worry*)

One final thought before we embark on an analysis of the first twelve verses (we'll examine the final twelve next week): All the way through these verses we read of "the Lord," "His Spirit," "God" . . . and "me," "I," "my." To the psalmist, God is there; better than that, *God is here.* He is reachable, knowable, available, and real. All alienation is removed. All strained formalities and religious protocol are erased. Not only is He *here,* but He is *involved* and *interested* in each individual on this speck-of-a-planet called Earth.

Let's start with the first question.

HOW WELL DOES GOD KNOW ME?

In the first *four* verses of David's song, we are given sufficient information to discover that *God is omniscient* . . . He knows everything. Read the following lyrics slowly and aloud:

> O Lord, Thou hast searched me and known me.
> Thou does know when I sit down and when I rise up;
> Thou dost understand my thought from afar.
> Thou dost scrutinize my path and my lying down,
> And art intimately acquainted with all my ways.
> Even before there is a word on my tongue,
> Behold, O Lord, Thou does know it all. [vv. 1–4]

The songwriter says that God *searches* him. The Hebrew term that led to this translation originally meant "to explore" and sometimes conveyed the idea of digging into or digging through something. To put it in popular terms, "O Lord—you *dig* me!" The thought is that God explores, digs into, and examines me through and through. In the next sentence David pictures himself in two phases of life—passive (sitting down) and active (rising up). Our most common and casual moments are completely familiar to our Lord. Furthermore, even our *thoughts* are an open book. Thoughts come into our minds through a series of distant, fleeting conceptions as microscopic nerves relate to one another in the brain through a complicated process of connections. Even *those* are known by our Lord. That is what David means by God's understanding "my thought from afar." Plutarch, the first-century Greek biographer, had this in mind when he wrote:

> Man may not see thee do an impious deed;
> But God thy very inmost thoughts can read.

We can see thoughts enter people's heads as their faces "light up" or, in some other way telegraph the entrance of ideas. We can hear thoughts as they leave people's minds through their mouths. But we cannot see what happens *between* the entrance and the exit. God can. In fact, God understands what prompts us to think certain thoughts. He therefore understands the hidden, unspoken motives behind our actions.

One Christmas we bought our small children an "Ant City." It was a plastic ant bed filled with a narrow sheet of sand, built out of transparent material that allowed you to watch the inner workings of the insects. Normally, all you can see in an ant bed in the ground are these busy little creatures crawling in and out of their hole. But this interesting "Ant City" allowed us to watch what happened after the ants went into their holes—we could watch these small insects as they journeyed through their tunnels. That is exactly what verse 2 is saying about our thought-life before God. He monitors the entire process.

I appreciate the *New American Standard Bible's* rendering of the third verse: "Thou dost scrutinize my path. . . ." The verb *scrutinize* is a translation of the Hebrew word which means "to sift." It is the idea of submitting oneself to minute scrutiny. God carefully sifts away at our choices and decisions. As a result of this phenomenal insight, He is thoroughly acquainted with us—and I mean thoroughly! To put the finishing touches on the facts of God's omniscience, He knows our words even *before* we utter them, which causes David to write: "Thou does know it all. . . ." God knows every word of every language in every human being on every continent at every moment of every day. Think of it!

Matthew 10:30 adds the capstone: ". . . the very hairs of your head are all numbered." It is not that God concerns Himself with mental and verbal trivia; it is simply that He is omniscient, that He is fully and accurately aware of everything at all times, the visible as well as the invisible, the public as well as the private.

One articulate theologian explains God's omniscience like this:

> To say that God is omniscient is to say that He possesses perfect knowledge and therefore has no need to learn. But it is more: it is to say that God has never learned and cannot learn. . . . God perfectly knows Himself and, being the source and author of all things, it follows that He knows all that can be known. And this He knows instantly and with a fullness of perfection that includes every possible item of knowledge concerning everything that exists or could have existed anywhere in the universe at any time in the past or that may exist in the centuries or ages yet unborn. . . . Because God knows all things perfectly, He knows no thing better than any other thing, but all things equally well . . . He is never surprised, never amazed, He never wonders about anything nor . . . does He seek information . . . our heavenly Father knows us completely. No talebearer can inform on us, no enemy can make an accusation stick; no forgotten skeleton can come tumbling out of some hidden closet to abash us and expose our past; no unsuspected weakness in our characters can come to light to turn God away from us, since He knew us utterly before we knew Him and called us to Himself in the full knowledge of everything that was against us.[15]

How well does God know you? These first four verses enable you to realize that He could not possibly know you better! Just in case the grind of insignificance is still doing a number on you, ponder the fact that you are the object of the living God's attention every moment of every day of your life!

Now consider the next two verses of Psalm 139:

Thou hast enclosed me behind and before,
And laid Thy hand upon me.
Such knowledge is too wonderful for me;
It is too high, I cannot attain to it. [vv. 5-6]

David now mentions *God's omnipotence;* He is in full control, He is all-powerful. Knowing us as He does, He puts the necessary controls upon us. The fact that He "encloses" us could be misunderstood. This is the translation of a Hebrew term used for the besieging of a city in battle—closing off all escape routes. One Hebrew scholar says it means "to be hemmed in." The idea is that God has us in inescapable situations and there steadies us, directs us, restrains us, keeps us from running and escaping from that situation. This explains why His hand is upon us.

Perhaps the apostle Paul was in such a predicament when he said he and his companions were "burdened excessively, beyond our strength" (2 Cor. 1:8). The King James Version renders those words: "we were pressed out of measure, above strength." The Greek term means "to be weighed down." It's the idea of intense *pressure:* "we were under tremendous pressure." In pressurized situations today God shuts off all escape routes, but He stays near and steadies us with His hand so that you and I might learn valuable lessons instead of running from the pressure. Annie Johnson Flint describes scenes familiar to all of us—times of inescapable pressure:

Pressed out of measure and pressed to all length;
Pressed so intensely it seems beyond strength.
Pressed in the body and pressed in the soul;
Pressed in the mind till the dark surges roll;
Pressure by foes, and pressure by friends;
Pressure on pressure, till life nearly ends.
Pressed into loving the staff and the rod;
Pressed into knowing no helper but God.
Pressed into liberty where nothing clings;
Pressed into faith for impossible things.
Pressed into living a life in the Lord;
Pressed into living a Christ-life outpoured.[16]

After contemplating all these truths, David exclaims, in effect, "It blows my mind!" (v. 6). So wonderful were these proofs of God's knowledge and control, he could not begin to contain his emotions. His *problem of identity* has begun to fade as the songwriter realizes God views His creatures as important and significant. He knows us. He scrutinizes our lives. He studies us and steadies us twenty-four hours a day. Although it blows our minds to comprehend it, it is true. How well does God know me? TOTALLY!

A related question follows on the heels of that first one.

HOW CLOSE IS GOD TO ME?

All right, so God knows me and controls me; so what? He can do that at a distance, through millions and millions of light years of space. What I want to know is this: *Is He near?* Perhaps that is your reaction to the first few verses of Psalm 139. What you'd like to know has to do with closeness. Is He really up close and in touch? Yes, God is near. He is no distant, preoccupied Deity. In fact, *He is omnipresent.* In verse 7, David states this in the form of two questions: "Where can I go from Thy Spirit? / Or where can I flee from Thy presence?"

The rebellious prophet Jonah must have wondered: "Can I find any place that will remove me from God?" He found out the hard way that the answer is an emphatic "No!" David puts it in terms anyone can understand.

> If I ascend to heaven, Thou art there;
> If I make my bed in Sheol, behold, Thou art there.
> If I take the wings of the dawn,
> If I dwell in the remotest part of the sea,
> Even there Thy hand will lead me,
> And Thy right hand will lay hold of me. [Ps. 139:8–10]

In the Hebrew Bible, the pronouns referring to God are abrupt and emphatic: "If I go up to heaven—THOU! If I go down to the grave—THOU!"

The next verse carries us out into the vast ocean on "the wings of the dawn." It's a beautiful expression, but what does it mean? Most likely it describes the rays of the morning sun that flash across the sky. Perhaps we could paraphrase it more technically by saying: "If I could travel the speed of light. . . ." Just think of that! By traveling at such speed, I would get to the moon in less than two seconds—Thou! (God would meet me.) It would take about four years to reach the first star at that speed, and again—Thou! (God would be there as well.) Omnipresence simply means there is no place He is *not*.

And the huge body of water we call an ocean may make me seem insignificant and remote—but still He is there. He never leaves me lonely—"even there Thy hand will lead me."

The first time I grasped the magnitude of these verses I was in the Marine Corps on a troop ship crossing the Pacific Ocean, bound for the Orient. It took seventeen days. The ocean swells on stormy days were forty to fifty feet high; and when our ship was down in the bowels of the swell, the crest loomed above like a giant domed building about to fall on us. As we would rise up to the peak, we could see nothing but water all around— deep, blue-black swells, never-ending across the horizon, 360 degrees around. I remember opening my Bible early one morning to Psalm 139:7–10 and, honestly, I almost shouted. Talk about an object lesson—I *was* one! I suddenly felt at ease in His presence. My loneliness seemed utterly foolish. His hand was leading me, His right hand was holding me right there in the "remotest part of the sea." Though I was literally insignificant by comparison, a calm, secure feeling swept over me.

That is the point David is communicating here. God is never absent.

And now in verses 11 and 12, he announces that not even darkness affects God's pervading presence:

> If I say, "Surely the darkness will overwhelm me,
> And the light around me will be night,"
> Even the darkness is not dark to Thee,
> And the night is as bright as the day.
> Darkness and light are alike to Thee.

There were times in my childhood when I would occasionally feel fearful at night. (You may recall having similar feelings.) At those times I would grab the covers and snatch them over my head. I can still remember tucking myself far down beneath them, thinking that I would be kept from harm. How childish . . . and yet, how much like adults!

Somehow, we may think, *If I do this in the darkness, it will go unnoticed.* This ancient song reminds us that it won't! Even the darkness is not dark to the Lord. According to Hebrews 4:13, there is not a creature hidden from Him. We need never feel lonely. He sees it all . . . and best of all, He cares.

That's enough for this week. We'll conclude this song next week. It has been rich to glean encouragement from the composer's thoughts, hasn't it? God cares for you and me. How very much He cares! He does so because we are important to Him. The grind of feeling insignificant is diminished as the truth of David's song emerges.

R EFLECTIONS ON INSIGNIFICANCE

1. Tonight, step outside. If the air is clear and the sky cloudless, look up. Why not go ahead, lie down flat on your back, and stare at those incredible stars? Stay long enough to allow your mind to grasp the immensity of the galaxy above you. It is easy to forget that what you are observing may seem vast, but it is only one galaxy among many! Remind yourself that you are more significant to your God than any one *or all* of those planets and stars in the stellar spaces. After all, they are ultimately going to pass away, but you are eternal. Give Him your grateful thanks.

2. In the early part of Psalm 139, David mentioned God's knowing your actions, your location, your words, your thoughts, and your entire situation. He then exploded with one of his "It's too much, Lord!" exclamations. What seems "too much" to you? Which part of the song makes you shake your head in amazement? Have you told Him . . . or anyone else? Do so.

3. Many people I know are still a little fearful of the dark. Look back at verses 11–12. It's possible you, too, feel uneasy after nightfall. Commit both of these verses to memory. Start saying them to yourself whenever you step into the darkness. See if just the reminder of His presence in the darkness doesn't help relieve some of your fears.

Psalm

For the choir director.
A Psalm of David.

For Thou didst form my inward
    parts;
    Thou didst weave me in my
    mother's womb.
I will give thanks to Thee, for I am
    fearfully and wonderfully made;
Wonderful are Thy works,
And my soul knows it very well.
My frame was not hidden from Thee,
When I was made in secret,
And skillfully wrought in the depths of
    the earth.
Thine eyes have seen my unformed
    substance;
And in Thy book they were all written,
The days that were ordained for me,
When as yet there was not one of them.

How precious also are Thy thoughts to
    me, O God!
How vast is the sum of them!

If I should count them, they would
outnumber the sand.
When I awake, I am still with Thee.

O that Thou wouldst slay the wicked, O
God;
Depart from me, therefore, men of
bloodshed.
For they speak against Thee wickedly,
And Thine enemies take Thy name in
vain.
Do I not hate those who hate Thee, O
Lord?
And do I not loathe those who rise up
against Thee?
I hate them with the utmost hatred;
They have become my enemies.

Search me, O God, and know my heart;
Try me and know my anxious thoughts;
And see if there be any hurtful way in
me,
And lead me in the everlasting
way.   [139:13–24]

THE GRIND OF INSECURITY

Let's begin this week with a few words of review. Psalm 139 links us with God. It, like few other scriptures, connects us with our Creator. You'll recall it answers four of the most frequently asked questions that come to our minds about God:

How well does God know me? (vv. 1– 6)
How close is God to me? (vv. 7–12)
How carefully has God made me? (vv. 13–18)
How much will God protect/help me? (vv. 19–24)

Haven't you asked yourself such things before? Sure you have! Everyone has. Built into all of us is a curiosity that longs to be satisfied, especially regarding the One who created this world.

Last week we looked at the first twelve verses of this great song. From the first six verses we discovered that God *knows* us thoroughly and completely. We found that He knows our private, quiet moments just as well as He knows our public and active times. We learned that He not only knows our thoughts and our words, but He even knows them before they are lodged in our brains or expressed from our mouths . . . God knows everything about everyone, every moment of every day—God is *omniscient*. Furthermore, we learned that God is in full control. Nothing occurs outside the realm of His sovereign will—God is *omnipotent*.

In the next six verses we found that He who knows us is always *near* us. No place we may travel, regardless of the speed of our vehicle, causes us to be lost from His sight or distant from Him. Not even darkness separates us from Him. How amazing! Darkness is just like light to God. Nothing could begin to separate Him from us or, for that matter, make Him nearer to us. Both are impossible. God is *omnipresent*.

HOW CAREFULLY HAS GOD MADE ME?

"Okay," you reply. "The song makes beautiful poetry and declares great theology, but how can I be sure it is all true?" A subtle uncertainty grinds away in most of us. One of the best proofs that God is and does all these things is *the design of your body*. Consider how carefully He has made you. Verses 13–16 address this. In my opinion this section of biblical truth is one of the most remarkable revelations in all of Scripture. Remember, it was written by David in a day when anatomy and embryology were relatively unknown subjects—at best, primitive. Yet here in this ancient song the prenatal stages of development are set forth with phenomenal simplicity and insight. The point David declares is this: Only a God who knows us and is near us could be so intimately involved in making us.

Verse 12 tells us of darkness and the inability of humanity to hide from God. Previous verses speak of hidden or remote places as being well-known and under the perpetual surveillance of God. Verse 13 goes even further. It transports us into *the womb*, a place of intimacy and darkness. It is here that the songwriter builds his case.

Verse 13

> For Thou didst form my inward parts;
> Thou didst weave me in my mother's womb.

The *Thou* is highly emphatic. The idea is "You, Yourself, and no other. . . ." It is neither "nature" nor "Mother Nature" who forms the miracle in the womb; it is God alone . . . and no other. Linger over the term *form*. When this verb appears in the original Hebrew, it often carries the idea of "originate." God originates our inward parts. It may surprise you to know that those two words—*inward parts*—literally mean "kidneys." In ancient times the kidneys were symbolic of all our vital organs—kidney, heart, lung, liver, etc. In fact, the verse goes on to say that God did "weave me together" in the womb. The verb *sah-nack* suggests the idea of knitting together like an interwoven mass or thicket. God is involved in placing all the organs and various parts of our body together into such a well-knitted fashion, it forms a veritable "thicket" of muscle, tendons, bone, blood, veins, and arteries.

Let me paraphrase verse 13 in order to bring out some of the color in the original text:

> For God alone—none other—originated my vital organs (such as my kidneys). You knitted my inner being together in the womb of my mother.

Verse 14

Verse 14 causes the writer to burst forth in praise. Observe his spontaneous words of grateful amazement:

> I will give thanks to Thee, for I am fearfully and wonderfully
> made;
> Wonderful are Thy works,
> And my soul knows it very well.

Isn't this true? We are a species of wonder. No one would argue that the human body is a phenomenal combination of strength, beauty, coordination, grace, and balance on the outside. But if you think the outside is remarkable, just glance *inside*. Talk about something wonderful!

Verse 15

Verse 15 describes our origin:

> My frame was not hidden from Thee,
> When I was made in secret,
> And skillfully wrought in the depths of the earth.

We sometimes refer to our bodily shape as our "frame." The original Hebrew term here means "bony substance" or "skeleton." Our skeletons were not hidden from God when they were made "in secret . . . in the depths of the earth." This is an idiomatic expression for a protected place, a concealed and safe place—as one may hide his treasure by burying it. No doubt this "secret place" is a reference to the womb. The Hebrew word translated *skillfully wrought* literally means "variegated" . . . like a multicolored piece of cloth. Moses used the same Hebrew term in Exodus when he referred to the making of the curtains in the ancient tabernacle. The idea is similar to an embroidered piece of tapestry or a work of fine needlepoint. The picture must include the concept of our veins and arteries, "embroidered" like variegated threads within the body. God is *that* involved in the making of our bodies. He is like a careful, skillful artist who takes great pain with each color and stroke.

Again, a paraphrase:

> My skeleton and bones were not hidden from You when I was made in that concealed place of protection, when my veins and arteries were skillfully embroidered together in variegated colors like fine needlepoint.

The truth of all this was brought home to me several years ago in a conversation I had with a young man doing his medical internship. He was studying to be a surgeon. He commented on the beautiful "color scheme" God has placed within our inner bodies. He stated that there are definite colors in our various organs . . . that the veins and arteries almost make the inner network appear "variegated" in color. He smiled when I informed him that that is exactly what David wrote in his song centuries ago.

Verse 16

This verse adds the capstone:

> Thine eyes have seen my unformed substance;
> And in Thy book they were all written,
> The days that were ordained for me,
> When as yet there was not one of them.

God's eyes were fixed upon my "unformed substance," says David. The Hebrew verb from which this descriptive statement is taken means "to fold together, to wrap up." In its noun form it appears only here in the Old Testament, and it means "embryo." In other words, David is saying: "In my very first hours and days of life after conception—when I was still wrapped up in embryonic form—God was watching over me. He was never absent nor unconcerned." Frankly, it is impossible to read these verses and deny that an unborn fetus is a living human being. From the very earliest moments after conception, God is at work in the mother's womb. Talk about a case against abortion!

The verse goes on to address life *after* birth. Not only does God concern Himself with us between conception and birth, but He also sets His attention upon us between birth and death. Look closely at this sixteenth verse. Looking at life from God's vantage point, David says that our heavenly Father marks out our days and "ordains" them even before we are born ". . . When as yet there was not one of them." The original term translated *ordain* is often used in the Old Testament in connection with a potter who forms clay on his wheel, shaping and pressing and pulling at it until it takes the shape he has in mind. God forms our days so that they are exactly the kind of days we should have to become the kind of person He wants us to be. There is little room left for insecurity once we understand His constant interest in our lives.

Verses 17–18

David is again on the crest of ecstasy as he exclaims:

> How precious also are Thy thoughts to me, O God!
> How vast is the sum of them!
> If I should count them, they would outnumber the sand.
> When I awake, I am still with Thee.

In today's terms this great songwriter might say: "How valuable! How mighty and vast! Your thoughts and your plans for me are magnificent, O God! You carefully and meticulously form me in the womb, you arrange and appoint my days so that each twenty-four-hour period does its part in shaping me into Your kind of person . . . and (grace heaped upon grace!) when death invades, I awake in Your presence—still with Thee."

Let me put these inspired lyrics together so that the paraphrase includes much of what we have discovered:

> For You, God, and none other, originated my vital organs (such as my kidneys). You knitted me together in the womb of my mother. . . . My skeleton and bones were not hidden from You when I was made in that concealed place of protection, when my veins and arteries were skillfully embroidered together in variegated colors like fine needlepoint. Your eyes watched over me when I was just an embryo; and in Your book the days I should experience were all described and recorded—the kind of days that would shape me into the person You want me to be—even before I had been born. How priceless and mighty and vast and numerous are Your thoughts of me, O God! Should I attempt to count them, they would outnumber the sand on the seashore. And Your plan isn't limited just to *this* life. Should I die, I would awaken securely in Your arms—I would be with You more than ever before.

HOW MUCH WILL GOD PROTECT/HELP ME?

The grind of insecurity begins to slow down when we grasp how perfectly God designed each one of us, and especially when we cap it off with how much He helps us.

Verses 19–22

The songwriter doesn't mince his words in these verses:

> O that Thou wouldst slay the wicked, O God;
> Depart from me, therefore, men of bloodshed.
> For they speak against Thee wickedly,
> And Thine enemies take Thy name in vain.
> Do I not hate those who hate Thee, O Lord?
> And do I not loathe those who rise up against Thee?
> I hate them with the utmost hatred;
> They have become my enemies. [Ps. 139:19–22]

The subject on his heart is clearly expressed:

The wicked (v. 19a)
Men of bloodshed (v. 19b)
Thine enemies (v. 20)
Those who hate/rise up against Thee (v. 21)
My enemies (v. 22)

On six separate occasions David refers to the enemies of God in the strongest of terms. These were not moderate, passive foes of the Lord; they were unashamed, hateful, open, and blatant despisers of God and God's people. To associate with them would pollute the testimony of any saint—and David declares his independence of them, especially when he says, ". . . They have become my enemies" (v. 22b).

Exactly what does David ask of God? One specific thing is requested: "Slay the wicked!" (v. 19a). To him, the God of heaven is marvelous, pure, holy, just, and good. His desire was to be the same—just as we are told to be in Ephesians 5:1, which says: "Therefore be imitators of God, as beloved children."

David wanted to imitate God. He longed to be a godly man—perhaps more than any other king in the history of Israel, which may explain why he was called "a man after God's own heart." He wanted to be removed from every enemy of God, lest he become swayed and stained by their wickedness. This shouldn't be taken as a bloodthirsty, brutal plea . . . nor a self-righteous, super-spiritual prayer. He was supremely interested in being God's man, regardless. In his zeal for righteousness, he asked God's help in protecting him from those who stood against the things he held dear. To David, a man of war, the only solution for God was to "slay the wicked!" He did not hesitate to request that of Him.

Before I move on, let me ask you: With whom do you spend most of your time? How close are you to those who defy and deny the name of your Savior? How deep a friendship have you nurtured with people who are out-and-out enemies of righteousness? Could the answers to those questions explain your battle with insecurity?

Charles Spurgeon once wrote: "Godless men are not the stuff out of which true friends can ever be made."[17] True words! While I am not encouraging our isolating ourselves from all lost people, I *am* saying that a close companionship with haters of God will take a damaging toll on our spiritual life. The virus of the degenerate heart is dangerously contagious, and you cannot spend much time near those who have it without eventually suffering from the same disease. This is as true for the teenager who wants "popularity at any cost" as it is for the businessman who prostitutes his convictions for an extra buck. Spiritual compromise is a deadly problem! We have already looked at 1 Corinthians 15:33 on more than one occasion since we began our year-long scriptural safari, but it's worth repeating here: "Do not be deceived: 'Bad company corrupts good morals.'"

Verse 20

In Psalm 139:20, David lists two characteristics that identify God's enemies:

1. They speak against God (they are irreverent).
2. They take His name in vain (they use profanity).

Isn't it interesting that wicked people reveal their wickedness through their tongue? Irreverence and profanity are the trade-

marks of deep heart problems. Mark it down: a foul, irreverer
tongue is the byproduct of a foul, irreverent heart.

Because David trusted God to protect him by slaying his enemies, he did not try to take matters into his own hands . . .
nor did he attempt to clean up the lives of God's enemies. Both
would be futile efforts. He left the final decision with his
Lord—a very wise and biblical action to take, by the way.

Verse 23–24

Before David closes hymn 139, he makes a final request of
God in verses 23–24. The words are familiar to many Christians.

> Search me, O God, and know my heart;
> Try me and know my anxious thoughts;
> And see if there be any hurtful way in me,
> And lead me in the everlasting way.

David no longer looks *up* (as in verses 1–18) nor *around* (as in
verses 19–22); he now looks *within*. He wants to be God's man
at any cost, so he invites the Lord to make a thorough examination of him down deep inside. The word *search* was used earlier
in verse 1. The basic idea of the original Hebrew verb, you may
remember, means "to explore, dig, probe." David wants God to
penetrate his outer shell and dig down deeply within him. He
unveils his inner being, down where unspoken thoughts dwell
and unstated motives hide out in secret, and he invites God's
searchlight.

Now David goes even further. He asks the Lord to put him
to the test so as to discover any distracting thoughts. In other
words, he is saying, "Find out which thoughts carry me away
from fellowship with You, O God. Show them to me so that
I can understand them and their effect on my walk with You."
That was his desire. Insecurity has passed off the scene as he
stands open before his Lord.

The desired result of this probing is set forth in the last verse,
where David asks God to see if there is any way of pain or grief
in him. It is not that *God* might know the results, but that he

himself—David—might know what God discovered. When you submit yourself to the scalpel of the surgeon for an exploratory operation, you do it *not* just for the sake of the physician. *You* want to know the findings yourself, don't you? You are interested in what is discovered. David finally states that it is his desire to be led "in the everlasting way" . . . meaning the path of righteousness. I repeat, he wanted to be a man of God, regardless.

Do *you* want to be a person whose walk with God is intimate and deep? Honestly now, is Christianity simply a ticket to heaven for you, or is it the very root and foundation of your life? Is this business of Bible reading/study, prayer, church attendance, baptism, witnessing, the Lord's Table, and the singing of hymns just something to calm your guilt and/or occupy your Sundays? On the other hand, if Christ has gotten a solid grasp of your will and you've become genuinely serious about spiritual things, then you will take the truth of these verses and allow it to take root in your life. Becoming a godly person takes time, but along the way it includes occasions when you expose your entire inner being to God's searching and you welcome any insight He might give you, regardless of the difficulty involved in facing it. By and by, the daily grind of insecurity will fade and you will be saying to the Lord: "I gladly open all the closets of my life . . . every room and every corner. Scrutinize my thoughts and examine my motives, Lord. Show me what needs attention. Reveal to me what brings pain to You in my life."

R EFLECTIONS ON INSECURITY

1. What a rich, revealing song David composed! As you look back over that center section of Psalm 139 (verses 13–18), what helps you the most?

   - The thought that He was watching over you from the time of conception?

   - The way He wove your organs and muscles and personality together?

   - The fact that He determined your appearance and structure and height before birth?

   Why? What caused you to choose the one you did?

2. Think about the implications of the verses we just considered. Why are they so damaging to those who say there is no problem with having an abortion . . . "after all there isn't really a life until birth" we are told. Use verses 13–16 to refute that position.

3. The final "benediction" of the song (verses 23–24) is quite a vulnerable prayer. Have you prayed it this week? If not, do so now. Utter the words aloud. As God "searches" and "tries" you . . . pay attention. If He reveals a "hurtful way" to you, be ready to deal with it.

Psalm

Maskil of David, when he was in the cave.
A Prayer.

I cry aloud with my voice to the Lord;
   I make supplication with my voice to
     the Lord.
   I pour out my complaint before Him;
I declare my trouble before Him.
When my spirit was overwhelmed within
   me,
Thou didst know my path.
In the way where I walk
They have hidden a trap for me.
Look to the right and see;
For there is no one who regards me;
There is no escape for me;
No one cares for my soul.

I cried out to Thee, O Lord;
I said, "Thou art my refuge,
My portion in the land of the living.
Give heed to my cry,
For I am brought very low;
Deliver me from my persecutors,
For they are too strong for me.
Bring my soul out of prison,
So that I may give thanks to Thy name;
The righteous will surround me.
For Thou wilt deal bountifully with
   me." [142:1–7]

THE GRIND OF DEPRESSION

Who hasn't struggled with those demoralizing seasons of dark depression? Some get so low and stay there so long they decide that taking their lives is better than enduring it any longer. Others seem to go in and out . . . down, then back up again. Depression has been described as a black hole, an abysmal cave. It certainly includes discouraging feelings that refuse to go away. I know some who have fought the battle of depression for years! In Book I we addressed the grind of despondency. Depression is much deeper, more complicated, and usually lasts longer. Despondency leaves us feeling listless, blue, and discouraged, but depression is a feeling of severe oppresiveness that is far more serious. If it doesn't lift, professional help is often necessary, though not always. Mysteriously, there are occasions when hope returns rather suddenly and the light begins to shine again. Few joys are greater than that one!

My hope is that this song from David's pen will help bring some long-awaited light into your cave of depression. Before we begin to dig into the first verse of his great hymn, we come across some helpful information in the superscription: *"Maskil of David, when he was in the cave. A Prayer."*

THE OPENING STATEMENT

There are four important parts to this opening statement:
1. <u>"Maskil."</u> Thirteen of the songs in the Hebrews' hymnal

are so designated. As we learned in the previous volume, this is from the Hebrew root verb *sah-kaal,* meaning "to be prudent, wise, to give insight and instruction." It is an *instructive* psalm. It is designed to give us help and insight in a certain area of life. It will assist us so that we may know how to handle a particular situation wisely.

Since Psalm 142 deals with a time of depression in the writer's life, it is a *maskil* designed to give us insight into handling times of great, overwhelming distress.

2. "... of David." This assures us that David was the composer of the hymn. Although David did not write *all* the psalms, he wrote more in Israel's ancient hymnal than any other person.

3. "... when he was in the cave." The phrase regarding "the cave" appears in only one other superscription—Psalm 57. Unfortunately, David does not designate *which* cave. Two possibilities come to mind—either the cave of Engedi (1 Sam. 24) or Adullam (1 Sam. 22). It was probably the latter—for reasons I'll not take the time to develop here.

To appreciate that which gave birth to this song of depression, listen to the first two verses of 1 Samuel 22:

> So David departed from there and escaped to the cave of Adullam; and when his brothers and all his father's household heard of it, they went down there to him. And everyone who was in distress, and everyone who was in debt, and everyone who was discontented, gathered to him; and he became captain over them. Now there were about four hundred men with him.

Talk about adding insult to injury! Here's our friend David, running for his life from madman Saul, finally finding relief and solitude in a dark cave. His relief is short-lived, however, as his solitude is invaded by a solid stream of "everyone who was in distress, and everyone who was in debt, and everyone who was discontented . . . about four hundred men." Just imagine! Four hundred failures. Four hundred malcontents. Four hundred *plus one*—David.

The four hundred were an unorganized, inefficient, depressed mob without a leader, so David was "elected" to be in charge. Picture the scene in your mind. With a little imagination you could see how depressed he must have been. Surely he sighed as he thought, *What now?* or *Why me?* Well, whatever else he did, he also wrote a song—Psalm 142. In the depth of distress and at the end of his rope he talked with his Lord about his desperate situation. So much for the cave.

4. A Prayer. Spurgeon says: "Caves make good closets for prayer."[18] True words. This psalm is actually a prayer, so we should handle it with respect. Prayers were not recorded in Scripture for the purpose of analysis, but to bring insight and encouragement. This psalm is a good one to consider when you find yourself in the same state of mind as David. To put it bluntly, he was back in the pits.

In the first two verses we find David at the mouth of that gloomy cave. The depth of his anguish is clearly expressed. He comes face to face with his God in prayer. (Note: twice he calls "to the Lord" and twice he brings his complaint "before Him.")

> I cry aloud with my voice to the Lord;
> I make supplication with my voice to the Lord.
> I pour out my complaint before Him;
> I declare my trouble before Him.

Verse 1

What is translated in the first verse as "I cry aloud" literally means "I shriek." The original Hebrew term means "to sound as thunder, to bellow." From the interior of that cave, David thunders out his pitiful needs with heartrending groans. "I make supplication" could better be rendered "I implore favor." His self-image had been assaulted. He felt stripped, worthless, and useless—completely depressed. So he asks for evidence of God's favor. He needs to feel needed and necessary. He no longer had honor and respect; self-esteem was, it seemed, forever removed.

When we hit the bottom, we feel this way. Our self-image is shot! In order to be effective, we *must* view ourselves as God views us—favorable, loved, useful, and needed. I have found that my first step toward a solution is turning "to the Lord"—going "before Him" as David did. To stay at the bottom, lick my wounds, and roll in misery leads only to deeper despair. Call upon Him—*shriek* if you must—but don't sit for days in the silence of self-pity! God longs to hear your words. Your honest and forthright declaration is precisely what prayer is all about. It is a discipline that ignites incredible results.

I used to wonder why we ever needed to utter words in prayer since God already knows all our thoughts (Ps. 139:4). Then one day I stumbled across Hosea 14:1–2:

> Return, O Israel, to the Lord your God,
> For you have stumbled because of your iniquity.
> Take words with you and return to the Lord.
> Say to Him, "Take away all iniquity,
> And receive us graciously,
> That we may present the fruit of our lips."

Did you notice the prophet's command? His charge is to "take words with you. . . ." Saying our most troubling thoughts, expressing our deep-down feelings in words, is a definite therapy. This way we get those depressive feelings out into the open . . . we resurrect them from the prisonlike limbo of our inner being. David did exactly that. He "took words with him" as he came to terms with his depression.

Verse 2

In the second verse of Psalm 142 the man openly declares his problem to God: "I pour out my complaint before Him; / I declare my trouble before Him." Look at that term *trouble*. It comes from the Hebrew verb meaning "to be bound up, tied tightly, restricted, narrow, cramped"—or as we would say today, "I'm in a *tight fix*." When he says "I declare my trouble," the Hebrew word for *declare* literally means "to cause to be conspicuous." He wanted *nothing* hidden.

Putting all the preceding thoughts together, the first two verses could read:

> I shriek with my voice to the Lord;
> I implore favor with my voice to the Lord.
> I pour out, before Him, my complaint;
> My cramped, narrow way, before Him,
> I cause to be conspicuous.

Do you *really* level with God about how you feel and what you are experiencing? Do you get vividly specific? He wants to be your closest Friend, your dearest Counselor. He wants you to keep nothing from Him. Unfortunately, many who suffer lengthy battles with depression do not express what is plaguing them. Some find it almost impossible to articulate thoughts that are brimming with pain or hostility or grief. Most stay to themselves and say very little. David spoke openly of his anguish.

Verse 3

The third verse would speak more literally if we read it:

> When my spirit fainted away within me . . .
> (But You—You Yourself—know my pathway)
> In the way where I walk
> They have concealed a trap for me.

The verse begins with an unfinished sentence. David feels enveloped or wrapped up in his depression, so much so his inner spirit feels faint and feeble. Suddenly, he stops and admits that God knows everything, even his inner feelings. This seems to occur to David rather abruptly. (A parallel passage on this same subject is Job 23:10–17, which you should stop and read. It is magnificent!) David then adds that things on the *outside* of the cave are as depressing as on the *inside*. Traps were laid by Saul and his men. Spies were everywhere. He was a marked man.

Verse 4

Verse 4 rounds out the bleak picture:

> Look to the right and see;
> For there is no one who regards me;

There is no escape for me;
No one cares for my soul.

He invited the Lord to look to his right—the place for a protector and defender to stand—but no one was there. He was alone, humanly speaking. He could not escape. He felt that there was no one who cared for his soul. The poor man is so-o-o-o-o-o depressed!

Perhaps you feel down today, thinking that all hope is gone, that God has abandoned you, that the end has come. Yes, you may feel those things, but that doesn't mean your feelings are true. The Lord of heaven knows the pressure of your feelings. He understands the depths of your distress. Best of all, He is there. He cares. He understands: "The righteous will surround me, / For Thou wilt deal bountifully with me" (142:7).

What faith! David is looking ahead and claiming, by faith, a time of genuine victory. He is declaring that God will again use him and cause others to surround him and look to him for leadership. Why? Because God will deal bountifully with him . . . because God will use these distressing, difficult days to give him maturity and inner strength and stability. Inner healing will come, someday.

Let me repeat what I said earlier in Book I—God doesn't use us in the lives of other people because we *do* some things, but rather because we *are* something. People do not long to be around one who *does* a lot of things as much as they want to be around one who *is* what they admire. It is greatness of character and a life with depth that earns the respect of others. Those who have been honed and buffeted, bruised and melted in the furnace of affliction, and then emerge with emotional stability and inner strength—they are the ones who have a ministry in the lives of others. Their weakness is like a magnet . . . for when we are weak, He is strong.

So then, in summary, if you are in the cave of depression, try your best to look up. Call upon the Lord Jesus Christ. Hold nothing back. You can trust Him to handle whatever you toss in His direction. Tell Him exactly how your situation is affecting you. If you are able, spell out precisely what you need at this time. Rely on Him. Do not doubt and do not waver. Stand firm.

Remember, you are in His schoolroom. He is the Teacher. He is giving you a lengthy examination in the crucible of suffering . . . and no one can give a more complete exam than our Lord!

I commend this song to all who are undergoing the daily grind of depression today. It is food for your soul in the cave as the storm continues to roar.

Hang in there, my friend. He is preparing you for a unique message and an enviable ministry. Believe it or not, that dark cave of depression which seems endless is part of His divine plan. Who knows? The light you have been longing to see could return today.

REFLECTIONS ON DEPRESSION

1. Describe *your* cave today. Spend a few minutes thinking through the reason you find yourself submerged amidst such dark feelings and dismal outlook. Does it include:
   - something from your recent past?
   - something you feel angry about?
   - something between you and another person?
   - something you resent or thought had ended?
   - something you fear in the future?

   A time of personal analysis can yield a great deal of insight. Take the time to do just that.

2. Do not hesitate to follow David's model. "Cry aloud" with your voice to the Lord. "Pour out" your complaint . . . "declare" your trouble. You can even shriek! Trust me, He can handle *whatever* you serve across the net. He longs to hear you.

3. Have you sought the assistance, the friendship, the counsel of another? Why not start there? Furthermore, have you had a thorough physical exam within the past twelve or eighteen months? If not, do so. People who stay depressed over a long period of time usually become isolated, lonely sufferers. There is a better way. To stay all alone only deepens the cave and intensifies the sadness. Seek help. As I mentioned earlier, it may require some professional assistance. If so, don't hesitate. Caves can be awfully dark and demoralizing. Our minds tend to play tricks on us if we stay in them too long.

Psalm

Praise the Lord!
Sing to the Lord a new song,
And His praise in the
congregation of the godly
ones.
Let Israel be glad in his Maker;
Let the sons of Zion rejoice in their King.
Let them praise His name with dancing;
Let them sing praises to Him with timbrel
and lyre.
For the Lord takes pleasure in His people;
He will beautify the afflicted ones with
salvation.

Let the godly ones exult in glory;
Let them sing for joy on their beds.
Let the high praises of God be in their
mouth,
And a two-edged sword in their hand,
To execute vengeance on the nations,
And punishment on the peoples;
To bind their kings with chains,
And their nobles with fetters of iron;
To execute on them the judgment written;
This is an honor for all His godly ones.
Praise the Lord!   [149:1–9]

THE GRIND OF
PRAISE-LESS TIMES

There are times when the hardest words in the world to utter are *Praise the Lord* (also translated "Hallelujah!"). These words just don't flow from our lips. In fact, there are times we are turned off even when *others* use the words!

In the final five psalms, interestingly, each one begins with that statement of praise. Perhaps by focusing on one of the five, we will uncover some things that will help us live beyond the grind of praise-less times.

If you are a Christian and have spent much time in churches and Christian groups, you have heard "Hallelujah!" dozens, even hundreds, of times. But what does it actually mean? We hear it and we say it without realizing its significance. In the next few pages, I want to explore its meaning with you. These five concluding "Hallelujah Psalms" form the most beautiful scenery on the last leg of our journey through the ancient hymnal—a journey that has often included times of sadness, sin, gloom, loneliness, distress, and depression.

I recall returning to the United States after a lengthy tour of duty on Okinawa and other Oriental islands and countries. As our troop ship sailed under the beautiful Golden Gate Bridge, tears came to my eyes! All the loneliness, sadness, and distress of my previous months away from my homeland and wife and family faded from significance because of that final lap into the harbor of San Francisco. That is the way it is in our study of the songs in Scripture. The beauty and loveliness of the final scene tend to make us forget the many days the composers spent in heartache and sorrow.

Hallelujah is literally a Hebrew term, not English. It is a composite word, made up of two smaller terms—*hah-lale*, meaning "to boast," and *Yah-weh*, meaning "Jehovah." Putting them together, the exact meaning is "boast in Jehovah!" To *boast* is "to speak of or assert with excessive pride." Normally, it has to do with a display of pride in oneself. However, in the case of *Hallelujah!* it means a display of pride or an assertion of glory and honor in the Lord. So then, whenever we say "Hallelujah!" we are asserting "let's give glory and praise to the Lord . . . and none other!"

This explains why some versions of the Bible prefer to translate *Hallelujah!* "Praise the Lord!" That is what it means. Self is ignored. Magnifying the Lord is the single concern of these last five psalms. Whenever we say "Hallelujah!" let's realize what we are saying. During praise-less times, we are usually preoccupied with *ourselves*. We find it almost impossible to focus fully on *Yah-weh*.

Looking at Psalm 149 as a whole, I find three significant points of interest:

1. It is written to believers—godly ones, not carnal ones. In verses 1, 5, and 9, the *godly ones* are specifically mentioned.

2. It is written to *Jewish* believers. This becomes evident as you examine such terms as *Israel* (v. 2), *sons of Zion* (v. 2), *His people* (v. 4), and *the nations* (Gentiles, v. 7).

3. It falls into three sections. Each section has to do with certain times in which we are to praise our Lord: (a) verses 1–3, times of blessing; (b) verses 4–6, times of suffering; (c) verses 7–9, times of warfare.

IN TIMES OF BLESSING

> Praise the Lord!
> Sing to the Lord a new song,

And His praise in the congregation of the godly ones.
Let Israel be glad in his Maker;
Let the sons of Zion rejoice in their King.
Let them praise His name with dancing;
Let them sing praises to Him with timbrel and lyre. [vv. 1-3]

The songwriter gives us three commands as he discusses times of blessing. He tells us to sing (v. 1), to be glad (v. 2), and to praise His name (v. 3) when we are blessed by God. Let's look at each command and meditate upon what God is saying.

Sing

We are told to sing *a new song*. When God rewards us, He is pleased to hear us respond with fresh and spontaneous expressions of delight. We are to share this publicly "in the congregation of the godly ones." Often we openly share our times of stress and heartache—and we should—but seldom do we feel as free to share those occasions when His abundant blessings surround us.

Be Glad

Times of prosperity and/or promotion that God makes possible should never cause guilt. No reason for that. Be glad! Rejoice! Unfortunately, some in the Christian ranks have begun to believe that it is spiritual to suffer, but almost shameful to be made prosperous. However, let's never forget that our rejoicing should be directed toward Him who brought the blessings, and not ourselves or another. Psalm 75:6-7 makes that clear:

> For not from the east, nor from the west,
> Nor from the desert comes exaltation;
> But God is the Judge;
> He puts down one, and exalts another.

If it is you He has chosen to lift up and exalt, accept it humbly; rejoice in it without guilt! This brings us to the third command.

Praise

The third verse tells us, in effect, to really "let loose." Don't hold your praise to yourself; let it out! In the days of the psalmist, it was quite common for God's people literally to dance for joy and play on musical instruments when they were filled with praise. David danced in the street when the ark was brought back into the city of David (2 Sam. 6:12–15). Likewise, Miriam, Moses' sister, danced in praise of God after the Israelites crossed the Red Sea (Exod. 15:20–21). The dancing in Scripture was done out of praise in one's heart to God for His blessings and deliverance.

The whole point of these first three verses of Psalm 149 is that we are to enjoy our times of blessing in full measure. We are to give our Lord fresh, unrestrained exclamations of praise when He chooses to pour out His abundance upon us. Those are the times when it is easy to say, "Praise the Lord." However, we are also to *Praise Him in times of suffering.*

IN TIMES OF SUFFERING

> For [since] the Lord takes pleasure in His people;
> He will beautify the afflicted ones with salvation.
> Let the godly ones exult in glory;
> Let them sing for joy on their beds.
> Let the high praises of God be in their mouth.
> And a two-edged sword in their hand. [vv. 4–6]

I think it would help to begin verse 4 with "Since" rather than "For." This is permissible with the original language, and it helps to separate verse 4 from the preceding section, as I believe it should be.

God's Viewpoint (v. 4)

I notice two statements in verse 4 regarding the way God views those who are afflicted with suffering:

1. <u>He takes pleasure in them.</u> The Hebrew term is *rah-tzah*, meaning "to accept favorably, be pleased with, satisfied with." So often the one who is set aside feels completely unloved and useless—even rejected. He isn't contributing a thing because he can't. Not able to produce, he begins to feel as though he is nothing but a drag, a weary responsibility. That is why suffering is usually a praise-less grind! But this verse says quite the opposite! It says that God "accepts us favorably"—He is "pleased with us" even when we are laid aside and totally unproductive. That fact alone should encourage each one who is afflicted with pain and sidelined because of illness. You may be in a hospital room or alone at home. Take heart! God still accepts you and looks upon you with favor, even though you cannot produce anything at this present time.

2. <u>He beautifies them.</u> To be technical about it, the verse says that God "will beautify the afflicted ones with salvation" (deliverance). This is so true. When deliverance comes, when healing occurs, when the sunshine of hope splashes across the once-dismal room of the sufferer, beauty returns. The long facial lines of stress begin to fade, the light returns to the eyes, the whole countenance is lifted. God beautifies them!

In a broader, nontechnical sense, however, I want to suggest that God beautifies many who live long years *with* affliction. Some of the most beautiful people I have known are people whose lives have been scarred by disease, pain, and paralysis. Stationed upon their bed or limited to a chair, these "beautiful sufferers" have a radiance that shines like the quiet, faithful beam from a lighthouse across troubled waters. Often I go to minister to *them* . . . but I soon discover that the beauty of their lives ministers to *me!* Their attitude toward suffering prompts me to give praise to God.

Sufferer's Viewpoint (vv. 5–6)

The afflicted person is addressed in verses 5–6. Here God tells us how to handle times of suffering:

1. Exult (rejoice) in it
2. Sing about it (on the bed)

3. Praise God for it
4. Hold onto the two-edged sword through it

We have developed the first three already, but not the fourth. Hold fast to the sword! In other words, don't drop your defenses. Stay faithful to the Word of God—the sword of the Spirit (Eph. 6:17), the two-edged sword (Heb. 4:12).

Sickness and suffering have a tendency to weaken our faith if we fail to feed our thoughts with God's Word. Praise, like a fragrant blossom, wilts quickly. The sufferer is admonished to hold fast to the sword—good counsel. This is one of the reasons a visit with those who are ill should include sharing a portion of the living Book, the Bible. It helps the sufferer keep a firm grip on the two-edged sword. Finally, *we are to praise God in times of warfare.*

IN TIMES OF WARFARE

> To execute vengeance on the nations,
> And punishment on the peoples;
> To bind their kings with chains,
> And their nobles with fetters of iron;
> To execute on them the judgment written;
> This is an honor for all His godly ones.
> Praise the Lord! [vv. 7–9]

These final verses are the most difficult in the song to understand. As I stated earlier, it is important for us to interpret this psalm historically, with the believing Jew in mind. You see, the enemies of Israel were enemies of God, so Israel was trained to be a militant, aggressive force against wrong (they still are!) . . . to "execute vengeance on the nations and punishment on the peoples." This work of judgment was actually "written" (v. 9) in such passages as Deuteronomy 32:41–43; Joel 3; and Zechariah 14.

Practically, however, verses 7–9 exhort the Christian today to stand and fight against Satan and all his hosts of demons. Our warfare is not in the realm of the seen, but the unseen . . . not in the fleshly realm but the spiritual as we saw in our lengthy study of Psalm 91. This is precisely what 2 Corinthians 10:3–5 is saying:

> For though we walk in the flesh, we do not war according to the flesh, for the weapons of our warfare are not of the flesh, but divinely powerful for the destruction of fortresses. We are destroying speculations and every lofty thing raised up against the knowledge of God, and we are taking every thought captive to the obedience of Christ.

So then, let us be just as aggressive and militant against our spiritual foe as Israel was against her national foes. After all, "this is an honor for all His godly ones." To think that God would even allow us to be a part of His combat unit is an honor, indeed! May He be praised for equipping us for battle, empowering us for the fight, and encouraging us with the absolute promise of victory. Praise-less times are often times of demonic warfare . . . but the victory is ours! Read the following New Testament promises and rejoice.

> Therefore, my beloved brethren, be steadfast, immovable, always abounding in the work of the Lord, knowing that your toil is not in vain in the Lord. [1 Cor. 15:58]

> But thanks be to God, who always leads us in His triumph in Christ, and manifests through us the sweet aroma of the knowledge of Him in every place. [2 Cor. 2:14]

> And when you were dead in your transgressions and the uncircumcision of your flesh, He made you alive together with Him, having forgiven us all our transgressions, having canceled out the certificate of debt consisting of decrees against us and which was hostile to us; and He has taken it out of the way, having nailed it to the cross. When He had disarmed the rulers and authorities, He made a public display of them, having triumphed over them through Him. [Col. 2:13–15]

> Submit therefore to God. Resist the devil and he will flee from you. [James 4:7]

> You are from God, little children, and have overcome them; because greater is He who is in you than he who is in the world. [1 John 4:4]

CONCLUSION

Praise the Lord at all times! In times of blessing, praise Him! In times of suffering, praise Him! In times of warfare, praise Him! When we come to that enviable place in our Christian experience that we can honestly say "Praise the Lord!" in *every* situation—and genuinely mean it—we will have assimilated the full thrust of this magnificent hymn of praise—Psalm 149— and all the songs in Scripture. May that day come soon . . . and may it never end.

During the eighteenth century, Charles Wesley wrote numerous hymns. It has been estimated that during his lifetime he composed over eight thousand! "O for a Heart to Praise My God," one of his finest and oldest, has been put to the familiar tune of "O for a Thousand Tongues to Sing," another Wesley hymn. It is a fitting conclusion to our study of the songs in Scripture.

> O for a heart to praise my God,
>   A heart from sin set free,
> A heart that always feels Thy blood
>   So freely shed for me!
>
> A heart resigned, submissive, meek
>   My great Redeemer's throne;
> Where only Christ is heard to speak,
>   Where Jesus reigns alone.
>
> A heart in every thought renewed,
>   And full of love divine;
> Perfect, and right, and pure, and good,
>   A copy, Lord of Thine![19]

REFLECTIONS ON PRAISE-LESS TIMES

1. Do you remember the literal meaning of "Hallelujah"? Let's give it a whirl:

   hah-lale: _____

   Yah-weh: _____

   Put together: _____

2. What are the most common "praise-less" grinds in your life? Be specific. See if you can discover a pattern. Talk it over this week with close friends or a minister.

3. Whenever you encounter either a period of suffering or a time of warfare (as we saw in Psalm 149), just quietly utter, "Praise You, Lord!" and focus fully on Him. It can make an amazing difference. Furthermore, your countenance will be lifted up!

♫

Can you believe it?

If you have been following the game plan I suggested at the beginning of Book I —taking one reading per week— we have already traveled three-fourths of the way through the year together. And what a journey it has been!

We began with thirteen weeks in the songs of Scripture, followed by a second section of the next thirteen weeks in the sayings of Scripture. We discovered that by balancing our time in the Psalms and the Proverbs, we could maintain our spiritual equilibrium a bit better. The songs seem to turn our attention toward God, while the sayings tend to address more of our horizontal needs and relationships.

Now that we have completed our second segment of studies in the songs, we have one final section in the sayings before we bring our yearlong journey to an end — thirteen more readings and applications of Solomon's wisdom in light of today.

So hang on! We're off again on our scriptural safari, looking for practical insights that will help us live beyond the daily grind. Before we know it, the winding trail of Truth will make its final bend, so pay close attention!

THE
SAYINGS
IN
SCRIPTURE

WEEK 40
THROUGH
WEEK 52

The fear of the Lord is the
  beginning of wisdom,
  And the knowledge of the Holy
  One is understanding.
For by me your days will be multiplied,
And years of life will be added to
 you. [9:10–11]

The Lord will not allow the righteous to
 hunger,
But He will thrust aside the craving of
 the wicked. [10:3]

The way of the Lord is a stronghold to
 the upright,
But ruin to the workers of
 iniquity. [10:29]

When a man's ways are pleasing to the
 Lord,
He makes even his enemies to be at
 peace with him. [16:7]

Many are the plans in a man's heart,
But the counsel of the Lord, it will
 stand. [19:21]

The king's heart is like channels of water
 in the hand of the Lord;
He turns it wherever He wishes. [21:1]

THE GRIND OF SUBMISSION TO SOVEREIGNTY

At first glance the list of sayings on the previous page may appear more like a hodgepodge of random thoughts. A closer look, however, reveals a common theme—one we tend to forget or ignore. It is the theme of God's almighty sovereignty.

Since our generation is so hung up on human ingenuity and carnal cleverness, we tend to give people strokes that only God deserves.

- A battle is won . . . we hang medals on veterans.

- A degree is earned . . . we applaud the graduates.

- A sum of money is donated . . . we engrave contributors' names in bronze.

- An organization stays in the black through hard times . . . we give the CEO a bonus.

- A writer or scientist makes an outstanding contribution . . . we award the Pulitzer or Nobel prize.

- A sermon meets numerous needs . . . we thank the preacher.

There's nothing at all wrong with showing appreciation, just so we acknowledge the One who really deserves the maximum credit and give Him the greatest glory. But since He works out His will so silently (and often mysteriously), we feel a little spooky saying much about His almighty sovereignty.

Too bad. More needs to be said these days about God's sovereignty. Why? Because when so little is being said, man starts to strut his stuff. Look back at those timeless sayings from Solomon's pen. Read them slower this time.

Do you see what they are saying? God is in charge. Actually He is an unseen stronghold to the upright and an unseen obstacle in the way of the wicked (10:3, 29). He is *so* powerful that He can honor those who please Him by changing the attitudes of those who once felt enmity toward His followers (16:7). And get this: Once it is all said and done, after our plans have been hammered out, thought through, reworked, decided on, and distributed—it is ultimately *His* counsel that will stand.

That doesn't make you nervous, does it? You're not bothered by these comments about a doctrine that has become controversial, are you? Solomon didn't learn of God's sovereignty from John Calvin, remember; Calvin learned it from Scripture. Relax, this isn't simply "reformed doctrine," it is revelational doctrine. Frankly, I find it extremely comforting and enormously relieving. But for many (especially the hard-charging, do-it-yourself types) submission to sovereignty is an irksome daily grind. That's too bad.

Let's dig a little deeper into Proverbs 21:1:

> The king's heart is like channels of water in the hand of the Lord;
> He turns it wherever He wishes.

Immediately we can see it is a "comparative couplet" (see earlier discussion pp. 157–158 Book I). Something is compared to something else. Most comparative couplets end with the comparison and leave it at that. But this saying comes to a conclusion in what could be called the declarative part of the proverb . . . leaving the reader a timeless principle.

Observe the comparison: "The king's heart is like channels of water in the hand of the Lord." The Hebrew sentence doesn't begin with "the king's heart" but rather with "like channels." The Hebrew term translated *channels* is one that refers to small irrigation ditches that run from a main source—a reservoir—out into dry thirsty flatlands needing a cool drink. In other words: "Like irrigation canals carrying water is the heart of the king in Jehovah's hand. . . ."

What's the point? The king's heart (his inner being), the internal part of him that makes decisions, breathes out and communicates attitudes and policies, edicts and laws. As a result, he may appear to be in charge, but the entire matter from start to finish silently and sovereignly rests in the Lord's hand. The sovereign Lord, not the king or *any other* monarch or leader, qualifies to be the U.C. with U.A.—Ultimate Chief with Ultimate Authority.

How can anyone say such a thing, especially if the human authority is an unbeliever? Well, just finish reading Solomon's saying: "He [the Lord Himself] turns it wherever He wishes." Literally, He "causes it to be bent wherever He is pleased." God is calling the shots. Again, I ask you—Do you have struggles with that? If so, then you will really churn over this:

> "But at the end of that period I, Nebuchadnezzar, raised my eyes toward heaven, and my reason returned to me, and I blessed the Most High and praised and honored Him who lives forever;
>
> For His dominion is an everlasting dominion,
> And His kingdom endures from generation to generation.
> And all the inhabitants of the earth are accounted as nothing,
> But He does according to His will in the host of heaven
> And among the inhabitants of earth;
> And no one can ward off His hand
> Or say to Him, 'What hast Thou done?'" [Dan. 4:34–35]

Those are the words of a powerful king who was describing how God had worked him over prior to his coming full circle.

What is true of ancient kings is also true of modern bosses. Your boss. Or anyone else who thinks he is in full control. Yes, even you. God is ultimately going to have His way. You may decide to wrestle or attempt to resist, but I've got news for you; He's never met His match. He will win. He will have His way.

And just in case today is a high-level stress day when submitting to your sovereign Lord doesn't seem all that fair or fulfilling, take my advice: Do it anyway. You'll be glad later. Maybe sooner.

R EFLECTIONS ON SUBMITTING TO SOVEREIGNTY

1. Do some digging on your own this week. Find a couple or three reliable reference works and write out your own expanded definition of God's sovereignty. Begin with "Divine sovereignty is ＿＿＿＿＿＿＿＿＿＿＿＿＿

   ＿＿＿＿＿＿＿＿＿＿＿＿＿＿＿＿＿＿＿＿＿＿＿＿＿＿

   ＿＿＿＿＿＿＿＿＿＿＿＿＿＿＿＿＿＿＿＿＿＿＿＿＿＿

   ＿＿＿＿＿＿＿＿＿＿＿＿＿＿＿＿＿＿＿＿＿＿＿＿."

2. For the balance of the week, pick out two Bible characters whose lives were uniquely directed by God. Read up on both. *Joseph* is a beautiful example from the Old Testament. (Genesis 50:15–21 is a classic reference.) And from the New Testament, *Saul of Tarsus* is another worth examining. (Note especially Acts 9:1–20.) God's hand on Joseph's life illustrates how He can change a heart from resentment to forgiveness. His hand on Saul's life illustrates His sovereign ability to bring a proud, strong-willed type to his knees in utter humility.

3. This weekend, get alone. Find a quiet place where you can think. And pray. And reorder your life. Speak openly and audibly to the Lord and tell Him of your willingness to "lay down your arms." Acknowledge your stubborn streak. Express your desire to let Him have His way. Invite Him to take charge of each segment of your life. Yes, each one.

The hand of the diligent will rule,
But the slack hand will be put to
forced labor.   [12:24]

A slothful man does not roast his prey,
But the precious possession of a man is
diligence.   [12:27]

The soul of the sluggard craves and gets
nothing,
But the soul of the diligent is made
fat.   [13:4]

The way of the sluggard is as a hedge of
thorns,
But the path of the upright is a
highway.   [15:19]

He also who is slack in his work
Is brother to him who destroys.   [18:9]

Laziness casts into a deep sleep,
And an idle man will suffer
   hunger.   [19:15]

The sluggard says, "There is a lion
   outside;
I shall be slain in the streets!"   [22:13]

The sluggard says, "There is a lion in the
   road!
A lion is in the open square!"
As the door turns on its hinges,
So does the sluggard on his bed.
The sluggard buries his hand in the dish;
He is weary of bringing it to his mouth
   again.
The sluggard is wiser in his own eyes
Than seven men who can give a discreet
   answer.   [26:13–16]

THE GRIND OF
LAZINESS

Many people live under the false impression that work is a curse. Some attempt to quote Scripture to verify their position that work was the sad consequence of Adam's fall in the Garden of Eden. Wrong!

Before sin ever entered the human race—while total innocence prevailed—Adam was assigned the task of cultivating the Garden (Gen. 2:15). Work is not a curse. The curse that followed the Fall had to do with the hassles—the thorn- and thistlelike irritations that now accompany one's work—not work itself. Work, alone, is a privilege, a challenge to indolence, an answer to boredom, and a place to invest one's energy . . . not to mention to provide for our physical needs.

Throughout the Bible we are encouraged to be people of diligence, committed to the tasks in life that need to be accomplished. Some, however, do not consider this a privilege, but a drag. For those folks the daily grind of laziness is an undeniable reality. For this entire week, therefore, let's snap on our zoom lens and focus on this practical plague.

Of all the Scriptures that address the issue of laziness, none are more eloquent than the sayings of Solomon. Among the terms he uses for the lazy, "sluggard" seems to be his favorite. When I trace my way through the Proverbs, I find no less than *six characteristics* of the sluggard.

1. The sluggard has trouble getting started:

How long will you lie down, O sluggard?
When will you arise from your sleep?
"A little sleep, a little slumber,
A little folding of the hands to rest"—
And your poverty will come in like a vagabond,
And your need like an armed man. [6:9–11]

You may remember that in Book I we spent a week on procrastination, so there is no need to repeat what was presented in that study. Nevertheless, there is no getting around it: laziness focuses on the obstacles, the excuses that loom large on the front end of a task. Those who are lazy just can't seem to roll up their sleeves and plunge in full bore.

2. The sluggard is restless: He (or she) may have desires, but the trouble comes in implementing them:

The soul of the sluggard craves and gets nothing,
But the soul of the diligent is made fat. [13:4]

The desire of the sluggard puts him to death,
For his hands refuse to work;
All day long he is craving,
While the righteous gives and does not hold back. [21:25–26]

It is not uncommon for the lazy to be extremely skilled, creative people. They can talk and dream and even sketch out the game plan, but the discipline of pursuit is lacking. As we just read, the "craving" goes on "all day long," but little gets accomplished. When it comes to the sluggard's getting off dead center and getting the job done, forget it.

3. The sluggard takes a costly toll on others:

He also who is slack in his work
Is brother to him who destroys. [18:9]

That last word pulsates with liabilities. A lazy employee doesn't simply hold an organization back, he *destroys* its motivation and drive. A lazy player doesn't just weaken the team, he *destroys* its spirit, its will to win. A lazy pastor doesn't merely limit a church, he *destroys* its excitement, its passion to win souls and meet needs. Before long, everyone must do more to compensate for the sluggard's negative influence.

4. The sluggard is usually defensive:

> The sluggard is wiser in his own eyes
> Than seven men who can give a discreet answer. [26:16]

Can't you just hear it . . . all those rationalizing comments? Unfortunately, it is this clever ability to cover up or explain away that keeps the lazy person from coming to terms with reality.

5. The sluggard is a quitter:

> A slothful man does not roast his prey,
> But the precious possession of a man is diligence. [12:27]

In this saying, there is the telltale mark of laziness: an absence of thoroughness.

- He likes to catch fish, but not to clean them.

- He loves to eat, but don't expect him to help with the dishes.

- He can add a room onto the house, but getting it painted is another story.

He'd rather sleep than work; he'd rather focus on why something can't be helped . . . then blame the government for not caring (see Prov. 19:15).

6. The sluggard lives by excuses:

> The sluggard says, "There is a lion outside;
> I shall be slain in the streets!" [22:13]

That saying always makes me smile. Those lions in the street are nothing more than a fertile imagination gone to seed. The "lion" returns . . .

The sluggard says, "There is a lion in the road!
A lion is in the open square!"
As the door turns on its hinges,
So does the sluggard on his bed.
The sluggard buries his hand in the dish;
He is weary of bringing it to his mouth again. [26:13–15]

If it weren't so tragic, the analogy of a sluggard on a bed resembling a door on a hinge would be hilarious!

No one ever automatically or instantaneously overcame laziness. If this happens to be one of your daily grinds, today is the best day to start a new direction. The best place to start is by admitting it if you are lazy . . . stop covering it up. I dare you!

A young fellow rushed into a gas station to use the pay phone. The manager overheard his telephone conversation as he asked:

"Sir, could you use a hardworking, honest young man to work for you?" [pause] "Oh . . . you've already got a hardworking, honest young man? Well, thanks anyway!"

The boy hung up the phone with a smile. Humming to himself, he began to walk away, obviously happy.

"How can you be so cheery?" asked the eavesdropping service-station manager. "I thought the man you talked to already had someone and didn't want to hire you."

The young fellow answered, "Well, you see *I am* the hardworking young man. I was just checking up on my job!"

If you called your boss, disguised your voice, and asked about *your* job, what do you think would be the boss's answer?

R EFLECTIONS ON LAZINESS

1. Go back over that list of six characteristics. Spend enough time on each to see yourself mirrored in the scene. Which two represent your greatest area(s) of weakness? Admit them in writing:

   a. _____

   b. _____

2. Now that you have identified your style, spell out a game plan for correcting the tendency to be lazy. Be specific, practical, and realistic. Begin your strategy with such words as: "Today, I will begin to . . ." or "From now on, I am going to . . ."

3. Do you happen to have a lazy acquaintance who holds you back? Frequently, an unhealthy or unwholesome association will give us just the excuse we need to settle for too many limitations. Do you really need to spend that much time with him (or her)? If you do, be honest and confront the problem. Ask the person either to join you in a strategy to change or to step aside so you can.

If you are slack in the day of distress,
Your strength is limited.   [24:10]

Two things I asked of Thee,
Do not refuse me before I die:
Keep deception and lies far from me,
Give me neither poverty nor riches;
Feed me with the food that is my portion,
Lest I be full and deny Thee and say,
    "Who is the Lord?"
Or lest I be in want and steal,
And profane the name of my
    God.   [30:7–9]

THE GRIND OF IMBALANCE

The longer I live the more I realize the ease with which we can slip into extremes. I see it all around me and sometimes, to my own embarrassment, I find it in myself. A major prayer of mine as I grow older is, "Lord, keep me balanced!"

— We need a balance between work and play (too much of either is unhealthy and distasteful).

— We need a balance between time alone and time with others (too much of either takes a toll on us).

— We need a balance between independence and dependence (either one, all alone, leads to problems).

— We need a balance between kindness and firmness,
between waiting and praying, working and obeying,
between saving and spending,
between taking in and giving out,
between wanting too much and expecting too little,
between warm acceptance and keen discernment,
between grace and truth.

For many folks, the struggle with imbalance is not an annual conflict—it's a daily grind.

Solomon mentions one kind of test: adversity.

> If you are slack in the day of distress,
> Your strength is limited. [Prov. 24:10]

When things are adverse, survival is our primary goal. Adversity is a test on our resiliency, our creativity. Up against it, we reach down deep into our inner character and we "gut it out." We hold up through the crisis by tapping into our reservoir of inner strength.

But another far more subtle test is the opposite extreme: prosperity—when things begin to come easy, when there's plenty of money, when everybody applauds, when we get all our ducks in a row and the gravy starts pouring in. Now *that's* the time to hang tough! Why? Because in times of prosperity things get complicated. Integrity is on the block. Humility is put to the test. Consistency is under the gun. Of the two, I'm convinced prosperity is a much greater test than adversity. It is far more deceptive.

The one who wrote the following sayings understood all this much better than we. Listen to his wise counsel, actually a prayer:

> Two things I asked of Thee,
> Do not refuse me before I die:
> Keep deception and lies far from me,
> Give me neither poverty nor riches;
> Feed me with the food that is my portion,
> Lest I be full and deny Thee and say, "Who is the Lord?"
> Or lest I be in want and steal,
> And profane the name of my God. [30:7–9]

The man had lived enough years and seen enough scenes to boil his petition down to two specifics:

1. Keep me from deceiving and lying.
2. Give me neither too little nor too much.

It is that second request that intrigues us, isn't it? That is the one he amplifies. Why does he resist having too little? There would be the temptation to steal. Whoever doubts that has never looked into the faces of his own starving children. At that moment, feeding them could easily overrule upholding some high-and-mighty principle. Adversity can tempt us to profane the name of our God.

And why does he fear possessing too much? Ah, there's the sneaky one! It's *then*—when we're fat-'n'-sassy—that we are tempted to yawn at sacred things and think heretical thoughts like, *God? Aw, who really needs Him?* Prosperity can tempt us to presume on the grace of our God.

Think it over all week long. The adversary of our souls is the *expert* of extremes. He never runs out of ways to push us to the limit . . . to get us so far out on one end we start looking freaky and sounding fanatical as we cast perspective to the winds.

The longer I live, the more I must fight the tendency to go to extremes . . . and the more I value balance.

R EFLECTIONS ON IMBALANCE

1. Let's do a little honest appraisal, okay? To help keep your appraisal on a fairly reliable footing, two things will be needed:

   a. Your calendar
   b. Your checkbook

   Looking through your *calendar*, do you find a balance or imbalance? Too many things going on or too little time with others? And while you're looking, when was the last time you got away for an overnight . . . just to be refreshed? Is your time being kept in balance?

   Next, go back over the last several months in your checkbook. Go ahead, take a look! Do your expenditures reflect balance or imbalance? Too much (or not enough) on yourself? How about God's part? Is the way you spend your money an indication of balance?

2. Adversity or prosperity . . . toward which extreme are you? How are you handling the pressures? Does anyone know—I mean someone who can really pray you through these testy waters? Try not to underplay or overreact to the battle. You would be wise to memorize Proverbs 30:7–9 this week.

3. Let me put it straight: Is Christ truly Lord? Being the Bulwark of Balance, He is eminently capable of escorting you through life's daily grinds, including this one. It may be essential (you decide) for you to set aside one hour this week and turn all the details of your life over to Him, including your calendar and your checkbook.

Wisdom shouts in the street,
She lifts her voice in the
square;
At the head of the noisy
streets she cries out;
At the entrance of the gates in the city,
she utters her sayings;
"How long, O naive ones, will you love
simplicity?
And scoffers delight themselves in
scoffing,
And fools hate knowledge?"   [1:20–22]

"Because they hated knowledge,
And did not choose the fear of the Lord.
They would not accept my counsel,
They spurned all my reproof.
So they shall eat of the fruit of their own
way,
And be satiated with their own devices.
For the waywardness of the naive shall
kill them,
And the complacency of fools shall
destroy them."   [1:29–32]

THE GRIND OF
OPPOSITION

By opposition, I am not referring to external resistance from others but to internal resistance within one's self. I'm not talking about our encounters with someone or something else that withstands our efforts. What I have in mind is how we personally withstand or resist the things of God—His leading, His reproofs, His will, His wisdom. Some are so given to internal opposition that they regularly fail to learn the lessons Truth attempts to teach. While others glean God's message and follow His principles, many spurn His ways. You may find yourself in that latter category these days.

As a pastor, I have been amazed at the difference among Christians when it comes to acceptance of instruction. Some never seem to learn. While there are always those who are sensitive and open to spiritual things—in fact, a few can't seem to get enough!—there are those who are exposed to the same truths year after year, but they fail to soak in. Not until I came across three types of individuals in the sayings of Scripture did I understand why. All three have the same thing in common—they are people of opposition, but they oppose in different ways.

The Simple

The "simple" are called "naive ones" by Solomon. The Hebrew *pah-thah* means "to be spacious, wide." In noun form it is

frequently translated "door, entrance." It is the idea of being
completely open, believing every word, easily misled, even en-
ticed . . . an easy prey to deception. The naive are susceptible
to evil and wide open to any opinion. They are usually inadequate when it comes to coping with life's complexities, especially if it requires a great deal of mental effort.

Reading through Proverbs, I find that the simple:

—are insensitive to danger or evil:

> For at the window of my house
> I looked out through my lattice,
> And I saw among the naive,
> I discerned among the youths,
> A young man lacking sense,
> Passing through the street near her corner;
> And he takes the way to her house,
> In the twilight, in the evening,
> In the middle of the night and in the darkness. [7:6–9]

> Suddenly he follows her,
> As an ox goes to the slaughter . . . [7:22a]

—do not envision the consequences:

> "Whoever is naive, let him turn in here,"
> And to him who lacks understanding she says,
> "Stolen water is sweet;
> And bread eaten in secret is pleasant."
> But he does not know that the dead are there,
> That her guests are in the depths of Sheol. [9:16–18]

—are gullible . . . they lack caution:

> The naive believes everything,
> But the prudent man considers his steps. [14:15]

—fail to learn . . . they plunge in again and again!

> The prudent sees the evil and hides himself,
> But the naive go on, and are punished for it. [22:3]

The Scoffer

Here is a person quite different from the simple. The scoffer "delights in his scoffing." The Hebrew term *lootz* means "to turn aside, to mock." It is the thought of rejecting with vigorous contempt . . . to refuse and to show disdain or disgust for spiritual truth. Back in Book I, during our very first week together, we read God's warning against sitting "in the seat of scoffers" (Ps. 1:1); so this is not our first encounter with those who sneer at the sacred.

Our response is to "whip 'em into shape," to apply a lot of intense discipline so they will stop scoffing. More than likely, that's wasted effort. Solomon reminds us:

> He who corrects a scoffer gets dishonor for himself.
> And he who reproves a wicked man gets insults for himself.
> Do not reprove a scoffer, lest he hate you,
> Reprove a wise man, and he will love you. [9:7–8]

This explains why all these fall under the general heading of "the opposition." The scoffer won't listen to words of correction. He vigorously opposes it.

> A wise son accepts his father's discipline,
> But a scoffer does not listen to rebuke. [13:1]

Nor will he (or she) appreciate our attempts to bring about a change.

> A scoffer does not love one who reproves him,
> He will not go to the wise. [15:12]

The Fool

The Hebrew root term for fool is *kah-sal*, meaning "to be stupid, dull." Its Arabic counterpart means "to be sluggish, thick, coarse." Don't misunderstand. The fool has the capacity to reason, he just reasons wrongly. Fools are absolutely convinced of one thing: they can get along quite well *without* God. Scripture reserves some of its severest rebukes for fools.

- Fools traffic in wickedness . . . they play with it.

    Doing wickedness is like sport to a fool;
    And so is wisdom to a man of understanding. [10:23]

- Fools place folly on display . . . they flaunt it.

    Every prudent man acts with knowledge,
    But a fool displays folly. [13:16]

- Fools arrogantly "let it all hang out."

    A wise man is cautious and turns away from evil,
    But a fool is arrogant and careless. [14:16]

Strong words! Nevertheless, they need to be heard. They also help explain why the resistance factor is so obvious among some. Resistance is not only real to some and common among humanity in general, but it may also be *your* personal daily grind. If so, this is the week to come to terms with it. And that is true even if you have little insignificant-looking areas of opposition in only a few quiet corners of your heart. Few things please our Lord more than a teachable spirit.

Do you possess one?

R EFLECTIONS ON OPPOSITION

1. See if you can, in your own words, define the three types of individuals we found mentioned in the sayings of Scripture:

   • The simple _____

   _____

   • The scoffer _____

   _____

   • The fool _____

   _____

   Can you think of a biblical example of each?

2. Which one represents an area of struggle for you? Can you call to mind a recent occasion that illustrates this fact? If you have children, can you see this same trait being played out in one (or more) of them? Spend some time thinking how you can help counteract that tendency.

3. Since no one else (according to Proverbs) seems that effective when it comes to changing the simple, the scoffer, or the fool, the responsibility for such rests with the individuals themselves. What are some things you can *do* personally to turn the tide? Aside from wishing and praying, describe two or three action steps that will begin to move you from the ranks of opposition. When do you plan to start?

Wine is a mocker, strong drink
      a brawler,
And whoever is intoxicated
      by it is not wise. [20:1]

Who has woe? Who has sorrow?
Who has contentions? Who has
    complaining?
Who has wounds without cause?
Who has redness of eyes?
Those who linger long over wine,
Those who go to taste mixed wine.
Do not look on the wine when it is red,
When it sparkles in the cup,
When it goes down smoothly;
At the last it bites like a serpent,
And stings like a viper.
Your eyes will see strange things,
And your mind will utter perverse
    things.
And you will be like one who lies down
    in the middle of the sea,
Or like one who lies down on the top of a
    mast.
"They struck me, but I did not become ill;
They beat me, but I did not know it.
When shall I awake?
I will seek another drink." [23:29–35]

THE GRIND OF
ADDICTION

I smile inside every time I hear someone say the Bible is irrelevant. Right away, I know that person is not well acquainted with the pages of God's Book. As one who has been a student of Scripture for over three decades, I am still occasionally stunned at how up-to-date and on target it really is.

Take the daily grind of addiction—for many today, a grim reality. Is there any subject of greater relevance than this one? And yet, centuries ago, when the Lord was directing His messengers to record His truth, this was a subject He chose not to overlook. Here we sit on the verge of the twenty-first century swarming with evidence of modern technology everywhere we turn, yet the ancient sayings of a long-ago writer speak with fresh relevance.

His collection of wise sayings includes pertinent words and warnings for all who may be tempted by the taste of alcohol or, to apply it further, by the allurements of some drug. Chemical abuse is no longer in hiding, whispered about by a select body of professionals behind closed doors. It is now out of the closet. Support groups in communities, colleges, and churches are available all across the country. They have people in them who don't scold or scream, preach or moralize . . . they offer support. They take time. They encourage. They care. Most of them have been through the hellish nightmare of addiction, so they understand what it feels like to be trapped, held captive by a bottle, a pill, a snort, an injection . . . or even food.

Substance abuse is no longer limited to the sleazy back alley. It's now in the high-rise owned by the high roller, in nice homes where small children play, in efficient offices where business is transacted, in military barracks where boredom is high, and on professional sports teams where competition is fierce and where money is plentiful. It's even in prisons where men and women serve time.

Perhaps there's an addiction to some substance in your life as well. You may be an upstanding and admired citizen—you may even be active in your community or church—but the *real* you is dependent on a drink or a "high" you get from some other substance. You, of all people, understand the warnings of Solomon: "Wine is a mocker" and "At the last it bites like a serpent." You hardly need to be reminded that as a result of taking it in, "Your eyes will see strange things, and your mind will utter perverse things." Yet, in spite of the humiliation and the embarrassment, you're back at it the next day (as Solomon describes it), again thinking "I will seek another drink." To call this incredible craving a "daily grind" is to put it mildly. It is more like a devastating grip you simply cannot conquer . . . an evil force beyond your ability to control.

I would not be foolish enough to suggest that within a week's time you will be free—certainly not. (There are a few who testify of overnight transformations, but they are the exception, not the norm.) However, I can assure you of this: Within a week you can be moving in a new direction. No addiction—I repeat: NO addiction—is more powerful than the power of the Almighty. Never forget that His power stills storms and heals diseases and casts out demons. In fact, it is the same power that once raised Jesus from the dead.

You think His power can't handle your addiction? You're convinced that you are beyond hope? You're not sure this God who brought His Son back from beyond can give you the strength you need to say "No" one day at a time? Get serious! Then read the following verses and rejoice with new hope:

Fear not, for I am with you. Do not be dismayed. I am your God. I will strengthen you; I will help you; I will uphold you with my victorious right hand. [Isa. 41:10, TLB]

But remember this—the wrong desires that come into your life aren't anything new and different. Many others have faced exactly the same problems before you. And no temptation is irresistible. You can trust God to keep the temptation from becoming so strong that you can't stand up against it, for he has promised this and will do what he says. He will show you how to escape temptation's power so that you can bear up patiently against it. [1 Cor. 10:13, TLB]

In our church in Fullerton, we have a ministry for those who struggle with chemical abuse. The name of this wonderful support group is "Lion Tamer's Anonymous." The stories of recovery that emerge from the ranks of those courageous folks are nothing short of thrilling.

I recall one that involved a married couple with several small children. Both parents were addicted to cocaine. It was not unusual for them to be high on the drug for a day or two each weekend. Thanks to the compassionate and gentle, yet firm, determination of a few caring friends in our Lion Tamer's group, this couple has found ways to "escape temptation's power."

If some addiction has become your daily grind, I urge you to face it head-on . . . up-front. Do whatever is needed to break its grip. Yes, *whatever.*

R EFLECTIONS ON ADDICTION

1. To begin with, write out *The Living Bible* paraphrase of the two verses of Scripture you just read (Isaiah 41:10 and 1 Corinthians 10:13) on a three-by-five card or a small slip of paper. Keep it near your bed at night, on the table near where you sit to watch television, beside you where you work, and on the dashboard of the car you drive. Read the statements every day. By the end of the week, have them committed to memory. Personalize the two scriptures by inserting *your* name in place of "you" and "your."

2. Stop trying to ignore or excuse your addiction. As I mentioned a moment ago, face it. Confront the truth. Finish this sentence:

   I, _____, am addicted to _____.
      (your name)   (substance)

   Nobody ever began to overcome any habit who failed to admit it was true . . . so start there.

3. You need not only the prayers of others, but you need practical support as well. Locate a group, a professional hands-on person, or find a reliable clinic that specializes in helping people deal with your addiction. Reach out and admit your need for assistance. You may need to be hospitalized or go through an extensive program as an initial plan to get started. For sure, you must be accountable to a small group of caring individuals—preferably those who will not only help you work through your battle but those who will also support your faith. However, you must make the first move. Make it *today.* Good for you!

He who mocks the poor
    reproaches his Maker;
He who rejoices at calamity
    will not go
    unpunished.   [17:5]

Do not rejoice when your enemy falls,
And do not let your heart be glad when
    he stumbles;
Lest the Lord see it and be displeased,
And He turn away His anger from him.

Do not fret yourself because of evildoers,
Or be envious of the wicked;
For there will be no future for the evil
    man;
The lamp of the wicked will be put
    out.   [24:17–20]

If your enemy is hungry, give him food
    to eat;
And if he is thirsty, give him water to
    drink;
For you will heap burning coals on his
    head,
And the Lord will reward
    you.   [25:21–22]

THE GRIND OF REVENGE

Have you spent much time around someone who is eaten up with the cancer of revenge—someone who is nursing an attitude of resentment? It is a tragic thing to witness. These folks are walking time bombs. Festering bitterness searches for and usually finds ways to explode. Often, those who suffer the brunt of another's revenge are innocent bystanders. They just happen to be in the way when the volcano erupts. Since revenge fuels such an enormous and uncontrollable fire, it is a wonder more aren't hurt by it. It may be a popular reaction, but it is not a solution.

I think Sir Francis Bacon had the right idea when he said:

> Revenge is a kind of wild justice; which the more man's nature runs to, the more ought law to weed it out. . . . certainly, in taking revenge a man is but even with his enemy; but in passing over it, he is superior, for it is a prince's part to pardon.

It is possible that revenge happens to be your personal daily grind. If so, trust me, you have a lot of company in that struggle. It is a common ailment woven into the fabric of universal humanity. There isn't a culture where revenge isn't found. But that doesn't excuse it! This is the week to expose revenge in all its ugliness. Like a tumor that will ultimately turn a healthy body into a corpse if it is ignored, this disease-carrying growth must be removed. The sooner, the better.

But how? Here's where God's Word comes to our rescue! First, we must do something that is painful within ourselves— we must forgive our enemy; and second, we must do something that is profitable for our "enemy."

FORGIVE YOUR ENEMY

First things first. The revenge clings tenaciously within us because we have not forgiven the other person. Sounds simple—too simple—doesn't it? How do I know I've not forgiven someone else? I rejoice at the thought of calamity striking him or her . . . but Solomon's saying declares that such an attitude "will not go unpunished." The stinging acid of resentment will eat away at my own inner peace. Furthermore, by our rejoicing when our enemy falls, we somehow hold back God's anger (Prov. 24:17–18). In some mysterious way, the Lord's taking vengeance on our behalf is connected to our releasing all of that to Him. By our refusing to forgive, revealed in our looking with delight on the offender's calamity, we hinder the divine process. Vengeance is God's work, but it awaits our releasing it to Him.

> "'Vengeance is Mine, and retribution,
> In due time their foot will slip;
> For the day of their calamity is near,
> And the impending things are hastening upon them.'
> For the Lord will vindicate His people,
> And will have compassion on His servants;
> When He sees that their strength is gone,
> And there is none remaining, bond or free." [Deut.
>   32:35–36]

Because that is true, all thought of our taking revenge must be put to bed. When we do, we "leave room [or give a place] for the wrath of God" (Rom. 12:19) to go to work. Read the following slowly and very carefully:

> Never pay back evil for evil to anyone. Respect what is right in the sight of all men. If possible, so far as it depends on you, be at

peace with all men. Never take your own revenge, beloved, but leave room for the wrath of God, for it is written, "Vengeance is Mine, I will repay, says the Lord." [Rom. 12:17–19]

So much for the first part: forgive, forgive, forgive!

SHOW KINDNESS TOWARD YOUR ENEMY

Now then, the second step proves the validity of our forgiveness . . . we do something beneficial on behalf of the one we once resented.

> If your enemy is hungry, give him food to eat;
> And if he is thirsty, give him water to drink;
> For you will heap burning coals on his head,
> And the Lord will reward you. [Prov. 25:21–22]

- Your now-forgiven enemy is hungry? Provide a nice meal.

- Your now-forgiven enemy is thirsty? Prepare a cool drink.

"That's easy enough," you say. "But what does all this mean about heaping burning coals on his head?"

In ancient days, homes were heated and meals were fixed on a small portable stove, somewhat like our outside barbecue grills. Frequently, a person would run low on hot coals and would need to replenish his supply. The container was commonly carried on the head. So as the individual passed beneath second-story windows, thoughtful people who had extra hot coals in their possession would reach out of the window and place them in the container atop his head. Thanks to the thoughtful generosity of a few folks, he would arrive at the site with a pile of burning coals on his head and a ready-made fire for cooking and keeping warm. "Heaping burning coals on someone's head" came to be a popular expression for a spontaneous and courteous act one person would voluntarily do for another.

The saying was still popular in the New Testament era, since Paul referred to it in a context very similar to the ones we've been considering in the sayings of Solomon.

> "But if your enemy is hungry, feed him, and if he is thirsty, give him a drink; for in so doing you will heap burning coals upon his head." Do not be overcome by evil, but overcome evil with good. [Rom. 12:20–21]

I find it interesting that the only two places in Scripture where this custom is mentioned are in identical settings: demonstrating kindness toward someone who was once an offender—an enemy. That is worth some thought.

Equally significant is Paul's concluding remark. Instead of being "overcome by evil" (that's what happens when the cancer of revenge continues to spread its tentacles), we are told to "overcome evil with good."

The daily grind of revenge will continue to siphon our peace, our joy, and our love until we forgive—and I mean *completely* forgive—and ultimately prove our forgiveness through acts of kindness, courtesy, and thoughtfulness.

R EFLECTIONS ON REVENGE

1. Do you have someone's face on the dart board of your mind? Be honest, now . . . 'fess up! Have you been entertaining thoughts of revenge toward another individual? Do you smile with cruel cynicism when you read the popular bumper sticker: "I don't get mad . . . I get even." As is true of all other transgressions, confession is the first step toward cleansing. Are you willing to admit to yourself and to the Lord that you've looked forward to the day when calamity would strike that person?

2. This is the week to work through whatever it takes to get rid of your secret. The ugly tumor of revenge *must* come out. If you can't seem to handle the surgical procedure alone, call for help. A minister, a priest, a counselor, a friend, a family member, a teacher—somebody who will not only hear you but help you. You'll need to talk it through (remember Proverbs 20:5 which we considered in the second section of Book I?) and hammer out a way to find peace within. Call on the Lord for His help. Take your time. Do a thorough job of cleaning all the corruption out of the wound. Don't be surprised if tears flow.

3. When the week has come to an end, begin to think of a way to "heap burning coals" on the head of that person. It may be in the form of a kind letter you write. Perhaps you could put in a good word for him (or her). Or send a gift—something tangible. Don't fake it. If you cannot pull it off with a pure motive, wait. The time will come when you will have an opportunity to do so.

D o not envy a man of violence,
    And do not choose any of his
        ways.
    For the crooked man is an
        abomination to the Lord;
But He is intimate with the
    upright.   [3:31–32]

———————

For jealousy [envy] enrages a man,
And he will not spare in the day of
    vengeance.
He will not accept any ransom,
Nor will he be content though you give
    many gifts.   [6:34–35]

———————

A tranquil heart is life to the body,
But passion [envy] is rottenness to the
    bones.   [14:30]

———————

Do not let your heart envy sinners,
But live in the fear of the Lord always.
Surely there is a future,

And your hope will not be cut off.
Listen, my son, and be wise,
And direct your heart in the
    way. [23:17–19]

––––––––––

Do not be envious of evil men,
Nor desire to be with them;
For their minds devise violence,
And their lips talk of trouble. [24:1–2]

––––––––––

Do not fret because of evildoers,
Or be envious of the wicked;
For there will be no future for the evil
    man;
The lamp of the wicked will be put
    out. [24:19–20]

––––––––––

Wrath is fierce and anger is a flood,
But who can stand before jealousy
    [envy]? [27:4]

THE GRIND OF
ENVY

Envy is one of the great enemies of inner peace. It steals contentment from the heart. Petrarch was so right when he said:

> Five great enemies to peace inhabit within us: avarice, ambition, envy, anger, and pride. If those enemies were to be banished, we should infallibly enjoy perpetual peace.

Envy is the desire to equal another in achievement or excellence or possessions. The ancients referred to it as a malignant or hostile feeling. Augustine lists it among "the passions [that] rage like tyrants and throw into confusion the whole soul . . . with storms from every quarter." He then describes such a soul as having an "eagerness to win what was not possessed. . . . Wherever he turns, avarice can confine him, self-indulgence dissipate him, ambition master him, pride puff him up, envy torture him, sloth drug him. . . ."[1]

An apt term: *torture.* Such is the toll envy takes on its victims.

Jealousy and *envy* are often used interchangeably, but there is a slight difference. Jealousy begins with full hands but is frightened or threatened by the loss of its plenty. It is the resistance to losing what one has, in spite of the struggle to keep it. Envy is not quite the same. Envy begins with empty hands, mourning what it *doesn't* have. In *Purgatorio,* Dante portrays it as "a blind beggar whose eyelids are sewn shut." One who is envious is unreasonable because he is sewn up within himself.

Such torture can scarcely be exaggerated. Jealousy wants

to possess what it already has; envy wants to have what another possesses.

Interestingly, both emerge in Scripture from the same Hebrew term *qua-nah*, which means "to be intensely red." It is descriptive of one whose face is flushed as a sudden surge of blood announces the rush of emotion. To demonstrate the grim irony of language, *zeal* and *ardor* and *envy* all come from a common linguistic root. The same emotion that "enrages a man" (Prov. 6:34) also floods him with zeal to defend his country or adore his wife and family.

On several occasions the sayings of Scripture include warnings against our being consumed by envy. As you read earlier, we are not to envy one who is violent, or to choose any of his ways. An abrupt burst of anger may get quick results, but in the long run, the long-term consequences far outweigh the initial benefits (Prov. 3:31–32). In fact, the cultivation of envy brings "rottenness to the bones" (Prov. 14:30).

I find it extremely significant that the most-often repeated warnings regarding envy have to do with our being envious of the sinner, of evil men and their wayward lifestyle (Prov. 23:17; 24:1, 19). That should not surprise us. A favorite unguarded mind game so many folks play is to imagine how stimulating it would be to live it up . . . to throw restraint to the winds and "let it all hang out." Face it, sin has its sensual and seasonal pleasures. They may be short-lived and passing (Heb. 11:25), but they're certainly not dull and boring!

Furthermore, the wicked appear to get away with murder. Haven't you noticed? They maneuver their way through life with relative ease, they get out of trouble by lying and cheating, they can own and drive whatever, live wherever, and con whomever they wish out of whatever they want. And it seems as though they usually get away with it! And all this without accountability or responsibility. If something gets to be a hassle, bail out of it! If somebody gets in the way, walk over him! When we compare that self-satisfying lifestyle to the disciplines of devotion and the restraints of righteousness, it doesn't take an advanced degree from Dartmouth to see how envy can creep in.

And while we're at it, envy isn't limited to inner tortures over the ungodly. We can be just as envious of our fellow Christians.

It happens so quickly! That age-old, red-face flush can happen in dozens of life's scenes:

- When we hear a more polished speaker
- When we watch a more capable leader
- When we visit a bigger church
- When we read a better book
- When we meet a more beautiful, thinner woman (or a more handsome or charming man)
- When we observe a more effective evangelist
- When we ride in a more luxurious car
- When we listen to a more popular singer

The envy-list has no end. Not even preachers are immune!

Perhaps *this* is your daily grind. It is possible that the grind is intensifying as your age is outrunning your accomplishments. There was once a time when you could push that feeling away and keep a lid on it as you stored it in your attic of future dreams. Hope kept it diffused. No longer.

The reality of truth refuses to let you push envy aside any longer. The fact is . . . you won't be able to have or own or enjoy most of the things you see and hear others enjoying. And it is robbing you of that "perpetual peace" as envy tortures you with its malignant whisperings. What is worse, instead of your being happy for the other person whom God has blessed, you are suspicious or resentful, maybe downright angry. "Envy," reminds Solomon, "enrages a man."

This is the week to come to terms with envy. How much more peaceful to be contented with our lot! How much better to "rejoice with those who rejoice"! A mark of maturity is the ability to appreciate another more gifted than we . . . to applaud another more honored than we . . . to enjoy another more blessed than we. Such a wholesome response underscores our confidence in and allegiance to the sovereignty of God, who "puts down one and exalts another" (Ps. 75:7).

All week long let's expose our inner struggle with envy to the Physician of our souls. Like revenge, envy is another tumor we dare not ignore. Let's invite the Physician's scalpel and allow Him to excise it. If ignored, envy can become a terminal illness of the soul.

REFLECTIONS ON ENVY

1. Before the week ends, get a Bible concordance and look up every reference in Scripture under the headings of "envy" and "envious." Read each verse you locate slowly and aloud. Let the Spirit touch your inner spirit with the full impact of His truth. It may hurt, but it will ultimately help bring healing.

2. Do a little analysis of *your* battle with envy. Does it spring most often from a comparison of material possessions? *Why?* Does it increase when you are around more educated or capable people? *Why?* Does it emerge when you think of "what might have been" in your own life? *Why?* Could it be that envy is at the root of your underlying critical spirit? Could this explain why you have become more suspicious of those whom God has chosen to bless? Since "jealousy [*qua-nah*] is as severe as Sheol [the grave]" (Song of Solomon 8:6), it can leave its victim immobilized. Talk to God about this.

3. This weekend, take a little extra time to turn your attention from others' achievements and blessings to your own. Count them one by one. Make a mental list of what the Lord has done *for* you and *through* you. Don't miss your years of service, your health, or your continued ability to be of help to others. Pray for contentment. Pray for healing from the plague of comparison. Pray for a grateful spirit. Finally, be big enough to pray for at least three other people who are being used by God in a greater or broader way than He has chosen to use you. Pray for their success, their continued effectiveness, and their protection from enemy attacks.

A man's discretion makes him
slow to anger,
And it is his glory to overlook a
transgression. [19:11]

Deliver those who are being taken away
to death,
And those who are staggering to
slaughter, O hold them back.
If you say, "See, we did not know this,"
Does He not consider it who weighs the
hearts?
And does He not know it who keeps your
soul?
And will He not render to man according
to his work? [24:11–12]

To show partiality is not good,
Because for a piece of bread a man will
transgress. [28:21]

The righteous is concerned for the rights
   of the poor,
The wicked does not understand such
   concern.   [29:7]

There is a kind of man who curses his
   father,
And does not bless his mother.
There is a kind who is pure in his own
   eyes,
Yet is not washed from his filthiness.
There is a kind—oh how lofty are his
   eyes!
And his eyelids are raised in arrogance.
There is a kind of man whose teeth are
   like swords,
And his jaw teeth like knives,
To devour the afflicted from the earth,
And the needy from among
   men.   [30:11–14]

THE GRIND OF
INTOLERANCE

Tolerance provides "wobble room" for those who can't seem to measure up. It also allows needed growing room for the young and the restless. It smiles rather than frowns on the struggling. Instead of rigidly pointing to the rules and rehearsing the failures of the fallen, it stoops and reaches out, offering fresh hope and acceptance.

Intolerance is the antithesis of all that I have just described. Unwilling to "overlook a transgression" (Prov. 19:11), it tightens the strings on guilt and verbalizes a lot of shoulds and musts. The heart of the intolerant has not been broken, not really. For many, it has become unbreakable, judgmental, without compassion.

Don't misunderstand; most of this lack of tolerance is not overt, but subtle. You can detect it in a look; it is not usually spoken. To draw upon Solomon's saying, instead of delivering those who are going under, those "staggering to slaughter," the intolerant excuse their lack of assistance by saying, "We did not know this" (Prov. 24:11–12). But the Lord knows better. The Lord is well aware of even the slightest spirit of partiality hidden in our hearts.

Is intolerance one of your daily grinds? Be honest; do you have difficulty leaving room for differing opinions or others who can't measure up? Could it be that you have tasted for so long the ecstasies of conquest that you've forgotten the agonies of defeat? I can think of any number of ways intolerance rears its head:

- The healthy can be impatient with the sickly.
- The strong have trouble adapting to the weak.
- The fleet do not do well with the slow.
- The productive lack understanding of the drudge.
- The wealthy can scarcely imagine the pain of being poor.
- The quick minds know nothing of the embarrassment of being a slow learner.
- The coordinated shake their heads at the awkward.
- The pragmatic criticize the philosophical.
- The engineer has little appreciation for the artist.
- The stable and secure haven't a clue on how to understand the fragile and fearful.

Karl Menninger wrote with keen perception:

> When a trout rising to a fly gets hooked on a line and finds himself unable to swim about freely, he begins with a fight which results in struggles and splashes and sometimes an escape. Often, of course, the situation is too tough for him.
>
> In the same way the human being struggles with his environment and with the hooks that catch him. Sometimes he masters his difficulties; sometimes they are too much for him. His struggles are all that the world sees and it naturally misunderstands them. It is hard for a free fish to understand what is happening to a hooked one.[2]

Perhaps you fall into the category of a "free fish." Having never felt the sting of a hook or the choking panic of being caught, you would do well to keep your pride in check! Solomon muses over certain kinds of people who are "pure in their own eyes," whose "eyelids are raised in arrogance." Interestingly, their teeth become swordlike, sharp as knives. And whom do they devour, according to the saying of Scripture? "The afflicted . . . the needy" (Prov. 30:14). Why, of course! The intolerant invariably choose to devour those they consider "beneath them."

This is an excellent time—all week long—to bring even the slightest intolerance that may be lurking in your life out in the open and place it before the Lord. Reflecting back on our study of Psalm 139, call to mind those last two verses, especially David's petition: "Search me, O God . . . And see if there be any hurtful way in me, / And lead me in the everlasting way." What a perfect occasion to talk with the Lord about your intolerance!

Before closing off our study, let's consider one more saying worth our examination:

> The generous man will be prosperous,
> And he who waters will himself be watered. [Prov. 11:25]

True, the initial interpretation of Solomon's words is related to being generous with one's money, but broaden it to include being generous of spirit—broad-shouldered and big-hearted. Such an individual will not be restrictive in spirit or demanding, but "generous" of soul. The good news is that the same will come back to him. Others, in turn, will be accepting and tolerant in return.

It may be hard for a free fish to understand what is happening to a hooked one, but it isn't completely impossible. Our Lord knew no sin, did no sin, had no sin. Although He was never "hooked," His heart went out to those who were ashamed of their sin. On one occasion He even stood in defense of a woman caught in the very act of adultery.

Remember His words of tolerance bathed so beautifully in grace? After shaming those self-appointed judges who were ready to stone her, He looked deeply into the fallen woman's eyes and gently reassured her, "Neither do I condemn you; go your way; from now on sin no more" (John 8:11). Not a hint of intolerance.

If intolerance has become a daily grind, it is imperative that you deal with it. I'm thinking not only of you but of others who suffer the blunt edge of your habit. Those around you who are forced to live with your rigidity would be relieved to know that you are aware of your problem and that you plan to ignore it no longer. This week could be a turning point for you.

REFLECTIONS ON INTOLERANCE

1. Do your best to describe the contrast between tolerance and intolerance. Two clarifications need to be thought through:

   a. When does tolerance become wholesale permission? How far is too far?

   b. There must be times when intolerance is appropriate, since Jesus drove the moneychangers out of the temple. Name another time or two in Scripture when our Lord refused to give ground. What does that imply?

2. Is there someone you know who could use an arm around a shoulder, a word of encouragement, and a few hours of companionship? Perhaps this person didn't measure up to the expectations of you or others, or holds to a different opinion on a controversial subject, or recently went through a time of personal disappointment that took the wind out of his or her sails. Would you risk making contact? Reach out and demonstrate compassion on that person's behalf. Listen to where he or she is coming from. *Really* listen. Call to mind Solomon's counsel regarding our being slow to anger: "It is his glory to overlook a transgression" (Prov. 19:11). Model that this week. As you do, you may be allowed to witness genuine healing.

3. Finally, it is time for some reflection. Since it is true that intolerance and arrogance are often related, could it be

that you have forgotten those occasions when *you* blew it . . . when you were like that trout, hooked and unable to get free? For the next ten minutes, vividly recall the pain of feeling alone, ashamed, and misunderstood. Think of a person or two who laid aside all pride as he (or she) invested time and demonstrated compassion. Ask the Lord to give you the courage to do the same. Time may be more of the essence than you realize.

Four things are small on the earth,
But they are exceedingly wise:
The ants are not a strong folk,
But they prepare their food in the
summer;
The badgers are not mighty folk,
Yet they make their houses in the rocks;
The locusts have no king,
Yet all of them go out in ranks;
The lizard you may grasp with the hands,
Yet it is in kings' palaces.   [30:24–28]

THE GRIND OF
EXCUSE-MAKING

Ants, badgers, locusts, and lizards . . . sounds like roll call for Noah's Ark! Or an advertisement for a new jungle movie. But no, these four creatures are discussed in Proverbs 30:24–28— another of those amazing sayings from Scripture that speaks volumes to us today.

According to the opening statement in verse 24, each of these four creatures is "small on the earth, but . . . exceedingly wise." Each represents a contrast. We shouldn't think that size means insignificance. Within each is a remarkable ability . . . and, likewise, a hidden peril. As we shall see, each teaches a lesson we would do well to learn.

The Ant

We have already looked at the ant in Book I, so there's no need to linger here over details already discussed. Suffice it to say that without some higher-ranking authority to drive them on, without great strength (one human foot can stomp several of them into oblivion!), the ant nevertheless works, works, works.

The Badger

This creature isn't big either, but it is extremely independent. A member of the weasel family, badgers grow to be not more than thirty inches long. They are sleek, low-slung (Corvette-like) ground dwellers. As nocturnal prowlers, they are seldom seen. Badgers are fierce fighters with powerful jaws; long, sharp teeth; and two-inch claws. Extremely rugged and resilient, they can whip creatures up to four times their size!

However, they are great at bluffing their opponents. A badger stands, snarling and arching its back . . . but at the precise moment it is about to get caught or chewed up and spit out, it suddenly retreats!

Here's how: Badgers are unlike all other animals whose hair is "set" in such a manner that it lies in only one direction. Remember how we can rub a cat "the wrong way" or do the same with a dog? Not so with a badger! Badgers' hair can go *both* ways. Its skin is so loose and its hair so thick and flexible that another creature can't get a good grip on it. This makes a badger the classic *escape artist!* When confronted, it may choose to fight. More often, however, (being clever) it will choose to retreat.

Now, we're beginning to uncover a clue in this list of small creatures. Both the ant, which can slip into an anthill, and the badger, which escapes when confronted, are good illustrations of one of man's (and woman's!) favorite indoor sports: *making excuses.* Some get so good at it, no one can get a grip on them. It may appear to be small and insignificant as grinds go, but excuse-making can take a heavy toll.

The Locust

We're getting smaller again. This insect is about the size of a grasshopper. They may have "no king" (unlike Canadian geese in flight or a pride of lions on a savanna which follow a definite leader); nevertheless, locusts are a team that can "go out in ranks." The gregarious locust swarm can wreck havoc on endless miles of crops. Interestingly, they can be mild and quiet, then suddenly become restless and irritable. They can turn in their moods and suddenly become violent, taking flight and traveling incredible distances.

Some swarms sound like a huge commercial jetliner overhead. And when they have finished with their attack on crops, every plant—every single plant—is stripped down to a barren, bleeding stalk, as if a fire had swept across the scene. One particular swarm was spotted as far as twelve hundred miles out at sea, flying northward from West Africa toward the British Isles. Another swarm covered a breadth of air space no less than two thousand square miles.

Amazing creature, the locust . . . and how moody! Quiet and placid, yet within moments, irritable and restless.

The Lizard

According to this saying, we're able to grasp the lizard with our hands, yet it is ever so slippery. The next thing we know, it winds up "in kings' palaces." How? Well, that's the lizard's secret; it's a master of disguises. It can blend in so perfectly with its background, no one even notices its presence. Operation camouflage. Slippery when grabbed, it squirts away, and to everyone's surprise, it shows up elsewhere in all its glory!

Ants, badgers, locusts, and lizards present a small but very clever message to all who live with the daily grind of excuse-making. We can easily escape, slip away, change our moods, and go right on without accepting or even acknowledging the confrontation. The devastation of living like that can be enormous. For example, those who continue to live financially irresponsible lives often wind up declaring bankruptcy. Or husbands and wives who prefer to overlook their part in marital conflicts go from one marriage to the next with little change in their habits. Unfortunately, making excuses never solves conflicts; it only postpones the consequences.

This is a good week to take a straight look at your tendency to dodge the hard questions . . . to ignore the warnings of a friend . . . to slip from the grip of one whose criticism may hurt at the moment, but later could prove extremely beneficial. Honestly now . . .

- Are you slippery?
- How about moody and evasive?

- Is it your tendency to bluff?
- Do you enjoy camouflage?
- Have you a favorite anthill of escape?
- Does confrontation annoy or frighten you?

All this week, work hard at coming to terms with your excuse-making lifestyle. Living beyond that daily grind starts with facing up to the truth.

REFLECTIONS ON EXCUSE-MAKING

1. Which creature are you more like:

   The ant? Why?
   The badger? In what way?
   The locust? How?
   The lizard? Explain.

2. Think of situations where you most often feel the need to slip away and run. See if you can detect a familiar pattern—a recurring scene. Now for the tough one: *Why?* What makes you so hard to nail down? Is there something to hide? Something you fear? Are you afraid to let others get close? What's the reason behind that pattern?

3. No relationships are more significant to our development than those of early childhood. It is during those years that we form our first habits in handling life situations. Reflect back:

   - Was your mother or father moody?
   - Was evasiveness permitted? Modeled?
   - Can you recall how confrontation may have been mishandled back then?
   - Were you taught to live without accountability?
   - Did you develop excuse-making in your early years?

   For the balance of this week, discuss this with a few friends. Be vulnerable. Talk openly about your ant-badger-locust-lizard makeup.

Honor the Lord from your
wealth,
And from the first of all your
produce;
So your barns will be filled with plenty,
And your vats will overflow with new
wine.   [3:9–10]

It is the blessing of the Lord that makes
rich,
And He adds no sorrow to it.   [10:22]

How much better it is to get wisdom than
gold!
And to get understanding is to be chosen
above silver.   [16:16]

The rich rules over the poor,
And the borrower becomes the lender's
slave.   [22:7]

Do not be among those who give pledges,
Among those who become sureties for
debts.

If you have nothing with which to pay,
Why should he take your bed from under
 you?   [22:26–27]

Do not weary yourself to gain wealth,
Cease from your consideration of it.
When you set your eyes on it, it is gone.
For wealth certainly makes itself wings,
Like an eagle that flies toward the
 heavens.   [23:4–5]

He who tills his land will have plenty of
 food,
But he who follows empty pursuits will
 have poverty in plenty.
A faithful man will abound with
 blessings,
But he who makes haste to be rich will
 not be unpunished.   [28:19–20]

A man with an evil eye hastens after
 wealth,
And does not know that want will come
 upon him.   [28:22]

THE GRIND OF
FINANCIAL
IRRESPONSIBILITY

Few "grinds" in life are more nerve-racking and energy-draining than those growing out of financial irresponsibility. Many are the headaches and heartaches of being overextended. Great are the worries of those, for example, who continue to increase their indebtedness or spend impulsively or loan money to others indiscriminately.

These words may bring a sting to your conscience if they describe your situation. What's worse, they may describe where you have found yourself off and on for as long as you can remember. It may not bring much comfort to know that *you are not alone,* but there is perhaps no more common problem among Americans than this one. So common is it that places of business must protect themselves from this phenomenon by operating under strict guidelines. All this reminds me of a sign that made me smile. It hangs in a Fort Lauderdale restaurant:

> IF YOU ARE OVER 80 YEARS OLD
> AND ACCOMPANIED BY YOUR PARENTS,
> WE WILL CASH YOUR CHECK

Some wag once described our times with three different definitions:

> *Recession:* When the man next door loses his job.
> *Depression:* When you lose your job.
> *Panic:* When your wife loses her job.

Many families have reached the place where the wife's working is no longer an optional luxury, it's a necessity.

To the surprise of no one, the sayings of Scripture having to do with money are numerous. Long before Ben Franklin penned his wit and wisdom in *Poor Richard's Almanac,* Solomon's words had been around for centuries, available for all to read. And when you attempt to categorize them, you realize just how varied the subjects are that have to do with financial matters.

Solomon's sayings cover a broad spectrum, including getting money (earning and inheriting), releasing money (spending, squandering, loaning, and giving), investing money, saving money, and handling money wisely. The synonyms used in Scripture are many: money, wealth, riches, lending, borrowing, spending, giving, losing, silver, gold, plenty, abundance, want, poverty, and a half dozen others.

Having traced the subject through Solomon's sayings, I have discovered the following principles of money management. There are six of them.

1. <u>Those who honor God with their money are blessed in</u> <u>return.</u>

> Honor the Lord from your wealth,
> And from the first of all your produce;
> So your barns will be filled with plenty,
> And your vats will overflow with new wine. [3:9–10]
>
> It is the blessing of the Lord that makes rich,
> And He adds no sorrow to it. [10:22]
>
> Adversity pursues sinners,
> But the righteous will be rewarded with prosperity. [13:21]

I have said for years that you can tell much more about an individual's dedication to God by looking at that person's checkbook than by looking at his or her Bible. Again and again throughout Scripture, we read of the blessings God grants (not all of them tangible, by the way) to those who "honor the Lord" with their finances.

2. <u>Those who make riches their passion lose much more than</u> <u>they gain.</u>

Do not weary yourself to gain wealth,
Cease from your consideration of it.
When you set your eyes on it, it is gone.
For wealth certainly makes itself wings,
Like an eagle that flies toward the heavens. [23:4–5]

Can't you just picture the scene? For that reason I think it is appropriate that an eagle appears on much of our American currency! Who hasn't been tempted by some get-rich-quick scheme? And think of the thousands of people who are drawn into the broad and juicy appeal of the investors who promise they can make a killing for them on their "deal." Beware of words like "it's a once-in-a-lifetime" opportunity! When you hear such stuff, listen for the flapping of eagles' wings. And heed instead the wisdom of Solomon's words!

He who tills his land will have plenty of food,
But he who follows empty pursuits will have poverty in plenty.
A faithful man will abound with blessings,
But he who makes haste to be rich will not be unpunished.
   [28:19–20]

A man with an evil eye hastens after wealth,
And does not know that want will come upon him. [28:22]

3. Wisdom gives wealth guidance. If you have a choice between wisdom and wealth, count on it; *wisdom* is much to be preferred!

Take my instruction, and not silver,
And knowledge rather than choicest gold.
For wisdom is better than jewels;
And all desirable things can not compare with her. [8:10–11]

Riches and honor are with me,
Enduring wealth and righteousness.
My fruit is better than gold, even pure gold,
And my yield than choicest silver. [8:18–19]

How much better it is to get wisdom than gold!
And to get understanding is to be chosen above silver. [16:16]

Wisdom provides the recipient of increased finances with the restraints that are needed. Furthermore, it helps one maintain that essential equilibrium, for much wealth can be a heady trip. Since riches never made anyone honest or generous or discerning, wisdom must come aboard to steer our vessel around those disastrous shallow reefs. The reason for this brings us to a fourth principle of money management.

4. Increased riches bring increased complications. As I examine the biblical record, I find several such complications mentioned in the Book of Proverbs:

- A false sense of security

> The rich man's wealth is his fortress,
> The ruin of the poor is their poverty. [10:15]

> A rich man's wealth is his strong city,
> And like a high wall in his own imagination. [18:11]

- A sudden burst of many new "friends"

The poor is hated even by his neighbor,
But those who love the rich are many. [14:20]

Wealth adds many friends,
But a poor man is separated from his friend. [19:4]

A man of many friends comes to ruin,
But there is a friend who sticks closer than a brother. [18:24]

- The possibility of arrogance and pride

The poor man utters supplications,
But the rich man answers roughly. [18:23]

The rich man is wise in his own eyes,
But the poor who has understanding sees through him. [28:11]

- Increased moral temptations

Do not desire her beauty in your heart,
Nor let her catch you with her eyelids.
For on account of a harlot one is reduced to a loaf of bread,
And an adulteress hunts for the precious life.

Can a man take fire in his bosom,
And his clothes not be burned?
Or can a man walk on hot coals,
And his feet not be scorched? [6:25–28]

A man who loves wisdom makes his father glad,
But he who keeps company with harlots wastes his wealth. [29:3]

5. <u>Money cannot buy life's most valuable possessions.</u>
It is strange how so many live under the delusion that a fat bank account will make possible "the best things in life" when, in fact, it will provide no such thing. Don't misunderstand. There is nothing wrong with having wealth if it has been earned honestly and if one's perspective stays clear. However, "the good life" should not be equated with "the true life," which Paul calls "life indeed" (1 Timothy 6:19). Money will only buy things that are for sale . . . and happiness or a clear conscience or freedom from worry is not among them. Money can be used to purchase lovely and comfortable dwellings, pleasure vacations, and delightful works of art. But the priceless things in life are not for sale.
What are some of those priceless possessions?

- Peace

> Better is a little with the fear of the Lord,
> Than great treasure and turmoil with it. [15:16]

- Love

> Better is a dish of vegetables where love is,
> Than a fattened ox and hatred with it. [15:17]

- A good name . . . reputation and respect

> A good name is to be more desired than great riches,
> Favor is better than silver and gold. [22:1]

- Integrity

> Better is the poor who walks in his integrity,
> Than he who is crooked though he be rich. [28:6]

6. If handled wisely, money can be the means of great encouragement, but if mishandled, great stress.

> Adversity pursues sinners,
> But the righteous will be rewarded with prosperity.
> A good man leaves an inheritance to his children's children,
> And the wealth of the sinner is stored up for the righteous.
> [13:21–22]

Who can measure the encouragement our money can bring to others? If reared correctly, our children can benefit from and know the joy of receiving an inheritance from their parents. God's Word admonishes parents to provide for their families. Ministries of every kind are dependent upon the financial generosity of those who support them. The hungry can be fed, the poor can be clothed, the homeless can be sheltered, the abused can be comforted, the untaught can be educated . . . the list of possibilities is endless.

There is the flip side, however:

> The rich rules over the poor,
> And the borrower becomes the lender's slave. [22:7]

> Do not be among those who give pledges,
> Among those who become sureties for debts.
> If you have nothing with which to pay,
> Why should he take your bed from under you? [22:26–27]

This hardly needs to be explained. Pause over those key words . . . especially *slave*. No other term better describes the feeling of being financially irresponsible!

If this happens to be your "grind," let me encourage you to ignore it no longer. No more excuses! There are too many helpful books and reliable resources available for you to continue on in an irresponsible manner. Begin the process of change this week.

R EFLECTIONS ON FINANCIAL IRRESPONSIBILITY

1. Select three or four from the many sayings about money matters you just read that speak most pointedly to you. Write them on separate three-by-five cards and commit them to memory. You might also tape one of them on the front of your checkbook! All week long reflect on the truth of what you are committing to memory. Use those truths in several conversations this week.

2. One of the most helpful, practical tools you can use in getting a handle on your money is a budget. Don't let the week draw to a close before you have established a simple and easy-to-follow personal budget. If you need help, ask someone you respect for advice. If that person cannot help, surely he or she can steer you in the right direction by referring you to help from another source. But don't let the week run its course before you have *written down* a realistic financial game plan you will put in motion.

3. There are several splendid books available today on the subject of handling money wisely. There are also seminars and conferences, plus audio and video tapes provided by reliable authorities in the field of finances. This week, take a giant step toward conquering the dragon of financial ir-responsibility by doing one (or more) of three things:

   a. Purchase and begin reading a book on money manage-ment.
   b. Listen to a set of tapes on the subject.
   c. Look into a financial seminar that would best meet your need and make definite plans to attend.

An excellent wife, who can find?
For her worth is far above
jewels.
The heart of her husband trusts
in her,
And he will have no lack of gain.
She does him good and not evil
All the days of her life.
She looks for wool and flax,
And works with her hands in delight.
She is like merchant ships;
She brings her food from afar.
She rises also while it is still night,
And gives food to her household,
And portions to her maidens.
She considers a field and buys it;
From her earnings she plants a vineyard.
She girds herself with strength,
And makes her arms strong.
She senses that her gain is good;
Her lamp does not go out at night.
She stretches out her hands to the distaff,
And her hands grasp the spindle.
She extends her hand to the poor;
And she stretches out her hands to the
needy.
She is not afraid of the snow for her
household,

For all her household are clothed with
   scarlet.
She makes coverings for herself;
Her clothing is fine linen and purple.
Her husband is known in the gates,
When he sits among the elders of the
   land.
She makes linen garments and sells them,
And supplies belts to the tradesmen.
Strength and dignity are her clothing,
And she smiles at the future.
She opens her mouth in wisdom,
And the teaching of kindness is on her
   tongue.
She looks well to the ways of her
   household,
And does not eat the bread of idleness.
Her children rise up and bless her;
Her husband also, and he praises her,
   saying:
"Many daughters have done nobly,
But you excel them all."
Charm is deceitful and beauty is vain,
But a woman who fears the Lord, she
   shall be praised.
Give her the product of her hands,
And let her works praise her in the
   gates.   [31:10–31]

THE GRIND OF MOTHERHOOD

Without taking away from the joys, rewards, and those extra-special moments of motherhood, the daily tasks of that assignment can be *grinding!* Washing mounds of laundry; ironing; folding; cleaning; shopping; cooking; car pooling; being a referee, a coach, an encourager, a counselor, a cop; staying pretty; remaining tactful, lovable, compassionate, cheerful, responsible, balanced, and sane(!)—all have a way of making today's mothers feel strung out and spent. And it is all so daily . . . so relentlessly repetitive.

There is so much to know as well as to learn about this matter of being a good mother. It doesn't simply "just happen" once you have a child. It's as absurd to think that giving birth automatically makes you a good mother as it is to think that having a piano automatically makes you a good musician. There's an enormous amount of work to it, more than most will ever realize . . . (certainly more than most *husbands* realize, right?).

Among the eloquent sayings of Scripture is a most outstanding treatise on the mother's role. It is both profound and practical . . . full of wise counsel and strong encouragement. Anyone who reads this section realizes that God believes in the woman who gives her home the priority it deserves. He also sees her as a person, distinct and different from her husband, who finds fulfillment in her varied responsibilities and roles.

Right away, you sense God's affirming respect as the writer introduces this woman as "an excellent wife." She is rare, for he asks, "Who can find" one with such magnificent qualities? And in case you wonder if you are valued in God's eyes, just ponder this statement: ". . . for her worth is far above jewels" (31:10b).

Her relationship with her husband is nothing short of delightful:

> The heart of her husband trusts in her,
> And he will have no lack of gain.
> She does him good and not evil
> All the days of her life. [31:11–12]

> Her husband is known in the gates,
> When he sits among the elders of the land. [31:23]

> Her children rise up and bless her;
> Her husband also, and he praises her, saying:
> "Many daughters have done nobly,
> But you excel them all." [31:28–29]

There are affirmation and respect in those words. There is also supportive companionship, which causes this woman to work *with* her man, not against him . . . to do him "good and not evil" as she remains his partner.

I find this same woman quite capable. Perhaps a better word is *enterprising!* Look at the list of her activities mentioned from verses 13–27.

- She looks for good products.
- She works with her hands.
- She considers a field and buys it.
- She earns a wage.
- She plants a vineyard with her money.
- She makes her own clothes.
- She runs her own clothing business on the side.
- She is deeply committed to her home and family.

But this woman is not simply a "workhorse" . . . she is resourceful, compassionate, and secure. For example:

She is like merchant ships;
She brings her food from afar.
She rises also while it is still night,
And gives food to her household,
And portions to her maidens. [31:14–15]

She girds herself with strength,
And makes her arms strong.
She senses that her gain is good;
Her lamp does not go out at night. [vv. 17–18]

She extends her hand to the poor;
And she stretches out her hands to the needy.
She is not afraid of the snow for her household,
For all her household are clothed with scarlet. [vv. 20–21]

Give her the product of her hands,
And let her works praise her in the gates. [v. 31]

Within the heart of this mother is a depth of character.

Strength and dignity are her clothing,
And she smiles at the future.
She opens her mouth in wisdom,
And the teaching of kindness is on her tongue. [31:25–26]

"Many daughters have done nobly,
But you excel them all." [v. 29]

What a beautiful portrait! Can't you see her smiling as she looks toward the distant horizon of her life? She is neither insecure nor afraid. Her world is bigger than the immediate demands of today. Her strength is an inner strength, a sense of confidence in God. No wonder her children ultimately "bless her"! No wonder her husband happily "praises her"!

On top of it all she "fears the Lord." She walks with God. She holds Him in highest regard. She maintains a close relationship with the One who gave her her life, her health, her personality, her husband, her children, her ideas, her creativity, her determination to excel.

Somehow, you get the impression that this woman does not feel like a victim of four walls, a slave to a husband and houseful of kids. She certainly is no social invalid who feels inadequate and overwhelmed. No, not in the least. She has found some of the secrets of being herself, yet remaining extremely involved with and committed to her family, of enjoying her husband and the children, yet finding another dimension of fulfillment beyond them. And it's not because she is rich with servants at each door. Remember, she does her own shopping, makes her own clothes, works for a wage, and looks well to the many ways of her household. Quite a lady!

And may I add another dimension that is implied but not mentioned here? She is married to some kind of man! He must be incredibly secure and truly generous. He is not only willing to let her find fulfillment beyond him . . . he *affirms* her doing so. Don't forget, he praises her; he openly declares:

> "Many daughters have done nobly,
> But you excel them all." [31:29]

This man is worth a second look, fellow husbands. Maybe it is just male ego on my part, but I believe part of the reason why this "excellent wife," who was worth more than precious jewels, found fulfillment in her role as wife, mother, businesswoman, seamstress, investor, hostess, and friend of the needy was that her husband supported and affirmed such things in her. He found delight in her activities. He encouraged her to be the best mother possible, to reach out to others, to be all God meant her to be.

For those women who are blessed with partners like that, motherhood is a glory, not a grind.

REFLECTIONS ON MOTHERHOOD

1. Go back over these sayings in Proverbs 31. Take your time. Do a little honest appraisal. If you are a woman, take note of several behind-the-scene secrets of this woman's life.

   - Her positive attitude
   - Her indomitable spirit
   - Her secure determination
   - Her boundless energy
   - Her inner strength

   If you are a husband, review the comments I made in the next-to-last paragraph of this chapter. Are you like that? What could be done to help you be more of a support and encouragement?

2. In what ways are you gifted or skilled? Are you a good cook? Do you enjoy venturing into new (and sometimes risky) areas? Are you insightful as a counselor or teacher? How about sewing . . . are you a proficient seamstress? Does the idea of a small business intrigue you—say one you could do out of your home? Could it be that you have become so immersed in the daily demands of just "mothering," you have somehow lost the creative joys of being a whole person? Discuss this with your husband and/or a good friend.

3. Finally, think about the level of your commitment to the home. Do you really—honestly and truly—look well to the ways of your household? Do they know—does each member of your family realize—how much you value them and how committed you are to them? Could there be something you might do or change or say to communicate how deeply you care? Don't wait. Before the week has passed, fulfill that objective.

There are six things which the
Lord hates,
Yes, seven which are an
abomination to Him:
Haughty eyes, a lying tongue,
And hands that shed innocent blood.
A heart that devises wicked plans,
Feet that run rapidly to evil,
A false witness who utters lies,
And one who spreads strife among
brothers.   [6:16–19]

THE GRIND OF DISPLEASING GOD

Even though we have mentioned various shades of this subject and have glanced at these sayings on more than one occasion in our study together, we need to face the music directly. Who hasn't struggled with the daily grind of displeasing the Lord? Is there a grind that brings greater ache of soul? I don't think so.

No one begins the day thinking about how he (or she) might displease God. On the contrary, most people I know face the dawn with high hopes of pleasing Him. In our minds we establish a game plan that will include a good attitude, a day of wholesome activities. We prepare ourselves for possible temptations and trials by meeting early with our God and giving Him our day in advance. And yet . . . before the morning is half done, we can fall into a syndrome of carnality that is downright discouraging, if not altogether demoralizing.

Perhaps it will help us this week to focus in on a specific target. Rather than praying in general terms, "Lord, help me to please You," it may be more beneficial to name seven specific areas where we need help. The list of seven is inspired— Solomon calls them the "seven which are an abomination" to our Lord. At the end of each of the seven discussions that follow, you will find a suggested prayer.

1. <u>Haughty eyes.</u> Our eyes reveal the truth of our souls. They convey so many of our unspoken emotions. Eyes announce anger, impatience, sorrow, sarcasm, guilt, and especially pride. It's that last one God hates with intensity.

"God, guard me all this week from hidden arrogance!"

2. A lying tongue. Not all lies are big and bold. Half-truths flow so freely. Exaggerations, too. And false words of flattery are commonly heard. Since we looked at the tongue so closely in Book I, have you been more conscious of your words? Are you more aware of your tongue's power?

"God, alert me to the destructive force of my tongue. Stop me from every form of lying!"

3. Hands that shed innocent blood. Solomon clearly states that the Lord considers murder an abomination. You may have been victimized by someone. It could be going on right now. As time passes, unless forgiveness replaces resentment, your bitterness could grow into rage . . . and you could "shed innocent blood." You may have a major battle with abusing your child. If so, you *must* get help!

"God, direct me to wholesome and healthy ways to solve and dissolve my uncontrolled anger. Keep me from the sin of shedding innocent blood!"

4. A heart that devises wicked plans. Because we have examined the heart so carefully, we are aware of its power and its importance. Nothing we do or say occurs until it has been filtered through the heart within us. It is there that "wicked plans" are laid. It is there we map out our yielding to temptation, our release of restraint, our scheme to get even with someone else.

"God, cleanse my heart from any hurtful way . . . remove every ugly thought or scheme I have been pondering!"

5. Feet that run rapidly to evil. Old habits are hard to break. Because we have "gotten away with it" before, the skids of sin are greased. In fact, we become increasingly less fearful of God's stepping in the longer we get away with continued, familiar paths of sin. "Because God does not punish sinners instantly, people feel it is safe to do wrong" (Eccles. 8:11, TLB).

"God, halt me in my tracks!"

6. A false witness who utters lies. Rare are the truth tellers. Many are those who deliberately misrepresent the facts. When we have the opportunity to defend another's character or set the record straight in a group that is bad-mouthing a certain individual, the temptation to chime in and agree (or remain silent and allow the character assassination to continue) is great. But the Lord *hates* such actions.

"God, free me from whatever fears I have so that my witness will be true, based on accurate facts!"

7. <u>One who spreads strife among brothers</u>. Juicy information is so difficult to contain. This is especially true if there is an element of verbal malignancy in the talk. How easy to "spread strife" among our brothers and sisters . . . how hard to be a peacemaker! But Solomon pulls no punches. He calls this one of those abominations God despises. This is the third in the list having to do with the tongue.

"God, silence me from any hint of gossip!"

We frequently think of the love of God, but all too seldom meditate on the things He hates. We should! Believe me, when God's Word says He hates these things, there is intensity in the statement. That means each one deserves an intensity of our effort to correct and control each one named.

REFLECTIONS ON DISPLEASING GOD

1. Go back to the closing prayers in each of the seven areas mentioned in the sayings. Interestingly, there are *seven* specific things God hates . . . one for each day in the week. You can probably anticipate this project. On Sunday, take that first subject area on God's "hate list" (*haughty eyes*) and pray the prayer I've suggested throughout the day. Concentrate on overcoming that all day Sunday. On Monday, take the second; Tuesday, the third . . . follow the plan all week long.

2. Since three of these seven have to do with the tongue, we must give great attention to this powerful force. All week pay special attention not only to what you say but how and when you say it . . . and why . . . and to whom. Talk less and say more.

3. Which one thing mentioned in the list could be called your most frequent battleground? Be absolutely relentless as you roll up your sleeves and take on this hateful, ugly enemy of righteousness. Displeasing God is habit-forming! But so can be our pleasing Him. Tell at least two other people of your major struggle. Request their prayers. Trust God to use their intercession and your concentrated effort to defeat this enemy.

Proverbs

The proverbs of Solomon the son
of David, king of Israel:
To know wisdom and instruction,
To discern the sayings of
understanding,
To receive instruction in wise behavior,
Righteousness, justice and equity;
To give prudence to the naive,
To the youth knowledge and discretion,
A wise man will hear and increase in
learning,
And a man of understanding will acquire
wise counsel,
To understand a proverb and a figure,
The words of the wise and their riddles.

The fear of the Lord is the beginning of
knowledge;
Fools despise wisdom and instruction.

Hear, my son, your father's instruction,
And do not forsake your mother's
teaching;
Indeed, they are a graceful wreath to
your head,
And ornaments about your neck.
My son, if sinners entice you,
Do not consent.
If they say, 'Come with us,
Let us lie in wait for blood,
Let us ambush the innocent without
cause;
Let us swallow them alive like Sheol,
Even whole, as those who go down to the
pit;

We shall find all kinds of precious.
    wealth,
We shall fill our houses with spoil;
Throw in your lot with us,
We shall all have one purse."
My son do not walk in the way with
    them.
Keep your feet from their path,
For their feet run to evil,
And they hasten to shed blood.
Indeed, it is useless to spread the net
In the eyes of any bird;
But they lie in wait for their own blood;
They ambush their own lives.
So are the ways of everyone who gains
    by violence;
It takes away the life of its possessors.

Wisdom shouts in the street,
She lifts her voice in the square;
At the head of the noisy streets she cries
    out;
At the entrance of the gates in the city,
    she utters her sayings:
"How long, O naive ones, will you love
    simplicity?
And scoffers delight themselves in
    scoffing,
And fools hate knowledge?
Turn to my reproof,
Behold, I will pour out my spirit on you;
I will make my words known to
    you." [1:1–23]

THE GRIND OF
SUBSTITUTING
KNOWLEDGE FOR
WISDOM

Many, many weeks ago in Book I, when we first looked at the sayings of Scripture we began with the first chapter of Proverbs. It occurs to me that it would be worthwhile to return to it for a final time as we consider our tendency to *substitute knowledge for wisdom*. This is not only a daily grind; it is a lifetime tendency!

How easy it is to acquire knowledge, yet how difficult and painstaking is the process of gaining wisdom. Man gives knowledge; God gives wisdom. Knowledge is gleaned from getting an education—either by listening to and reading what the learned have to say or simply by gathering facts here and yon from your own experience. But what about the wisdom that is from above? As you already know, there is no course, no school, no earthly reservoir where such can be received. Unlike knowledge which can be measured in objective analyses and IQ tests and rewarded with diplomas and degrees, wisdom defies measurement; it is much more subjective, takes far more time, and has a great deal to do with attitude. One can be knowledgeable, yet distant from the living God. But those who are wise not only know the Lord by faith in His Son, Jesus Christ, they also hold Him in awesome respect. "The fear of the Lord" is still a telltale mark of wisdom.

So how does one obtain wisdom? Now that we have come to an end of our search through the sayings of Scripture, how can we continue our pursuit of God's wisdom? What are some ways to guard against falling back into our habit of substituting knowledge for wisdom?

I have four thoughts to suggest:

1. Read the Book of Proverbs regularly.

> The proverbs of Solomon the son of David, king of Israel:
> To know wisdom and instruction,
> To discern the sayings of understanding,
> To receive instruction in wise behavior,
> Righteousness, justice and equity;
> To give prudence to the naive,
> To the youth knowledge and discretion,
> A wise man will hear and increase in learning,
> And a man of understanding will acquire wise counsel,
> To understand a proverb and a figure,
> The words of the wise and their riddles.
> The fear of the Lord is the beginning of knowledge;
> Fools despise wisdom and instruction. [vv. 1–7]

The Book of Proverbs has thirty-one chapters—a natural fit into each month. It includes descriptions of over 180 different types of people. There is no mumbo-jumbo, no Rubic's-cube theology to unscramble, no weird, abstract theories to unravel, just straight talk for all of us who live imperfect lives on Planet Earth. Since Solomon declares that his writings have been recorded to help us "know wisdom," I suggest we take him up on it and glean new dimensions of wisdom by sitting at his feet. Read one chapter of the Book of Proverbs every day for the rest of your life and chances are good you'll not often be tempted to substitute knowledge for wisdom.

2. Hear and heed the counsel of those you respect.

> Hear, my son, your father's instruction,
> And do not forsake your mother's teaching;
> Indeed, they are a graceful wreath to your head,
> And ornaments about your neck. [vv. 8–9]

Wisdom isn't limited to the sayings of Scripture. It is possible that God has given you a godly set of parents, several trusted mentors, and one or two wise friends. They have been through experiences and endured some trials you have not yet encountered. They have had time to weave all that through the varied fabrics of life, which gives them a discernment and depth you may lack. The things they can pass along to you are "a graceful wreath . . . and ornaments" of wisdom available to you. Listen to them. Learn from them. Linger with them.

3. <u>Choose your friends carefully.</u>

My son, if sinners entice you,
Do not consent.
If they say, "Come with us,
Let us lie in wait for blood,
Let us ambush the innocent without cause;
Let us swallow them alive like Sheol,
Even whole, as those who go down to the pit;
We shall find all kinds of precious wealth,
We shall fill our houses with spoil;
Throw in your lot with us,
We shall all have one purse,"
My son do not walk in the way with them.
Keep your feet from their path,
For their feet run to evil,
And they hasten to shed blood.
Indeed, it is useless to spread the net
In the eyes of any bird;
But they lie in wait for their own blood;
They ambush their own lives.
So are the ways of everyone who gains by violence;
It takes away the life of its possessors. [vv. 10–19]

The longer I live the more careful I am with my choice of friends. I have fewer than in my youthful years, but they are deeper friends . . . treasured relationships.

As we read in Solomon's counsel, do not consent to relationships that drag you down and hurt your walk with God. Those who "ambush their own lives" (v. 18) will get you involved in counterproductive activities that will keep wisdom at arm's distance. You don't need that.

4. Pay close attention to life's reproofs.

Wisdom shouts in the street,
She lifts her voice in the square;
At the head of the noisy streets she cries out;
At the entrance of the gates in the city, she utters her sayings:
"How long, O naive ones, will you love simplicity?
And scoffers delight themselves in scoffing,
And fools hate knowledge?
Turn to my reproof,
Behold, I will pour out my spirit on you;
I will make my words known to you." [vv. 20–23]

If you have been on this journey since Book I, perhaps you recall the time we spent analyzing these words. Wisdom is personified as one who "shouts in the street" and "lifts her voice in the square." In other words, she is available. She speaks loud and clear. But, where? How? She tells us! "Turn to my reproof." It is there (in life's reproofs) she pours out her spirit on us and makes her words known to us.

God never wastes our time, allowing us to go through the dark and dismal valleys or endure those long and winding painful paths without purpose. In each one there are "reproofs" with wisdom attached. Many and foolish are those who simply grit their teeth and bear it. Few but wise are those who hear wisdom's voice and listen to her counsel.

For the rest of our years on this old earth, let's do our best to be numbered among that latter group.

R EFLECTIONS ON SUBSTITUTING KNOWLEDGE FOR WISDOM

1. As we have discovered through the course of this book, the secret of memory is review, review, review. Today is a good day to set up a plan for reviewing the sayings of Solomon. If you wish to read through the Book of Proverbs on a daily basis, think about the best time and place for doing so. To keep the readings fresh, you might want to pick up a copy of the Scriptures in a different version or perhaps a paraphrase. As you read through the Book of Proverbs, you may also want to review some of the pertinent discussions in this book.

2. All of us have at least one wise person we really admire. If at all possible, arrange a time to get together . . . perhaps once a month or once every other month. If that won't work, how about listening to audio tapes that person has made or reading some things he (or she) has written? You may find that cultivating a close companionship and accountability with a small group of trusted friends is the best way to fulfill your desire for a life of wisdom.

3. As a final, end-of-the-book project, bow and thank the Lord for His faithfulness to you. His Word has been our guide. His mercy and grace, our encouragement. His love, our motivation. His Spirit, our Helper. His power to bring about changes within us, our hope. Express to Him how grateful you are for all He has taught you in these pages and for His patience with you as you attempt to live beyond the daily grind.

CONCLUSION

Perhaps it has been a full year since you began your journey with me through the songs and sayings in Scripture. At least that was my original plan for you as we set out together in our first week of reading with Book I. I hope you have learned as much as I have! In the process of gleaning truth, encouragement, insight, and renewed strength from the Psalms and the Proverbs, I hope you have come to know yourself better—a better understanding of one's self is always a byproduct of time spent in God's relevant revelation.

Most of all, however, I hope you have come to know our Lord in new and fresh ways—and have found Him to be interested in the nuts and bolts of your everyday existence. In fact, it seems there is nothing He is not interested in, certainly nothing He is not aware of! If He has the hair on our heads numbered, He must care intimately and intensely about the things that concern us . . . especially those daily grinds that eat away at us.

My objective all along has been twofold: first, to provide you with comments and explanations of the songs and sayings so you could have a better grasp of the biblical text; and second, to assist you with applications and suggestions of each so you could put the truth into action.

Nothing would please me more than to know that my objective was accomplished, namely, that you increased your knowledge of these immortal psalms and proverbs and that you have begun to turn that knowledge into wisdom in practical ways.

I must confess to you that when I began to write this book, I looked upon the assignment with a heavy sigh. The journey before me seemed long and arduous. I found myself struggling with (occasionally even *dreading!*) the exacting task of another book, especially a two-volume work of this magnitude. My "daily grind" became the writing of these volumes, strange as that may sound. But I knew they should be written. What a pleasant surprise awaited me!

The more I got into the work, the greater became my motivation. To tell you the truth, it wasn't long before I could hardly sleep due to my excitement. Ideas came with increasing, sometimes furious, speed. It got to the place where I could not write fast enough! The remarkable fact is that all this took place while I was getting as little as three and often not more than five hours of sleep a night. This took place while I was maintaining the leadership over the ministry of our church as well as doing some special projects with my daily radio outreach, "Insight for Living." And considering that I wrote this book immediately on the heels of my previous one, *Growing Wise in Family Life,* I have been all the more amazed at the energy and creativity that surged through me during the entire process. I realize now that I was being given a literal illustration of the message of this book. What I first saw as a demanding, pressing assignment God turned into a joyful, fulfilling, and growing experience.

Life is full of such serendipities. What we dread, He is able to transform . . . and frequently *does!* What we lack in energy or ability, He supplies in abundance. What we alone are unable to handle, He handles for us—His helping hand makes up the difference. The book you hold in your hands is a tangible proof of what you just read.

I am smiling as I write these concluding words; to my own surprise I have been the first recipient of blessing from this project. The songs and sayings I had hoped would help you have helped me already. The reflections that I felt might be of encouragement to you have been encouraging me for weeks. Of this I am certain: they work!

Now I can say beyond the shadow of a doubt that living beyond the daily grind is not just a title; it is reliable truth. It is, in fact, the life God has designed for us to live. That is why He gets all the glory for removing all the grind.

NOTES

Introduction

1. C. S. Lewis, *Reflections on the Psalms* (London: Geoffrey Bles, 1958), 2–3.

Section Three

1. In an unpublished speech by Dr. Howard G. Hendricks, Dallas Theological Seminary, Dallas, Texas.

2. A. W. Tozer, *The Pursuit of God*, special edition (Wheaton, IL: Tyndale House Publishers), 17–18.

3. Robert Robinson [1757], "Come Thou Fount of Every Blessing."

4. William O. Cushing [1823–1902], "Under His Wings."

5. Martin Luther [1529], "A Mighty Fortress," translated by Frederick H. Hedge [1805–1890].

6. Charles Haddon Spurgeon, *The Treasury of David*, vol. 2 (Byron Center, MI: Associated Publishers and Authors, 1970), 4:233.

7. Kenneth S. Wuest, *The New Testament, An Expanded Translation*, vol. 3 (Grand Rapids, MI: Wm. B. Eerdman's Publishing Company, 1959), 463.

8. Charles Haddon Spurgeon, *The Treasury of David*, vol. 2, 5:281, 282.

9. Daniel Webster, from the tract "The Book of All Others for Lawyers" by Henry G. Perry, published by American Tract Society, Oradell, New Jersey.

10. Charles R. Swindoll, *Growing Wise in Family Life* (Portland, OR: Multnomah Press, 1988).

11. Charles Haddon Spurgeon, *The Treasury of David*, vol. 2, 7:86.

12. Graham Scroggie, *The Psalms*, revised edition (London: Pickering & Inglis, 1948, 1965, 1967), 273.

13. F. B. Meyer, *Moses* (Grand Rapids, MI: Zondervan Publishing House, 1953, 1954), 31, 32.

14. F. B. Meyer, *Christ in Isaiah* (Grand Rapids, MI: Zondervan Publishing House, 1950), 9, 10.

15. A. W. Tozer, *Knowledge of the Holy* (Harper & Brothers Publishers, 1961), 61–63.

16. Annie Johnson Flint, "Pressed." From *Poems That Preach*, compiled by John R. Rice (Murfreesboro,TN: Sword of the Lord Publishers, 1952).

17. Charles Haddon Spurgeon, *The Treasury of David*, vol. 2, 7:229.

18. Charles Haddon Spurgeon, *The Treasury of David*, vol. 2, 7:293.

19. Charles Wesley [1707–1788], "O for a Heart to Praise My God."

Section Four

1. Augustine, *Confessions;* cited in *The Great Thoughts*, compiled by George Seldez (NY: Ballantine, 1985), 25.

2. Karl A. Menninger in *The Chosen* by Chaim Potok (frontispiece). A Fawcett Crest Book, published by Ballantine Books. Copyright 1967 by Chaim Potok.